Napier University
Learning Information Services
STANDARD LOAN
Please return or renew this item by th...
Renew online at http://nuin.napier.ac.uk
Item is subj...

KT-198-144

FOCUS ON VOCABULARY

Mastering the Academic Word List

DIANE SCHMITT

NORBERT SCHMITT

NAPIER UNIVERSITY LIS

CRL
428.1 SCH

Focus on Vocabulary: Mastering the Academic Word List

Copyright © 2005 by Pearson Education, Inc.
All rights reserved.
No part of this publication may be reproduced,
stored in a retrieval system, or transmitted
in any form or by any means, electronic, mechanical,
photocopying, recording, or otherwise,
without the prior permission of the publisher.

Pearson Education, 10 Bank Street, White Plains, NY 10606

Executive Editor: Laura Le Dréan
Development manager: Paula H. Van Ells
Senior development editor: Joan Poole
Vice president, director of production and design: Rhea Banker
Senior production editor: Jane Townsend
Art director: Ann France
Vice president, marketing: Kate McLoughlin
Senior manufacturing buyer: Edith Pullman
Photo research: Dana Klinek
Text design: Ann France
Text composition: Laserwords
Text font: 10/13 New Aster
Cover design: Elizabeth Carlson
Cover image: Lawrence Lawry. Reprinted by permission of Getty Images.
Photo and Illustration credits: See page 239.

Library of Congress Cataloging-in-Publication Data

Schmitt, Diane.
   Focus on vocabulary: mastering the academic word list / by Diane and
Norbert Schmitt.
      p. cm.
   Includes index.
   ISBN 0-13-183308-1
   1.   Vocabulary—Problems, exercises, etc. 2.   Reading (Higher Education)—
Problems, exercises, etc.   I. Schmitt, Norbert. II. Title.
PE1449.S343 2005
428.1—dc22

                         2004021593

ISBN: 0-13-183308-1

LONGMAN ON THE **WEB**

Longman.com offers online resources for
teachers and students. Access our Companion
Websites, our online catalog, and our local
offices around the world.

Visit us at **longman.com**.

Printed in the United States of America
4 5 6 7 8 9 10–BAH–09 08 07 06

Thanks to Averil Coxhead for providing us and teachers everywhere with a principled word list to guide our teaching of academic vocabulary.

Contents

To the Teacher vi
To the Student x
About the Authors xv
Authors' Acknowledgments xv

UNIT 1 *Our Changing Society* 1

CHAPTER 1: Technology and Society 2
Reading: Human Societies—From the Iceman to Us 3

CHAPTER 2: Social Experience and Personal Development 11
Reading: Social Forces That Shape Our Lives 12
Reading: Emotions in Global Perspective: Do We All Feel the Same? 20

CHAPTER 3: The Changing Nature of the Family 22
Reading: Family Structure 23

CHAPTER 4: Strategy Practice 31

UNIT 2 *Consumer Behavior and Marketing* 36

CHAPTER 5: Influencing the Consumer 37
Reading: Marketing's Impact on Consumers 38

CHAPTER 6: Who Buys What? The Family's Influence 45
Reading: Consumer Socialization of Family Members 46
Reading: Different Views on Purchasing Behavior 54

CHAPTER 7: How We See Ourselves 56
Reading: How Perspectives on the Self Influence Consumer Behavior 57

CHAPTER 8: Strategy Practice 65

UNIT 3 *Workplaces and Work Spaces* 69

CHAPTER 9: How Office Space Affects Behavior 70
Reading: Work Space Design 71

CHAPTER 10: The Modern Office: Symbols of Status 79
Reading: The Meaning of the Chair 80
Reading: Office Designs That Work 88

CHAPTER 11: Sitting Comfortably 90
Reading: The Ergonomics of Sitting 91

CHAPTER 12: Strategy Practice 99

UNIT 4 *Use and Abuse of Natural Resources* 103

CHAPTER 13: Water for Sale 104
Reading: Exploding Sales for Bottled Water 105

CHAPTER 14: The Aral Sea—An Environmental Disaster 113
    Reading: The Dying Lake 114
    Reading: Creating More Fresh Water Through Desalination 121

CHAPTER 15: International Conflict over Natural Resources 123
    Reading: Water Politics in the Middle East and North Africa 124

CHAPTER 16: Strategy Practice 133

UNIT 5 *We Are What We Eat* **137**

CHAPTER 17: Food Roots and Foodways 138
    Reading: Food Habits and Beliefs 139

CHAPTER 18: Getting Back to Nature 147
    Reading: Organic Farming Versus Traditional Farming Methods 148
    Reading: Genetically Modified Foods 155

CHAPTER 19: Microorganisms: The Spice of Life? 157
    Reading: Food Microbiology 158

CHAPTER 20: Strategy Practice 166

UNIT 6 *Encounters with Music and Sound* 169

CHAPTER 21: Music as Social Conscience 170
    Reading: Opposing War Through Music: Classical and Modern Examples 171

CHAPTER 22: Noise Hurts 179
    Reading: Noise Pollution 180
    Reading: The Science of Sound 187

CHAPTER 23: Ultrasonics: Super Sound? 189
    Reading: Ultrasonics 190

CHAPTER 24: Strategy Practice 198

UNIT 7 *Animal Nature* 201

CHAPTER 25: Endangered Elephants 202
    Reading: Saving the African Elephant: Using International Law and Trade 203

CHAPTER 26: Animals: How Human? 211
    Reading: Chimpanzees: Our Closest Relative 212
    Reading: Kanzi: A Case Study of Ape Language Development 220

CHAPTER 27: Living Together: Advantage or Disadvantage? 222
    Reading: The Costs and Benefits of Social Behavior 223

CHAPTER 28: Strategy Practice 231

INDEX OF ACADEMIC WORDS 235

CREDITS 239

To the Teacher

Second-language learners have long realized the importance of vocabulary for improving language proficiency. However, very often vocabulary does not receive sufficient attention in language classrooms. Research indicates that learners need to have access to a minimum of 3,000 words in order to even begin to comprehend authentic texts (Laufer, 1992), and students wishing to study in English at the university level may need up to 10,000 words (Hazenberg and Hulstijn, 1996). In order to help students attain vocabularies of this size, teachers need to provide explicit instruction on the more frequent words, and they also must help students to develop learning strategies that will enable them to acquire less frequent vocabulary.

In addition to developing a wide vocabulary, learners wishing to operate in academic environments in English also need to become familiar with a special type of formal vocabulary that is common in academic discourse. Commonly known as *academic vocabulary*, these words are found in a wide variety of academic disciplines. They are not specific to any one discipline but are the "support vocabulary" (sometimes referred to as "sub-technical vocabulary") necessary for speaking or writing precisely in a variety of fields. Examples include the words *analyze, predominant*, and *theory*. In a typical academic textbook, these words make up around 10 percent of the total text (Coxhead, 2000). In addition to facilitating the precise statement of ideas, these words contribute to the more sophisticated tone that is characteristic of academic texts.

Focus on Vocabulary assists students in learning this academic vocabulary. However, there is still the question of *which* academic vocabulary to teach. We have relied upon empirical research to determine the target words presented in this book. Coxhead (2000) compiled a corpus of 3.5 million words of written academic discourse, composed of 414 academic texts written by more than 400 authors on 28 topic areas. From this broad corpus, she identified 570 word families that are used frequently in academic texts across a wide range of topics, thus creating the Academic Word List (AWL). We have deleted 66 of the most frequent words from the AWL, which we feel students should already know (for example, *area, create, require*, and *similar*). This leaves 504 words, and these words are the ones featured in *Focus on Vocabulary*.

There is always a compromise between teaching many words in a cursory fashion, and teaching fewer words in greater depth. The words in the AWL constitute a significant percentage of those used in academic texts (around 10 percent). Therefore, students need to learn these words and learn them well. In order to help students gain a reasonable mastery of these words, we have drawn on the latest vocabulary research to design the most beneficial exercises. The key rationale behind the pedagogy in this book can be summarized in the following points.

- *Words must be encountered numerous times in order to be learned*. Nation (1990) reviewed the literature and concluded that it takes from five to sixteen or more repetitions for a word to be learned. In every chapter in *Focus on Vocabulary*, each target word appears at least four times, and most appear many more times elsewhere in the book. The Strategy Practice chapters and separately bound Unit Tests provide additional recycling opportunities.

- *Different contexts provide different kinds of information about a word*. For example, it is possible to learn one meaning from a particular context (for example, *to **monitor** an election* in an international relations context) yet require a different context in order to learn a separate meaning (for example, *a computer **monitor*** in an information technology context). Because of this, we have provided exposures to the target academic vocabulary in the reading passages and in a number of different exercise types. The exercise sentences model as many different contexts as possible.
- *Students learn best when their attention is focused on the material to be learned* (Schmidt, 1990). To make the academic words more noticeable, we have placed them in **bold** type in the chapters in which they are the target words. However, to avoid excess clutter, recycled target vocabulary is not boldfaced in subsequent chapters.
- *Learning a word entails more than knowing its meaning, spelling, and pronunciation* (Schmitt, 2000). There are a number of other types of word knowledge, including a word's collocations, grammatical characteristics, register, frequency, and associations. In order to use a word with confidence, a learner must have some mastery of all of these types of word knowledge. Some can be taught explicitly, such as meaning and spelling, while others, such as frequency and register information, can be truly acquired only through numerous exposures to a word. The extensive recycling in *Focus on Vocabulary* helps learners develop intuition about types of word knowledge that are less suited to conscious learning. At the same time, the exercises focus on elements that can be explicitly taught. Every chapter focuses on meaning, the derivative forms of a word (word families), and collocation.
- *Learners typically do not know all of the members of a word family, even if they know some of these word forms* (Schmitt and Zimmerman, 2002). However, learners must know the correct form of a word (noun, verb, adjective, adverb) for a particular context. Thus, every chapter has a section devoted to the derivative forms of the target academic words.
- *An understanding of collocations is equally important for the natural use of words*. These word partnerships are difficult to teach, but collocations are so important to the appropriate use of vocabulary that we have included a section on collocations in each chapter. The exercises explicitly teach a number of collocations for the target academic words. However, as it is impossible to teach all of the collocations for a word, the exercises are best viewed as practice that will make learners more aware of collocations in general and that may help them develop their collocation intuition more rapidly.
- *Collocations should be presented in authentic contexts*. In order to ensure that the information in this book reflects the actual usage of academic words, we have researched the 179-million-word New Longman Corpus. This has allowed us to empirically determine how the target academic words behave in real contexts. This was particularly useful in identifying the collocations of the academic words, because intuitions are often unreliable in this area. In addition, the examples and sentence exercises in this book are based on the patterns and constructions found in the corpus, and so are authentic in nature.

Focus on Vocabulary is divided into seven units, each on a specific subject. Within each unit, there are four chapters—three main chapters plus a Strategy Practice chapter that presents additional techniques for building academic vocabulary.

MAIN CHAPTERS

Each of the three main chapters is organized as follows.

Getting Started provides warm-up questions about the chapter topic. The main purpose is to activate students' prior knowledge about the topic before they read the passage. However, the questions usually ask something about the students' lives or ideas, so they can be used as more general discussion questions as well.

Target Words presents 24 target words and asks students to assess their knowledge of each word both before and after they work through the chapter. The assessment test is taken from Schmitt and Zimmerman (2002) and reflects the view that vocabulary learning is incremental. Thus, even if students do not achieve productive mastery of every word after the chapter is finished, the test may show partial improvement (for example, a student may progress, from *no knowledge* to *receptive knowledge*). By avoiding a *no knowledge/full mastery* dichotomy, the test can measure smaller degrees of learning. Every student should be able to learn enough about the target words to show some improvement on this test: Such progress helps to maintain and enhance motivation.

Reading presents an academic reading passage, usually from an actual college textbook. We have simplified some of the non-academic vocabulary and the phrasing in the passages, but otherwise they remain authentic. Exposure to academic vocabulary in extended, nearly authentic texts is beneficial. There is a great deal of academic vocabulary in these texts that is not specifically targeted in the chapter, and this provides natural recycling (in new contexts) of words students have already studied. Also, students appreciate that the readings closely match their expectations of what academic reading is like. In addition, the passages lend themselves to a wide range of reading-based tasks.

Word Meaning features a variety of exercises designed to help students learn the meaning of each of the 24 target words. Some of the tasks are deductive in nature, and some are inductive, catering to a range of learning styles.

Word Families provides practice in recognizing and using the various derivative word forms that make up a word's family, for example, *access, accessible, accessibility*.

Collocation exercises are designed to improve students' intuition about the natural partnerships words form (*emotional stability, political stability*).

Expansion provides various reading, discussion, and writing activities that recycle the target words and expand students' word knowledge in new ways.

STRATEGY PRACTICE CHAPTERS

The fourth chapter in each unit includes the following features.

Using Your Dictionary—Dictionaries are the one resource students worldwide use to improve their vocabulary. However, many students never learn to use them systematically. This section provides tips and practice for using dictionaries effectively.

Strategy—This section provides an introduction to a number of different vocabulary learning strategies, such as *using affixes* and *the keyword technique*, along with advice on how to use the strategies effectively.

Word Knowledge—In the main chapters, we focus on meaning, derivatives, and collocation. In this section of the Strategy Practice chapters, we explore other kinds of word knowledge, including frequency and academic phrases.

The Strategy Practice section also provides additional chances for students to use the academic words they have studied.

ASSESSMENT

Focus on Vocabulary is accompanied by a separate booklet with a Student Book Answer Key and Unit Tests. The tests give students additional vocabulary practice and assessment.

Focus on Vocabulary draws on our vocabulary research and many years of experience teaching vocabulary. We hope that you enjoy using it in your classes and that it helps your students learn the academic vocabulary they need to flourish in an academic environment.

Good Luck!

REFERENCES

Coxhead, A. (2000). A new academic word list. *TESOL Quarterly, 34*: 213–238.

Laufer, B. (1992). How much lexis is necessary for reading comprehension? In P. Arnaud and H. Bejoint (Eds.), *Vocabulary and applied linguistics* (pp. 126–132). Basingstoke, UK: Macmillan.

Hazenberg, S., and Hulstijn, J. (1996). Defining a minimal receptive second-language vocabulary for non-native university students: An empirical investigation. *Applied Linguistics, 17*: 145–163.

Nation, I.S.P. (1990). *Teaching and learning vocabulary*. New York: Heinle and Heinle.

Schmidt, R. (1990). The role of consciousness in second language learning. *Applied Linguistics, 11*: 129–158.

Schmitt, N. (2000). *Vocabulary in language teaching*. Cambridge, UK: Cambridge University Press.

Schmitt, N., and Zimmerman, C. B. (2002). Derivative word forms: What do learners know? *TESOL Quarterly, 36*: 145–171.

To the Student

WHY STUDY ACADEMIC VOCABULARY?

When studying in English, you will be required to read texts, write essays, respond to exam questions, and participate in class discussions. The English used in academic environments differs somewhat from the English you hear in informal social situations. A key component of academic style is the use of academic vocabulary. By focusing your vocabulary study on words that occur frequently in academic contexts, you will be able to develop your own academic style and achieve academic success.

Focus on Vocabulary is based on the Academic Word List, a list of 570 words that occur frequently across a range of academic subjects. If you learn these words in addition to a 2,000-word basic vocabulary, you will be able to understand more than 86 percent of the words you encounter in your academic reading.

WHAT DOES IT MEAN TO KNOW A WORD?

Although you will encounter most new academic vocabulary when you read, you will also need to be able to use those words when you speak, listen, and write. In order to use academic words effectively in your oral and written work, you must know more than simple word meanings. You must expand your knowledge of a word so that you know which meaning fits a particular context. You must learn which word form to use (for example, a noun or a verb) in a specific sentence. In addition, you must learn how to combine academic words with other words to form commonly used collocations. Many elements of word knowledge are required in order to choose the best word for a particular situation.

Complete the following Word Knowledge Quiz. It will help you understand the amount of word knowledge needed in order to truly understand a word. When you finish, check your answers on page xiv.

Word Knowledge Quiz

1. **Word Meaning**—Many words in English have more than one meaning. The word *bank* occurs frequently in English. Place a checkmark (✓) next to the correct meanings of *bank* below.

   _____ **a.** a business that keeps and lends money

   _____ **b.** land along the side of a river or lake

   _____ **c.** a place where human blood is stored until someone needs it

   _____ **d.** a large amount of clouds, mist, or fog

   _____ **e.** a large box or container in which things can be stored or moved

   _____ **f.** a large number of machines arranged close together in a row

   _____ **g.** the money that people can win in a gambling game

   _____ **h.** a slope made at a curve in a road to make it safe for cars to go around

2. **Spelling and Pronunciation**—Many words have similar spellings but are not pronounced in the same way. Look at the words in Set 1. Notice that the letters *ough* are pronounced in three different ways in these words. In Set 2, the letters *ch* are pronounced in three different ways.

For each set of words, write the word pairs that share the same sounds or pronunciations for *ough* or *ch*.

Set 1

th<u>ough</u>   th<u>ough</u>t   t<u>ough</u>   d<u>ough</u>   c<u>ough</u>   r<u>ough</u>

_____   _____   _____

_____   _____   _____

Set 2

<u>ch</u>aracter   <u>ch</u>air   ma<u>ch</u>ine   coa<u>ch</u>   heada<u>ch</u>e   mousta<u>ch</u>e

_____   _____   _____

_____   _____   _____

3. **Word Families**—Most words are part of a "family" of words that have a shared meaning. For example, the word forms *appear* (a verb) and *appearance* (a noun) are related. In each of the following sentences, one word form is incorrect. Cross it out and write the correct word form in the blank.

   a. A develop country needs to build up its industry. _____

   b. Here is a plan to develop the economic rapidly. _____

   c. I need to obtain more knowledgement in earth science. _____

   d. She worked on loan applications for a corporate. _____

4. **Collocation**—Some words appear together frequently. They are "word partners," or collocations. In the sentence below, circle the letter of the word that is <u>not</u> a good partner for the word *changed*.

   Napoleon *changed* French society _____ by creating the Civil Code and the Commercial Code.

   a. radically   **b.** dramatically   **c.** deeply   **d.** considerably

5. **Synonyms**—Do you understand slight differences in meaning well enough to select the right word for a particular sentence? The words *change, adapt,* and *modify* have similar meanings, but they are not exactly the same. Select and write the word that best fits each sentence below.

   a. The author wanted to _____ his book for children.

   b. The social worker tried to _____ the child's bad behavior.

   c. You can't _____ your mind after signing the contract.

(continued)

6. **Frequency**—All of the words in each group below have a similar meaning. However, some of the words are much more common in English than the others. Can you rank the words according to how frequently they occur in English? For each row of words, write 1 for the most frequent word, 2 for the next most frequent word, and 3 for the least frequent word.

   a. _____ device   _____ gadget   _____ machine

   b. _____ errand   _____ job   _____ task

7. **Associations**—As you get to know a word better, it becomes "linked" in your mind with other words. These links, or associations, can help you use the word faster and more naturally. Ninety-eight native English speakers were asked to name words that they associated with the word *hungry*. Circle the words you think they associated with *hungry*.

empty	food	house	starving
sad	winter	thirsty	tired

The exercises in *Focus on Vocabulary* will help you increase your understanding of each kind of word knowledge listed above. Some of these topics (word meanings, word families, and collocations) will be focused on in the main chapters, while others will be highlighted in the Strategy Practice chapters. As you work your way through the book, you will learn many new academic words. However, you will find that you learn more than just the words' meanings; you will also gain a broad understanding of the way the words function in academic texts.

VOCABULARY CARDS—A KEY VOCABULARY LEARNING STRATEGY

Focus on Vocabulary will teach you many strategies for learning academic words. Using vocabulary cards is one such strategy. Look at the example of a vocabulary card below. This card was created by a Japanese student who wanted to understand and remember the word *horror*. Study the card and read the directions for creating vocabulary cards of your own.

(Front of card)

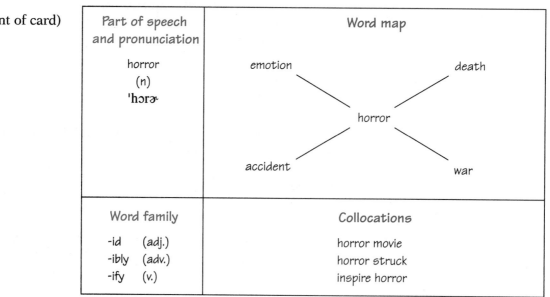

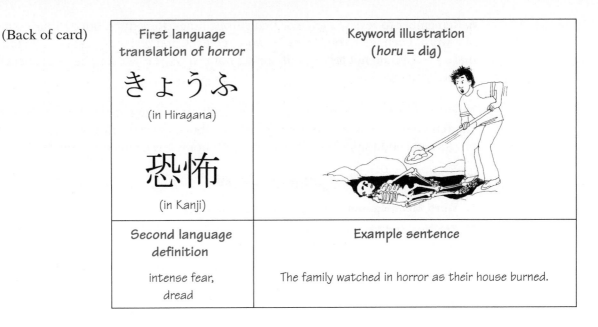

(Back of card)

First language translation of *horror*	Keyword illustration (*horu* = dig)
きょうふ (in Hiragana) 恐怖 (in Kanji)	
Second language definition intense fear, dread	Example sentence The family watched in horror as their house burned.

HOW TO CREATE AND USE VOCABULARY CARDS

To make your own vocabulary cards for the words in this book, follow these steps.

1. Write the English word in the top left corner of the front of the card. Then write the word's meaning in the top left corner of the back of the card. Include anything that tells the meaning, for example, first language translations or English definitions. With this information, you can start using the card to learn the word. The card pictured above is for a Japanese student learning the English word *horror*; therefore, it has two Japanese translations, one in Hiragana spelling and one in Kanji spelling.

2. When you review the card, add new information to it in the different sections. This will make you think more deeply about the word and will expand your word knowledge. Include the following kinds of information on your card:

- an example sentence for the word
- notes on how to form the other members of the word family
- a word map with related words
- a list of collocations
- any other information you find interesting or important

3. Consider adding a memory picture to the card. This is called the *keyword technique*. In the sample card above, the student drew a picture of someone digging up a skeleton because the English word *horror* sounds like the Japanese word *horu* (meaning "dig"), and a skeleton evokes horror. You will learn more about how to use the keyword technique in Chapter 24.

4. Keep filling out the different sections until you know the word well. For some words, you may need to complete all of the sections. For other words, you may need less information.

5. Keep your cards in a box or folder. Take some cards out and study them often. They are portable, so you can even take them with you and study them on the way to and from school or work. As you learn a word better, move its card toward the back of your box so you will not study it as often. Put cards for new words toward the front, where you will see them more often.

6. Remember to review each word numerous times. Repetition builds your memory of a word. Even after you "know" a word, go back and review it occasionally to make sure you do not forget it. If you do not review, you will lose all of the benefits of your previous study!

As you study the academic words in this book, try making vocabulary cards to help you remember the words. Studying with vocabulary cards will enrich the learning process and add to the knowledge gained by doing the exercises in the book.

Answers to the Quiz on pages x–xii

1. Word Meaning—All meanings are correct except e.

2. Spelling and Pronunciation

Set 1

The following word pairs share the same pronunciation for *ough*:

though /ðoʊ/	thought /θɔt/	tough /tʌf/
dough /doʊ/	cough /kɔf/	rough /rʌf/

Read the words aloud to compare the three pronunciations.

Set 2

The following word pairs share the same pronunciation for *ch*:

character /ˈkærɪktɚ/	chair /tʃɛr/	machine /məˈʃin/
headache /ˈhɛdeɪk/	coach /koʊtʃ/	moustache /ˈmʌstæʃ/

Read the words aloud to compare the three pronunciations.

If you are unfamiliar with phonetic spellings, please look at the chart on page 134 in Chapter 16, which gives an explanation of the various phonetic symbols.

3. Word Families
   a. ~~develop~~   developing
   b. ~~economic~~   economy
   c. ~~knowledgement~~   knowledge
   d. ~~corporate~~   corporation

4. Collocation—c

5. Synonyms
   a. This type of literary transformation is usually described by the word *adapt*.
   b. *Modify* means to change, but usually in a way that leads to improvement.
   c. *Change* is used to describe an adjustment in mental thinking or perspective, especially in the phrase "change your mind."

6. Frequency
   The figures in parentheses show how often these words occur per million words. The words are listed in order of decreasing occurrence.
   a. machine (140.26)   device (55.16)   gadget (2.24)
   b. job (306.27)   task (139.91)   errand (2.69)

7. Associations
   The associations the students gave included:

   food   thirsty   tired   empty   starving

About the Authors

▶ Diane Schmitt began teaching English in Japan and currently lives and teaches in the United Kingdom. She is Academic Team Leader for EFL/TESOL at Nottingham Trent University, where she coordinates all English language instruction at the university. She also contributes to the master's program in English Language Teaching. Her research interests include issues related to the acquisition of English for academic purposes and second-language testing. She is a regular contributor to English teaching conferences.

▶ Norbert Schmitt began his EFL teaching career in Japan, where he taught all levels of students for six years. After completing his Ph.D., he began lecturing at the University of Nottingham, where he is currently Reader of Applied Linguistics and Co-Director of the Centre for Research in Applied Linguistics. He is an active researcher in all aspects of second-language vocabulary studies and has published several books and numerous research papers in this area. He frequently presents at language-teaching conferences and consults on vocabulary learning and testing issues internationally.

AUTHORS' ACKNOWLEDGMENTS

We would like to thank Laura Le Dréan and the team at Longman who have helped to bring this project to fruition. In particular, we are grateful to Longman for allowing us access to their corpus and for providing the concordancing software. We would also like to thank the students and teaching staff at Nottingham Trent University for their continuous encouragement as they piloted successive versions of the material in this book.

Finally we would like to thank the following reviewers for their valuable comments: Thomas Adams, University of Pennsylvania, Philadelphia, PA; Richard Atkinson, Le Collège de Limoilou (Cégep), Charlesbourg, Quebec, Canada; Susan Carkin, Utah State University, Logan, UT; Michael Climo, Los Angeles Mission College, Sylmar, CA; Thomas Davis, Seattle Central Community College, Seattle, WA; Lynne Diaz-Rico, California State University, San Bernardino, CA; Anthony Halderman, Cuesta College, San Luis Obispo, CA; Marlise Horst, Concordia University, Montreal, Québec, Canada; Gwen Kane, Middlesex Community College, Edison, NJ; Jane Leshinsky, International Language Center, Denver, CO; Madeline Medeiros, Cuesta College, San Luis Obispo, CA; Christine Meloni, George Washington University, Washington, DC; Margaret Plenert, California State University, Fullerton, CA; Hollis (Mel) Shaw, Houston Community College, Houston, TX; Kathy Sherak, San Francisco State University, San Francisco, CA; Debbie Stone, Bellevue Community College, Bellevue, WA; Mary Westervelt, University of Pennsylvania, Philadelphia, PA; Maria Zlateva, Harvard University, Cambridge, MA.

1

Our Changing Society

1

Technology and Society

GETTING STARTED

Discuss the following questions with your classmates.

▶ What aspects of our society have changed the most during the past fifty years?

▶ What is one important cause of social change?

▶ In what ways are societies today better or worse than they were 300 years ago? Give some examples.

TARGET WORDS — Assessing Your Vocabulary Knowledge

When you study vocabulary, it is important to notice both the number of new words you are learning and how much your knowledge of previously studied words is increasing. Use the following scale to determine your knowledge of the academic words in this chapter.

1 I don't know this word.

2 I have seen this word before, but I am not sure of the meaning.

3 I understand the word when I see it or hear it in a sentence, but I don't know how to use it in my own speaking and writing.

4 I know this word and can use it in my own speaking and writing.

Look at each of the target words in the box. Use the scale to give yourself a score for each word. After you finish the chapter, score yourself again to check your improvement.

TARGET WORDS

_____capacity	_____diverse	_____evidence	_____item
_____complex	_____element	_____evolve	_____manipulate
_____consequences	_____encounter	_____furthermore	_____neutral
_____contemporary	_____environment	_____generation	_____source
_____contrast	_____estimate	_____global	_____symbolize
_____decline	_____eventually	_____interact	_____transform

The following passage is adapted from an introductory textbook on sociology. The passage introduces the concept of society and societal change. As you read, pay special attention to the target vocabulary words in **bold**.

HUMAN SOCIETIES—FROM THE ICEMAN TO US

1 *"I thought at first it was a doll's head,"* said Helmut Simon, a German tourist who, in 1991, made one of the scientific finds of the century. Simon was hiking across a huge glacier in southwest Austria near the Italian border when he stumbled upon a familiar shape protruding from the melting ice. He soon realized that it was not a doll but a human body: the so-called "Iceman," who died some 5,300 years ago, making him the oldest member of our species to be discovered essentially intact.

2 Imagine you were born some 300 years ago, in the year 1700. Although this is very recent in terms of the billions of years of the existence of Planet Earth, you would still have been living in a remarkably different world. You would never have been to a shopping mall. You would never have **encountered** the world of cars, railways, airplanes, telephones, cameras, computers, and televisions. And more than this, the idea of voting for your government, going to college, choosing your religion, or even choosing your identity would all have been rare. Welcome to the modern world!

3 Life has certainly changed in 300 years, and sociology was born out of a concern with this rapidly changing character of the modern, industrial world: with where we have come from and where we are heading. For sociologists, the term *society* means "all the people who **interact** in a defined space and share culture." In this sense, both a continent like Europe and specific individual countries such as Norway or Japan may be seen as societies.

4 Even humans living thousands of years ago were members of early human societies. **Evidence** of this comes from the discovery of the Iceman. Examining the Iceman's clothes, scientists were astonished at how advanced this "caveman's" society was. The Iceman's hair was neatly cut, and his body had numerous tattoos that probably **symbolized** his standing in the community. He wore a skillfully sewn leather coat over which a grass cape provided even

The Austrian Iceman

greater protection from the weather. His shoes, also made of leather, were stuffed with grass for comfort and warmth. He carried with him an axe, a wood-handled knife, and a bow that shot feathered arrows with stone points. A primitive backpack held additional tools and personal **items**, including natural medicines made from plants. It is **estimated** that he died some 5,300 years ago—before a great empire existed in Egypt, before the flowering of culture in ancient Greece, and before any society in Europe built a single city. As people who take for granted rapid transportation and instant **global** communication, we can look on this ancestor as a connection to our distant past.

5 Sociologists have identified great differences among societies that have flourished and **declined** throughout human history. They have observed how societies change over centuries as the people in them gain greater ability to **manipulate** their natural **environment**. Societies with basic technology can support only a small number of people who enjoy few choices about how to live. Technologically **complex** societies—while not necessarily "better" in any absolute sense—develop large populations; people in these societies are likely to lead **diverse**, highly specialized lives.

6   The greater the amount of technological skill and knowledge a society has, the faster the rate at which the society changes. Technologically simple societies, then, change very slowly. Take, for example, some of the clothing worn by the Austrian Iceman. It differs only slightly from clothes used by shepherds in the same area of the world early in the twentieth century. In **contrast** to simpler societies, industrial, technologically advanced societies change so quickly that people witness remarkable **transformations** within their lifetimes. Again, consider some familiar **elements** of **contemporary** culture that would probably puzzle, delight, and possibly frighten people who lived just a few **generations** ago: fast food, faxes, mobile phones, computer games, artificial hearts, fiber optics, test-tube babies, and many, many others. Indeed it is a strange modern world we live in—even when compared with the world of the recent past.

7   Consider also the countless **consequences** of technological change. When our ancestors first harnessed the power of the wind by using a sail, they set the stage for the invention of kites, sailing ships, windmills, and, **eventually,** airplanes. We are only now beginning to see how our modern lives are being changed by recent technologies like atomic energy or the computer.

8   Sociologists divide societies into five types according to their technologies: (1) hunting and gathering societies, (2) horticultural and pastoral societies, (3) agrarian societies, (4) industrial societies, and (5) post-industrial societies. *Hunting and gathering societies* use simple technologies to gather food from nature, such as hunting animals and picking berries. *Horticultural and pastoral societies* grow their own plants and raise animals to eat. *Agrarian societies*—which first appeared around the time of the Iceman—use technologies such as animal-drawn plows to farm on a larger scale. Agrarian societies were also the first to develop such technological innovations as irrigation, the wheel, writing, numbers, and expanded uses for metals. *Industrial societies* use technology that powers sophisticated machinery with advanced **sources** of energy. Before the industrial era, the major **source** of energy was the muscle power of humans and animals. In industrial societies, people learn mechanical skills so that they can operate the machinery needed to produce material goods. These societies **transformed** themselves more in a century than previous societies had in thousands of years. *Post-industrial societies*—like the ones many of us live in today—have developed technologies that support an information-based economy. People in these societies create, process, store, and apply information through the use of computers, fax machines, satellites, and other forms of communication technology.

9   Technology has a big impact on a society, but in itself it is **neutral**. People are the ones who decide how to use technology and whether it is used for good or bad purposes. Armed with the **capacity** to reshape the world, human societies must understand both the social benefits and problems caused by the desire for technological change. **Furthermore**, it is important to note that the five types of societies described above do not **evolve** from one type to another in an automatic process. In fact, in modern times, all of these societies may be said to coexist.

Adapted from Macionis, J. J. and Plummer, K. (1997). *Sociology: A Global Introduction.* New York: Prentice Hall Europe, pp. 64–75.

UNDERSTANDING THE READING

Respond to the following in writing. Base your responses on the reading and your own personal experiences.

1. What do sociologists mean by the term *society*? Do you agree with this definition? Why or why not?
2. Describe three technological advances in recent years that have changed the society you live in.
3. How are technologically advanced societies different from societies with simpler technologies? Give an example of how they differ.

WORD MEANING

This book presents a variety of strategies for learning and remembering the meanings of academic words. Sometimes you will be able to find clues to a word's meaning in the sentence in which the word appears. In other cases, the sentence will not contain clear clues to word meaning. You may need to reread the section in which the word appears and think about the ideas presented in the text. If you still are unsure of the correct definition, you may need to look the word up in a dictionary. For more help in finding the right meaning of a word, read the *Using Your Dictionary* section on page 31 of Chapter 4.

Match the words with their definitions. If you are unsure about a word's meaning, try to figure it out from the context by rereading the passage on pages 3–4. Then check your dictionary. The first one has been done for you.

Set 1

___c__ **1.** source

_____**2.** diverse

_____**3.** estimate

_____**4.** encounter

_____**5.** complex

_____**6.** neutral

_____**7.** item

a. having many closely related parts or details

b. not supporting one purpose or cause above another

c. a thing, place, activity, etc. that something comes from

d. different or varied

e. a single thing in a set, group, or list

f. to judge an amount partly by calculating and partly by guessing

g. to meet someone or experience something without planning to

Set 2

_____**1.** interact

_____**2.** element

_____**3.** contemporary

_____**4.** generation

_____**5.** consequences

_____**6.** manipulate

_____**7.** contrast

a. the average period of time between the birth of a person and the birth of that person's children

b. a basic or important part of something

c. to talk or work together with others

d. to skillfully handle, control, or use something

e. a difference

f. the results of a particular action or situation

g. belonging to the present time; modern

Read the row of words and phrases below each numbered word. One word or phrase in each list is *not* a synonym (word or phrase with a similar meaning) for the numbered word. Cross it out. The first one has been done for you.

1. evolve
develop   change   ~~correct~~   grow

2. global
limited   international   overall   worldwide

3. environment

| setting | pollution | surroundings | situation |

4. evidence

| facts | information | proof | belief |

5. symbolize

| be an emblem of | change | stand for | represent |

6. transform

| change | make over | succeed | alter |

7. furthermore

| in addition | on the other hand | also | moreover |

8. eventually

| finally | sooner or later | in the end | in a short time |

9. decline

| go down | improve | weaken | fall |

10. capacity

| ability | power | progress | competence |

WORD TIP

▶ The word **generation** often becomes a label for a specific group of people. Examples:

*Baby Boom **Generation*** refers to people born after World War II up to 1964.

***Generation** X* is used to describe people born during the late 1960s and 1970s in the United States.

***Generation** 1.5* is a label for young people who have had much of their schooling in the United States though they were born elsewhere.

▶ When part of a title or label, **generation** may be capitalized.

WORD FAMILIES

Most words belong to a "family" of words with a shared meaning. For example, the word forms *serious* (an adjective), *seriousness* (a noun), and *seriously* (an adverb) are related to one another. To know which form to use, you must figure out the word's part of speech in a sentence. In the reading "Human Societies," forms of the word *technology* appear seventeen times. The differences in the spelling indicate different parts of speech as shown below.

Verb	Noun	Adjective	Adverb
X = no form	technology	technological	technologically

Notice the endings for *technolog**ical*** and *technolog**ically***. These spelling patterns are common at the end of certain adjective and adverb forms. If you aren't sure of the form of a word, you can look the word up in a dictionary. If you need more help in finding the correct word form, read the *Using Your Dictionary* section on page 31 of Chapter 4.

The table below contains word families for some of the target words in the reading. Complete the chart. An *X* indicates that there is no form or that the form is not common. Sometimes there may be more than one form possible. If you are unsure about a form, check your dictionary.

Verb	Noun	Adjective	Adverb
X		complex	X
diversify	1. diversity 2. diversification	diverse	diversely
estimate	1. estimate 2. estimation	estimated	X
X	eventuality		eventually
evolve		evolving	X
X	1. globe 2. globalization	global	globally
interact	interaction	interactive	interactively
symbolize	1. symbol 2.	symbolic	symbolically
transform	transformation		X

Choose the correct form of the word in **bold** in sentence **a** to complete sentence **b**. Use the word families table you just completed as a guide. The first one has been done for you.

1. **a.** Communication is one area in which there have been amazing developments in **technology**.

   b. ___Technologically___ advanced methods of growing food have still not prevented hunger in some parts of the world.

2. **a.** Visitors to a new country are encouraged to **interact** with the local people to learn more about their culture.

   b. Social _____ is an important part of childhood development.

3. **a.** Environmentalists work to save endangered plants and animals in part to protect biological **diversity** in the natural world.

   b. Major soft drink companies have _____ their product lines by adding bottled water as a new product.

4. **a.** The **estimation** that one-fifth of Americans are seriously overweight is shocking.

   b. Historians _____ that among the more than 1,500 people who died on the *Titanic,* class, age, and sex played a key role in who lived and who died.

5. a. The worldwide popularity of products like the Walkman is an example of **globalization**.

    b. Governments and environmental groups use the phrase "Think

    _____, act locally" to encourage people to think of ways to save resources every day.

6. a. Both a red cross and a red crescent are used to **symbolize** the international organization whose aim is to protect and provide assistance to victims of war.

    b. Being overweight was at one time a _____ of wealth because it showed that you had enough money to eat well.

7. a. Many people feel that the job of being a parent today is much more **complex** than it was in the past.

    b. The _____ of the relationship between technological development and environmental change is still not fully understood.

8. a. Since the fall of the Berlin Wall in 1989, many Eastern European Communist parties have **transformed** themselves into Socialist parties.

    b. The newly _____ factory now houses forty young professionals living in luxury apartments.

9. a. The **eventual** end of the strike occurred after long discussions between union leaders and the employer.

    b. One purpose of insurance is to protect people from _____ that they cannot otherwise prepare for in advance.

10. a. Languages as diverse as Danish and Chinese have influenced the **evolution** of the English language.

    b. Because medical technology is always _____, doctors must regularly attend training programs.

COLLOCATION

When you look at words in context, you can see patterns in the way they are used. These patterns are not based on rules of grammar, but on traditions of use by native speakers. Certain words tend to occur together, and this is called *collocation*.

> For example, we say: *tall girl, tall building* and *high wall, high point*
> But we do not say: *high girl, high building* or *tall wall, tall point*

Sometimes the link between word partners and their meaning is clear and unsurprising, for example, in the collocations *bright light* or *heavy load*. Other times, the link may be unexpected, as when we say *bright child* or *heavy heart*.

Here are some typical collocation patterns:

noun + verb	*birds sing*
verb + noun	*deliver babies*
adjective + noun	*specific information*
verb + adverb	*breathe heavily*
noun + noun	*bear market*

Because collocations are not based on rules of grammar, the patterns for each word are one of a kind. Therefore, you must build up your knowledge of collocations one at a time. This section introduces a sample of the patterns you need to know in your academic reading and writing. Apply your growing understanding of collocations to new words and words you already know.

The following exercise asks you to use collocations in sentences of your own. Study the way the collocations are used in the example sentences. Pay close attention to the words around the collocations, particularly articles and prepositions. For example, in item 1 below, notice the prepositions *for* and *of* after **damaging consequences**. *For* indicates the receiver of **damaging consequences**. *Of* indicates the creator (cause) of the **damaging consequences**. Imitate the patterns you observe when you use the collocations in your own sentences.

Each item below contains three sentences with the same collocation. Write a fourth sentence of your own using the same word partners. The first one has been done for you.

1. **a.** The news report resulted in **damaging consequences** for the company.
    b. Pollution in the oceans can have very **damaging consequences** for ocean life.
    c. The **damaging consequences** of unemployment affect all levels of society.
    d. <u>The failure of the bank will have damaging consequences for its customers.</u>

2. **a.** The **rapid decline** in housing prices had a negative effect on the economy.
    b. The team's failure to win any games led to a **rapid decline** in fan support.
    c. Because of the **rapid decline** in the patient's health, the doctor had to perform an emergency operation.
    d. _____

3. **a.** There is **mounting evidence** that some types of fish will disappear completely from the North Sea if overfishing is not stopped.
    b. The education department has **mounting evidence** that the newly introduced tests are not leading to higher standards of teaching and learning.
    c. There is **mounting** scientific **evidence** that global warming is damaging the earth's atmosphere.
    d. _____

4. **a.** University **sources confirmed** that tuition prices would rise next year.
    b. Government **sources confirmed** that the president would travel to the Far East in early spring.
    c. Media **sources confirmed** that fighting had restarted in the war zone.
    d. _____

5. **a.** The **basic elements** of an enjoyable movie are a good story and interesting characters.
    b. Soy products are a **basic element** of many Chinese and Japanese recipes.
    c. A **basic element** of the new economic plan was a reduction in taxes for the poor and elderly.
    d. _____

6. **a.** The United Nations issued a resolution to **protect** the **environment**.
 b. Every country needs to do its part to **protect** the **environment**.
 c. We can **protect** the **environment** by using nonpolluting sources of energy, such as wind power.

 d. _____

7. **a.** The **earning capacity** of a woman in her lifetime is generally much less than that of a man.
 b. Government officials argue that the cost of tuition for college students is offset by increased **earning capacity** after graduation.
 c. Variations in the **earning capacity** of stocks and bonds are related to rises and falls in the market.

 d. _____

8. **a.** There is often a **marked contrast** between the cost of living in cities and the cost of living in rural areas.
 b. Voters observed a **marked contrast** between the politician's pre-election promises and his voting record in Congress.
 c. Teachers have noticed a **marked contrast** in behavior between children who do not have breakfast before school and those who do.

 d. _____

EXPANSION

An important part of academic study is forming and supporting opinions about the topic you are studying. Read the statements below and indicate whether you agree **(A)** or disagree **(D)**. Then discuss your opinions and reasoning with a partner.

_____ **1.** The **globalization** of **contemporary** culture will **eventually** destroy the uniqueness of **diverse** societies.

_____ **2.** It is no longer realistic for the members of one **generation** to expect their standard of living to be significantly better than that of the previous generation.

_____ **3.** All governments should cut back on military spending. **Furthermore**, the money saved should be used to support the neediest members of society.

_____ **4.** Governments should charge higher taxes on luxury **items** so that necessities such as heating oil and clothing can be sold tax free.

_____ **5.** There is not enough **interaction** between teenagers and their parents these days.

_____ **6.** Taking a position of **neutrality** in times of disagreement is a sign of weakness.

_____ **7.** Newspapers unfairly **manipulate** public opinion by printing one-sided news stories.

_____ **8.** Young people today are likely to **encounter** more difficulties in their lives than their parents did **a generation** ago.

 Now choose one of the statements above and write a personal essay about it. Express your opinions and reasoning, and be sure to provide support for your opinions.

2 Social Experience and Personal Development

GETTING STARTED

Discuss the following questions with your classmates.

▶ Who influenced you most when you were growing up?

▶ Do you think this person (or group of people) had an important role in shaping the kind of person you are today? Why or why not?

▶ What kind of influence would you like to have on the next generation?

TARGET WORDS—Assessing Your Vocabulary Knowledge

Look at each of the target words in the box. Use the scale to give yourself a score for each word. After you finish the chapter, score yourself again to check your improvement.

1 I don't know this word.

2 I have seen this word before, but I am not sure of the meaning.

3 I understand the word when I see it or hear it in a sentence, but I don't know how to use it in my own speaking and writing.

4 I know this word and can use it in my own speaking and writing.

TARGET WORDS

_____ affect	_____ conflict	_____ ethnicity	_____ range
_____ apparent	_____ conform	_____ evaluation	_____ retain
_____ aspect	_____ contact	_____ gender	_____ rigid
_____ attitude	_____ distinction	_____ media	_____ significance
_____ concept	_____ document	_____ persist	_____ style
_____ confer	_____ dominance	_____ process	_____ vary

The following passage is adapted from an introductory textbook on sociology. The passage focuses on four factors that influence our social development today. As you read, pay special attention to the target vocabulary words in **bold**.

SOCIAL FORCES THAT SHAPE OUR LIVES

1   Every social experience we have **affects** us in at least some small way. In modern industrial and post-industrial societies, however, there are four familiar influences that have special **significance** in the socialization **process**. They are the family, schooling, peer groups, and the mass media.

THE FAMILY

2   The family is the most important agent of socialization because it represents the center of children's lives. Babies are almost totally dependent on others, and the responsibility of meeting their needs almost always falls on parents and other family members. At least until the start of schooling, the family is responsible for teaching children cultural values, **attitudes**, and prejudices about themselves and others.

3   Family-based socialization is not entirely intentional. Children learn continuously from the kind of environment that adults create for them. Whether children learn to think of themselves as strong or weak, smart or stupid, loved or simply tolerated, and whether they believe the world to be safe or dangerous largely stems from this early environment that adults create.

4   Parenting **styles** aside, parental attention is important in the social development of children. Physical **contact**, verbal stimulation, and openness from parents and others all encourage intellectual growth.

5   The family also **confers** on children a specific social position; that is, parents not only bring children into the physical world, they also place them in society in terms of race, **ethnicity**, religion, and class. In time, all of these elements become part of a child's self-**concept**, or idea of him or her self. Of course, some **aspects** of social position may change later on, but social standing at birth **affects** us throughout our lives. In many ways, then, parents teach their children to follow in their footsteps.

SCHOOLING

6   Schooling stretches children's social world to include people with social backgrounds that differ from their own. As children encounter social diversity, they learn the **significance** society gives to people's race and sex, and they often act accordingly: for instance, studies **document** the tendency of children to gather together in play groups composed of one race and **gender**.

7   Formally, schooling teaches children a wide **range** of knowledge and skills. But schools provide a host of other lessons informally through what sociologists call the *hidden curriculum*. Activities such as spelling tests and sports teach children key cultural values such as competitive success. Children also receive countless formal and informal messages supporting their society's way of life as morally good.

8   Moving beyond the personal web of family life, children entering school soon discover that **evaluations** of skills like reading and arithmetic are based on impersonal, standardized tests. Here, the focus changes from *who* they are to *how* they perform. Of course, the confidence or anxiety that children develop at home can have a **significant** effect on how well they perform in school.

9   School is also most children's first experience with **rigid** formality. The school day runs on a strict timetable, and children are encouraged to **conform** to impersonal rules and be on time. Not surprisingly, **conformity** and punctuality are the same kinds of behavior expected by most of the large organizations that will employ these same children later in life.

10   Schools also socialize children with regard to **gender**. Although **gender** roles are evolving, in the first years of school, boys often take part in more physical activities and spend more time outdoors, while girls tend to be less active. **Gender distinctions** continue into the later grades and **persist** right through college:

women, for example, encounter pressure to choose degrees in the arts or humanities, while men are steered toward the physical sciences.

THE PEER GROUP

11 By the time they enter school, children have also discovered the *peer group*, a social group whose members have interests, social position, and age in common. A young child's peer group is generally made up of neighborhood friends; later, peer groups are composed of friends from school or elsewhere.

A peer group

12 Unlike the family and the school, the peer group allows young people to escape from the direct control of adults. With this newfound independence, members of peer groups gain valuable experience in forming social relationships on their own and developing a sense of themselves apart from their families. Peer groups also give young people the opportunity to discuss interests that may not be shared by adults (such as fashion and popular music) or are not approved of by parents (such as violent movies or video games).

13 For the young, the attraction of the peer group lies in the ever-present possibility of activity not permitted by adults; for the same reason, parents express concern about who their children's friends are. In a rapidly changing society, peer groups often rival parents in influence, as the **attitudes** of parents and children separate along the lines of a "generation gap." The **dominance** of peer groups is typically strongest during the teenage years, as young people begin to break away

from their families and think of themselves as responsible adults. At this stage of life, young people often show anxious **conformity** to peers because this new identity and sense of belonging eases some of the anxiety brought on by breaking away from the family.

14 The **conflict** between parents and peers may be more **apparent** than real, however, for even during the teenage years, children remain strongly influenced by their families. Peers may guide short-term concerns such as fashion and musical taste, but parents **retain** greater influence over the long-term goals of their children. One study, for example, found that parents had more influence than even best friends on young people's educational aspirations.

THE MASS MEDIA

15 The fourth major influence on social development is the mass **media**—impersonal communications directed to a vast audience. The term *media* is a Latin word meaning "middle," suggesting that the **media** function to connect people. Today, more than ever, the mass **media**—television, radio, and newspapers—have a great impact on our lives. For this reason, they are an important element in the socialization **process**. Television, introduced in 1939, has rapidly become the **dominant** means of communication throughout the world. Just how dependent on television are we? Figures **vary** by group, nation, class, and **gender**, but "average homes" may well keep a television on for seven hours or more each day. Years before children learn to read, watching television has become a regular habit and, as they grow up, young girls and boys spend as many hours in front of a television as they do in school. Indeed, children spend as much time watching television as they do interacting with their parents.

16 Family, schooling, peers, and mass **media** all have an impact on how we are socialized as children. Each of these social influences has the power to shape our thoughts, feelings, and actions. Yet, as free humans, we also have the ability to act back on society and, in so doing, shape our own lives and the world we live in, as is evident in the changes that have occurred in **gender** roles in the last thirty years.

Adapted from Macionis, J.J. and Plummer, K. (1997). *Sociology: A Global Introduction*. New York: Prentice Hall Europe, pp. 139–141.

Respond to the following in writing. Base your responses on the reading and your own personal experiences.

1. Describe each of the four factors that shape our social development. Give examples of how each factor shapes us.
2. How are the influence of family and the influence of peer groups related to each other?
3. In what ways can peer groups have a positive influence? In what ways can they have a negative effect? Give examples.

FOCUSING ON VOCABULARY

WORD MEANING

Many words have more than one meaning. When you come across an unfamiliar word in your reading, you can look the word up in a dictionary. If the word has multiple meanings, use context clues—words and phrases around the word—to figure out which meaning fits. For example, read the two definitions for *significance* in the following exercise. Go back to paragraph 1 of the reading and examine the context in which the target word appears: *. . . there are four familiar influences that have special **significance** in the socialization process*. Read both definitions and choose the one that fits the context. Substitute that meaning for the target word and see whether the sentence makes sense.

Each of the following target words appears in the reading on pages 12–13. Use the paragraph number in parentheses to locate each word in context. Read the dictionary definitions below. Write the letter of the definition that reflects how the word is used in the reading. The first one has been done for you.

   _b_   **1. significance** (1)
        a. the meaning of a word, sign, action, etc., especially when this is not immediately clear
        b. the importance of an event, action, etc., especially because of the influences it will have in the future

        2. process (1)
        a. a system or a treatment of materials that is used to produce goods
        b. a series of human actions or operations that are performed intentionally to reach a particular result

        3. attitude (2)
        a. the way that you behave toward someone or something, especially when this shows how you feel
        b. a style or behavior that shows you have the confidence to do daring things without caring what others think

        4. style (4)
        a. the particular way that someone behaves, works, or deals with other people
        b. a particular design or fashion, especially for something such as clothes, hair, furniture, etc.

_____**5. contact** (4)

    a. communication or meeting with a person, organization, country, etc., or the occasion on which the communication takes place

    b. the act or state of touching or being close to someone or something

_____**6. aspect** (5)

    a. the direction in which a window, room, or door faces

    b. one part of a situation, idea, plan, etc., that has many parts

_____**7. range** (7)

    a. a number of different things of the same general type

    b. the distance within which something can be seen or heard

_____**8. rigid** (9)

    a. physically stiff and not moving or bending

    b. strict or difficult to change

_____**9. distinction** (10)

    a. a clear difference between things

    b. the quality of being unusually good

_____**10. conflict** (14)

    a. a state of disagreement or argument between people, groups, countries, etc.

    b. a situation in which there is a choice between two or more opposing things

_____**11. apparent** (14)

    a. seeming to be real or true, although it may not really be so

    b. easily noticed or understood

_____**12. retain** (14)

    a. to keep something or continue to have something

    b. to keep facts in your memory

Each sentence below contains a paraphrase or set of synonyms for a target word. Read each sentence and then select the matching target word from the box. The first one has been done for you.

affect	conform	~~ethnicity~~	media
concept	document	evaluation	persist
confers	dominance	gender	vary

1. Employers cannot ask about _____*ethnicity*_____ on job

(race, nationality)
   application forms.

2. The older boy's _____ over the younger children

(power, control)
   worried some parents.

3. Overseas travel can _____ a person's view of

(influence, change)
   the world.

4. Ideas of correct parenting _____ from culture

(differ, contrast)
   to culture.

5. Parents _____ their children's early life through the
   (record, set down)
   family photo album.

6. The teacher's positive _____ of the student's work
   (assessment, judgment)
   increased her confidence.

7. Heavy rain will _____ throughout the weekend.
   (continue, carry on)

8. Many teenagers do not want to _____ to their
   (adapt, adjust)
   parents' style of dress or taste in music.

9. The event was widely publicized in the local _____.
   (newspaper, radio)

10. One goal of public schooling is to help children develop a(n)

    _____ of social responsibility.
    (idea, view)

11. A country's constitution _____ (on) its citizens
    (gives, bestows)
    certain rights and responsibilities.

12. Writers will often use plural forms to replace the pronouns "he" and "she" in

    order to avoid _____ bias in their writing.
    (sexual identity, female or male)

WORD TIP

> ▶ Note that social scientists often use the word **_gender_** to refer to a social or
> cultural distinction, while they use the word **_sex_** to refer to a biological distinction,
> male or female.
>
> **_Gender_** affects the total salary people will receive in their lifetime.
>
> Scientific and technological advances allow expectant parents to find out
> the **_sex_** of their baby before it is born.

WORD FAMILIES

Most of the target words introduced in this chapter are part of a word family. By
learning the other members of a word's family, you can recognize words more
quickly when you read or listen, and you can express yourself more clearly when
you write or speak. Spelling patterns can help you identify a word's part of speech.
For example, look at the first column in the table on page 17. Two of the verb forms
have the spelling pattern -*ate*. In the noun column, the spelling patterns -*tion* and -*ity*
occur twice. Getting to know these familiar spelling patterns will help you figure out
a word's part of speech and know how to use a word correctly in a sentence.

Study the members of the word families in the table on the facing page. Look for
spelling patterns for the verb, noun, adjective, and adverb forms of the words.
Complete the table. List the patterns in the spaces. The verb and noun columns have
been done for you.

Verb	Noun	Adjective	Adverb
conform	conformity	X	X
contact	contact	contact	X
X	distinction	1. distinct 2. distinctive	1. distinctly 2. distinctively
dominate	domination	1. dominant 2. dominating	X
X	ethnicity	ethnic	ethnically
evaluate	evaluation	evaluative	X
	persistence	persistent	persistently
X	rigidity	rigid	rigidly
X	significance	significant	significantly
	variation	varied	X
Spelling patterns			
-ate	-ity, -tion, -ance, -ence		

Read each sentence and identify the part of speech of the missing word. Write an appropriate form of the target word in the blank. Use the word families table above to help you. The first one has been done for you.

1. Because it burns more cleanly, natural gas has a _____significant_____ (**significance**) environmental advantage over oil.

2. Even a small _____ (**vary**) in the amount of medicine given to a person who is sick can have serious consequences.

3. Teenagers often rebel against the _____ (**conform**) of school uniforms by personalizing book bags and notebooks with decorations.

4. There are _____ (**persist**) rumors that the software company will soon go out of business.

5. Although the sound was coming from far away, he could still hear it _____ (**distinct**).

6. Britain was the _____ (**dominate**) international power during the nineteenth century.

7. _____ (**contact**) lenses made out of glass were first developed in Germany in 1887.

8. The subjective nature of literature makes it difficult to _____ (**evaluation**) the true worth of any particular story or poem.

9. The strength of a building or bridge largely depends on the
   _____ (**rigid**) of the materials used to build it.

10. While factors such as age and gender do significantly affect participation in
    sports, factors such as marital status and _____ (**ethnic**) do not.

COLLOCATION

You develop your knowledge of collocations by seeing and hearing words in many
contexts and noticing which words form partnerships with one another.
Remember that collocations can contain different parts of speech and perform
different grammatical functions within a sentence, as shown in the examples
below.

Examples:

a. Weak students often have a **bad attitude** toward completing homework.

   adjective + noun

b. People's **attitudes toward** the new theory changed after a surprising scientific
   discovery.

   noun + preposition

c. He had a complete **change** in **attitude** after failing the test.

   noun + noun

Each item below contains three example sentences with the same target word. In
each sentence, the target word is paired with a different word and forms a different
collocation. In the fourth sentence, the collocation has been left blank. Choose the
collocation from the examples that best fits the last sentence and write it in the blank.
You may need to change the form of one of the words to fit the sentence. The first
one has been done for you.

1. **a.** The National Park **retained control** of the land, even though it was being
      used for commercial farming.
   b. American universities **retain close ties** with past graduates through their
      alumni associations.
   c. Home-health nurses serve a vital function by allowing the elderly to **retain**
      their **independence** even after the effects of aging have set in.
   d. In order to _____*retain control*_____ over the crowd at the parade,
      the police set up barriers to prevent spectators from walking into the
      street.

2. **a.** The president of the university was happy to **confer** an honorary **degree**
      on the Nobel Peace Prize winner.
   b. Among many primitive tribes, being a skilled hunter **confers** a high **status**
      upon an individual.
   c. Each year, the Queen of England **confers titles** on British subjects who
      have provided particularly useful services to the country.
   d. Wearing a trendy brand of clothing can do much to
      _____ on teenagers in the eyes of their peers.

3. **a.** Poor physical conditions, a heavy workload, and **personality conflicts** with coworkers are all causes of stress at work.

    b. In unlocking the secrets of DNA, scientists have opened up new areas of **potential conflict** between scientific progress and ethics.

    c. The general had no wish to start an **armed conflict** that he was not certain of winning.

    d. The political leaders were unable to prevent the peaceful protests from developing into _____.

4. **a.** Finding a cure for cancer is a **continuing process**.

    b. The **decision-making process** in large organizations can be awkward and unmanageable.

    c. Quality control must be in place in all phases of the **production process**.

    d. The industrial revolution led to major changes in the

    _____ of a variety of man-made goods.

5. **a.** People who have a **positive attitude** toward life tend to live longer.

    b. Many people adopt a **wait-and-see attitude** toward new technology.

    c. Students often express **unfavorable attitudes** about videotaped lectures being offered in place of a live professor.

    d. The older generation often has a(n) _____ toward the fashion and music of the younger generation.

6. **a.** Although the history of the First and Second World Wars has been **amply documented**, new accounts of both wars are still being written.

    b. The contents of the art exhibition had to be **fully documented** for insurance purposes.

    c. The scientist's report **carefully documents** the development of the new drug.

    d. The causes of many social problems have not been

    _____ because research is still ongoing.

7. **a.** The supermarket was popular with international students because it stocked an **extensive range** of ethnic foods.

    b. The restaurant could only offer a **restricted range** of meals because the electricity had gone out earlier in the day.

    c. The college was able to offer a **surprising range** of degrees given its small size.

    d. The toys were only suitable for a(n) _____ age

    _____ as they had many small parts that could be swallowed by young children.

8. **a.** The goal of today's lecture is to **examine the concept** of culture in today's multicultural society.

    b. Efforts to **develop the concept** of a global village are being held back by ongoing ethnic and regional conflicts.

    c. The staff development workshop aimed to **introduce the concept** of relationship marketing to the sales team.

    d. During the first class, the teacher _____ of social change and handed out a list of required readings on the subject.

Complete the passage by filling in the blanks with the target words in the box. Use each word only once.

affects	aspects	gender	style
apparent	conform	media	varies

EMOTIONS IN GLOBAL PERSPECTIVE: DO WE ALL FEEL THE SAME?

1   We know that the people in our family, school, and peer group affect the person we become. In addition, the mass (1) _____, particularly television, affects our social development. Since every person's experiences and environment are somewhat different, does this mean that all people are completely distinct from one another? Or are there some (2) _____ that all people share? For example, do people the world over share similar feelings, and do they express them in the same way?

2   In fact, scientists have concluded that people throughout the world experience six basic emotions: anger, fear, disgust, happiness, surprise, and sadness. Moreover, people everywhere can easily recognize these emotions in the same distinctive facial expressions. This seeming, or (3) _____, similarity means that much of our emotional life is universal—rather than culturally variable—and that the display of emotion is biologically programmed rather than determined by our environment.

3   But even if the reality of emotions is rooted in our biology, there are three ways in which emotional life differs throughout the world. First, what causes a specific emotion (4) _____ from one society to another. Whether people define a particular situation as an insult (causing anger), a loss (calling forth sadness), or a mystical event (provoking surprise and awe) depends on the cultural surroundings of the individual.

4   Second, people (5) _____ to the norms of their culture when displaying emotion. Every society has rules about when, where, and to whom an individual may show certain emotions. For instance, people in the United States typically expect children to express emotions to parents, though adults are taught to guard their emotions in front of children.

5   Third, a society (6) _____ how people cope with emotions. Some societies encourage the expression of feelings, while others require a calmer (7) _____ of behavior. For example, in America, when someone encounters an old friend after a long period of time, the two may hug each other. In other countries, they may only shake hands. Societies also display significant

male/female differences in this regard. In England, most people consider emotional expression as feminine, expected of women but a sign of weakness in men. In other societies, however, this (8) _____ -typing of emotions is less pronounced or even reversed.

Adapted from Macionis, J.J. and Plummer, K. (1997). *Sociology: A Global Introduction*. New York: Prentice Hall Europe, pp. 164.

EXPLORING THE TOPIC

Think about what you have just read and what you know about how emotions are expressed in various cultures. Working with a partner, select two countries and write a comparison/contrast essay that focuses on how emotions are expressed in these two cultures. In what ways is the emotional expression similar? In what ways is the emotional expression different?

3 The Changing Nature of the Family

GETTING STARTED

Discuss the following questions with your classmates.

▶ How many people are there in your family? Is this a good number? Why or why not?

▶ What is the average family size in your country? Is there a trend toward having larger or smaller families?

▶ What are the advantages and disadvantages of larger and smaller families?

TARGET WORDS—Assessing Your Vocabulary Knowledge

Look at each of the target words in the box. Use the scale to give yourself a score for each word. After you finish the chapter, score yourself again to check your improvement.

1 I don't know this word.

2 I have seen this word before, but I am not sure of the meaning.

3 I understand the word when I see it or hear it in a sentence, but I don't know how to use it in my own speaking and writing.

4 I know this word and can use it in my own speaking and writing.

TARGET WORDS

_____assistance	_____cooperate	_____maintain	_____purchase
_____available	_____domestic	_____minority	_____rely
_____consist	_____function	_____negative	_____resource
_____consume	_____isolation	_____network	_____structure
_____contribute	_____labor	_____nuclear	_____transition
_____conversely	_____locate	_____promote	_____trend

The following passage is adapted from an introductory textbook on sociology. The passage focuses on a typical model of the family and how it is changing. As you read, pay special attention to the target vocabulary words in **bold**.

FAMILY STRUCTURE

1   Although the **function**, or purpose, of families around the world is similar, family **structure** differs significantly from society to society and even from group to group. Because family **structure** is such an important aspect of pre-modern and modern societies, it has always been a special focus in the social sciences.

KINSHIP VS. FAMILY

2   Sociologists and anthropologists make an important distinction between the family and the kinship group, although both are commonly called "families" in English. *Kinship* refers to a social **network** of people who are related by common ancestry or origin, by marriage, or by adoption. Kin can include close relatives such as parents, and distant relatives such as third cousins. Kin do not always live together or **function** as a group but they may recognize certain rights, responsibilities, and obligations to one another. For example, in American society, kin may come together for Thanksgiving or a family reunion.

3   In contrast, a *family* is a relatively small **domestic** group that *does* **function** as a **cooperative** unit. In the United States, the family is usually a group **consisting** of parents and their children. In many societies, though, the family includes relatives from three or more

A nuclear family

generations. For example, a group of brothers and their wives, their sons and their unmarried daughters, and their sons' wives and children may live together or near one another, **cooperating** to raise food, **maintain** the home, and care for children and the elderly. If the individuals **function** as a single unit, sociologists consider them to be a family. If, however, they simply live next door to one another and do not pool their **resources**, they are viewed as separate families even though they may be related.

4   During their lifetimes, most people are members of two different types of family groups: the family into which they were born and the family that they create when they marry and have children. Societies differ in the cultural emphasis they place on these two groups. Among the Pueblo Indians, for example, the family a person is born into is given a special significance, whereas the family a person marries into is treated more casually. When a Pueblo Indian couple marry, the woman stays in her mother's household, and her husband moves in. If the couple do not get along and divorce, the husband moves back to his mother's household with little fuss.

NUCLEAR AND EXTENDED FAMILIES

5   Although the culturally ideal Western family is the **nuclear** family—a two-generation family group that **consists** of a father and mother and their children, usually living apart from other relatives—variations on this pattern are common. Death and divorce can leave households with only one parent. An elderly grandparent may join the household. Economic problems may force a married child to bring his or her spouse and children to live with the family. When a family is a group that **consists** of three or more generations, it is called an *extended family*.

6   The two-parent **nuclear** family is most typical of the middle and upper classes, and while the single-parent family is found in all social classes, it is more common among the lower classes.

Single-parent families are generally the result of divorce and separation, out-of-wedlock birth, and male unemployment. The extended family is also more common among the lower classes, mainly because of economic conditions.

7   Most middle-class **nuclear** families can afford to hire someone to babysit for their children, to help them move to a new house, or to care for the sick. They are able to borrow money from the bank when they need it for emergencies or for luxury items, such as a new car. Thus there are few economic reasons for a middle-class family to be extended.

8   The **purchase** of certain products and services is a luxury that poorer families often cannot afford. Such families generally must **rely** on family members and relatives to provide the goods and services they cannot afford to buy. A cousin will babysit. A brother will lend money to his sister until the next payday. A grandmother will take the children to a doctor if necessary. Without this **network** of shared **assistance**, families with low incomes would not be able to provide for their needs or handle many types of emergencies. The more family members who are **available**, the more likely each one is to get **assistance**. Thus, large extended families with strong ties can be a real advantage—indeed, a necessity—for lower-income families.

THE GLOBAL TREND TOWARD NUCLEAR FAMILIES

9   Family **structure** around the world has been gradually changing in the direction of the **nuclear** family. This **transition** is thought to have begun in pre-industrial rural England; at that time and place, families of three or more generations were already a distinct **minority**.

10   Today, the **trend** toward the **nuclear** family seems to be closely associated with the urbanization, industrialization, and modernization of societies. As industry replaces agriculture as the main form of work, younger family members typically leave the farms and rural villages and move to the cities where jobs are **located**, often weakening ties with those left behind. Once in the cities, families continue to move for employment and other reasons (such as better housing conditions, retirement, and more comfortable weather). The agricultural family is likely to be extended and tied to a piece of land, while the industrial family is **nuclear** and much more mobile.

An extended family

11   The decline of the extended family is thus **promoted** by the changing nature of work. In rural societies, as among the poor in industrial societies, the extended family offers an economic advantage. Each member of the family does some productive work. Less able-bodied family members, such as children, the elderly, or members with a disability, can each **contribute** in some way to the economic interests of the family unit. In industrial societies, **conversely**, these family members are treated as less essential economically and are employed only under certain conditions (for example, when there is a **labor** shortage). They therefore produce little for the family unit, yet they **consume** at about the same rate as do producers. The extended family can therefore be a disadvantage in industrial societies.

12   The **transition** from the extended to the **nuclear** family has brought with it much greater freedom and personal mobility for the individual. In the extended family, an individual's needs are generally of lesser importance compared to the demands of the larger group. Privacy, for example, is hard to find. However, there are **negative** features to the **nuclear** family, too. Although individuals are freed from a wide variety of responsibilities and obligations, other family members are no longer as responsible for them. Because the family is now a smaller unit, emotional and economic support may be more limited as each family member has fewer people **available** to turn to for companionship or **assistance**. The result may be the increased social **isolation** of individuals.

Adapted from Popenoe, D. (1995). *Sociology*, 10th ed. Englewood Cliffs, NJ: Prentice Hall, pp. 310–313.

UNDERSTANDING THE READING

Respond to the following in writing. Base your responses on the reading and your own personal experiences.

1. What is the difference between a family and a kinship group?
2. In what ways do economic factors, such as income level and employment, affect family structure?
3. This reading was published in 1995. What new trends in family structure have you observed in the twenty-first century? Describe how the family is changing.

FOCUSING ON VOCABULARY

WORD MEANING

When you encounter an unfamiliar word, remember to look for context clues to determine the word's meaning. Look at the example. Suppose that you came across the word *isolation* in the following sentences, but did not know the exact meaning of the word.

> *People living in **isolation** are often lonely.*
> (You know that lonely people are often by themselves, or apart from other people.)

> *People with dangerous diseases are often held in **isolation** areas in hospitals so that other people do not catch their disease.*
> (You know that people with dangerous diseases must often be kept away from other people so that their disease will not spread.)

From the context of each sentence, you can determine that *isolation* means "the state or act of being apart from others."

Read the sentences below and circle the letter of the word or phrase that best matches the meaning of the target word in **bold**. Use context clues in the sentences to determine the correct meaning. Check your dictionary if you are not sure of the answer. The first one has been done for you.

1. Jobs requiring unskilled **labor** are often more physical than those requiring skilled **labor**, as can be seen when comparing the job of a farmhand with that of a computer operator.
   a. process
   b. employment
   c. workers *(circled)*

2. Exercise and sensible eating are necessary to **maintain** a healthy body.
   a. increase
   b. destroy
   c. keep up

3. Italians are a small ethnic **minority** in Canada.
   a. larger part of a big group
   b. a small part of a larger group
   c. exactly 50 percent of a group

4. Anger and hate are **negative** emotions.
  a. bad or harmful
  b. good or helpful
  c. somewhat good or helpful

5. Some supporters of democracy have tried to **promote** its development worldwide.
  a. encourage
  b. advertise
  c. diminish

6. Gold and diamonds are two of South Africa's most valuable natural **resources**.
  a. possessions with little value
  b. possessions with no value
  c. useful possessions

7. The **structure** of an English sentence includes a subject, verb, and object, or complement.
  a. element
  b. arrangement or organization
  c. process

8. The **transition** between high school and college can be difficult, which is why many students drop out.
  a. skill or ability
  b. confusion
  c. act or process of changing

9. At the beginning of the twenty-first century, most stock markets were in a downward **trend**.
  a. situation without change
  b. confused situation
  c. general way things are changing

10. Some Pueblo cliff dwellings are **located** in Mesa Verde National Park, Colorado.
  a. in a particular place
  b. convenient
  c. established

11. Janet is Steve's wife. **Conversely**, Steve is Janet's husband.
  a. in speaking of this
  b. because of this
  c. in an opposite way

Read the sentences below and use context to figure out the meaning of the target words in **bold**. Look for a core meaning that provides a general understanding of each target word. Write the meaning in your own words. The first one has been done for you.

1. a. People often **assist** the police by describing what happened during a crime.
  b. The rescue service provided **assistance** to the ship in trouble.

  assist _to help or support_

2. a. Before you write a check, you must be sure that you have enough money **available** in the bank to cover the amount.

   b. The government wished to increase the **availability** of affordable health care to poorer people.

   available _____

3. a. A month **consists** of 28–31 days.

   b. A square is a shape **consisting** of four equal sides and four 90-degree angles.

   consist _____

4. a. Doctors recommend that people **consume** two liters of water (about eight glasses) daily.

   b. Car manufacturers are now able to lower fuel **consumption** because technological advances have made engines more efficient.

   consume _____

5. a. **Cooperation** between teachers and parents can do much to improve a child's education.

   b. Conversation analysts have found that women tend to be **cooperative** in conversations, while men tend to be competitive.

   cooperate _____

6. a. Those who are unable to **contribute** money to the school building fund may help by giving their time.

   b. Employees may **contribute** a percentage of their monthly salary to a pension fund, which will be paid back to them after age sixty-five or at the time of retirement.

   contribute _____

7. a. The police were called to the family's home to settle a **domestic** argument.

   b. The artist painted a scene of happy **domesticity**—a large family sitting around the table eating a festive meal.

   domestic _____

8. a. The **function** of the telephone is to provide easy, convenient communication.

   b. Even though the factory was a century old, all of the equipment was still **functional** and worked perfectly.

   function _____

9. a. The Paris Metro—one of the best subway systems in the world—consists of a vast **network** of interconnected train lines.

   b. The inter-library loan **network** enables students and staff to borrow library books from other universities in the state.

   network _____

10. a. Many students prefer to rent formal clothing for dances and balls, because the cost of **purchasing** such items is so high.

   b. The family used most of its money for the **purchase** of food and clothing.

   purchase _____

11. a. These days, many families **rely** on both the husband and wife working in order to earn enough money for daily living.

   b. Bus use in the city is low because most commuters feel they cannot **rely** on a service that is regularly late.

   rely _____

▶ In introductory academic texts, subject-related vocabulary is often defined in the text. Paragraph 5 of "Family Structure" gives the definition of the term **nuclear family** between two dashes.

> Although the culturally ideal Western family is the **nuclear** family—a two-generation family group that consists of a father and mother and their children, usually living apart from other relatives—variations on this pattern are common.

▶ As you read, look out for other definitions of subject-related vocabulary within parentheses, commas, or dashes.

WORD FAMILIES

When using new words in writing, learners often select a word with the right meaning, but the wrong word form, or part of speech. Checking your writing to ensure that you have used the correct form is a very important step in editing your work.

You should choose the word form based on the function each word performs in your sentences. Does the word stand for a person, place, thing, or event (noun), does it describe a noun (adjective), is it an action or a state (verb), or does it describe an action (adverb)? Different word forms may have different spellings. If you do not know the correct spelling of a word form, use your dictionary to help you.

Read the sentences below. Some of the target words have been used correctly, but in six sentences a wrong word form has been used. If the wrong form has been used, cross it out and write the correct form. If the form is correct, put a checkmark (✓). The first two items have been done for you.

1. The building boom in the city has increased the ~~available~~ of cheap office space. _____availability_____

2. The **transitional** government carried out the work of the nation until the elections were held six months later. _____✓_____

3. Automobile associations believe that new roads must be built to solve traffic problems. **Converse**, environmentalists believe that new roads simply add to these problems. _____

4. Products that are sold for both **domestic** and restaurant use are sometimes packaged differently. _____

5. **Isolating** is one form of punishment that prisons use for difficult criminals.
   _____

6. After the storm, there was only one **functioning** telephone in the area.
   _____

7. Fifteen percent of the world's people **consuming** sixty-eight percent of the world's energy. _____

8. One objective of education in any country is the **promotion** of that country's cultural values. _____

9. Like the family, the workplace can only operate if there is a clear **structurally**. _____

10. An individual's daily **contributor** to the world's pollution problems may seem small, but when added together over years, it is significant. _____

COLLOCATION

Fluent users of a language have become used to the natural patterns in which words appear. As a language learner, it will be easier for others to understand you if you use these same natural patterns. A number of the words in this unit form word partnerships, or collocations. This means that when one word occurs in the pair, it naturally suggests the word or words around it. Remember that collocations often fall into the following simple patterns.

noun + verb   verb + noun   noun + noun
adjective + noun   verb + adverb

Match each target word in the box with the group of words that regularly occur with it. If the (~) symbol appears before a word in a list (e.g., ~*shortage*), the target word comes before the word in the list (e.g., ***labor** shortage*). In all other cases, the target word comes after the word in the list, as in *unskilled **labor***. The first one has been done for you.

consist	~~labor~~	minority	resources
consumer	location	network	trend

1. _____labor_____	2. _____	3. _____	4. _____
~shortage	sizeable	~primarily of	decide on a
~saving	ethnic	~exclusively of	ideal
~market	~groups	~largely of	pinpoint a
unskilled	~communities	~essentially of	perfect

5. _____	6. _____	7. _____	8. _____
~rights	reverse a	allocate	old boy
~confidence	downward	build up	extensive
~goods	follow a	waste	computer
~protection	observe a	exhaust	nationwide

Read the statements about family life in the following chart. Evaluate each statement. Is it an advantage of living in a **nuclear** family or an extended family? Place a checkmark (✓) in the appropriate box. If the factor is equally advantageous for both types of family structure, check the "equal advantage" box. Then discuss your opinions with a partner.

	Advantage of living in a **nuclear** family	Advantage of living in an extended family	Equal advantage for both family types
1. There are more people working, helping to **maintain** a steady income during economic slowdowns.			
2. Parents **rely** on their children to help with housework.			
3. There are fewer people who will ask for your **assistance**.			
4. There are more people around, so there is less chance of feeling lonely and **isolated**.			
5. Family members that **cooperate** with one another can do things that they could not do by themselves.			
6. **Domestic** decision making requires less discussion.			
7. Working family members contribute to the family's **purchasing** power.			
8. Expectations of relatives can have a **negative** impact on a couple's freedom.			

Write an essay about one of the topics below. Be sure to support your ideas with clear examples.

- How has family size changed in your home country since you were a child? Explain why these changes have occurred.
- What effects do changes in family size have on women? Explain. What effects do changes in family size have on children? Explain.

Strategy Practice

USING YOUR DICTIONARY—Word Meanings and Word Forms

Making good use of your dictionary will help you study and master academic vocabulary. In addition to giving you information about a word's meaning, dictionaries also explain pronunciation, grammar, word families, usage, and other information. If you do not have a dictionary, ask your teacher to recommend one. Each Strategy Practice chapter in *Focus on Vocabulary* presents aspects of dictionary use.

FINDING THE RIGHT MEANING

When you look up a word, you often find that it has more than one meaning. In many dictionaries, the first meaning is the most common one and therefore likely to be the one you need. However, this is not always the case, so you should read all of the meanings to be sure. To figure out which meaning is correct, think about the context in which you heard or read the unfamiliar word. Look for clues to the correct meaning by checking the words and sentences surrounding the new word. Use these context clues to figure out which dictionary meaning fits.

Read the entry below from the *Longman Advanced American Dictionary*. Then reread paragraph 6 of the Chapter 1 reading on page 4. Use the entry and context clues to respond to the following questions and exercises.

> **el•e•ment** /ˈɛləmənt/ *n.* [C] **1 [part]** one part or feature of a whole system, plan, piece of work etc., especially one that is basic or important: *The movie has **all the elements of** a great love story.* **2 an element of danger/truth/risk etc.** a definite amount, usually small, of danger, truth etc.: *There's an element of truth in what he says.* **3 [people]** USUALLY DISAPPROVING a group of people who can be recognized by particular behavior or beliefs: *The clubs also tend to attract a **criminal element** (=people who do illegal things).* **4 [chemistry]** a simple chemical substance such as CARBON, oxygen, or gold that is made of only one type of atom—compare COMPOUND¹ (2) **5 the elements** weather, especially bad weather: *The tent was their only protection from the elements.* **6 the elements of sth** the most basic and important features of something: *His imaginative stories use the elements of poetry—rhythm, rhyme, alliteration.* **7 be in your element** to be in a situation that you enjoy because you are good at it: *On the soccer field is where Christina really feels like she is in her element.* **8 be out of your element** to be in a situation that makes you uncomfortable because you are not good at it: *Miller is completely out of her element in this sci-fi role.* **9 [heat]** the part of a STOVE or other piece of electrical equipment that produces heat **10 [earth/air/fire/water]** one of the four substances from which people used to believe that everything was made

1. How many meanings does the dictionary entry give for the word **element**? _____

2. Which meaning matches the way **elements** is used in the reading? Write the number of the correct meaning. _____

3. What clues helped you figure out the meaning of **elements** in the passage?

_____

4. Write two sentences of your own to illustrate the meaning of **elements** in the reading. _____

_____

_____

_____

LOCATING WORD FORMS

You can use dictionaries to learn more about word forms and word families. Some word forms appear as their own entries in a dictionary. For example, study the separate entries for the three forms of **consume** below. Other word forms may not have their own entries. For example, find and circle the adverb **structurally** in the entry below.

con•sume /kənˈsum/ *v.* [T] **1** to completely use time, energy, goods etc.: *This year, health care costs will consume one-eighth of the average family's income.* **2** FORMAL to eat or drink something: *The college permits students who are 21 or older to consume alcoholic beverages in their dorm rooms.* **3 be consumed with guilt/passion/rage etc.** to have a very strong feeling that changes the way you behave and what you think about —see also CONSUMING **4** FORMAL if fire consumes something, it destroys it completely —see also TIME-CONSUMING

con•sum•er•is•m /kənˈsuməˌrɪzəm/ *n.* [U] **1** the idea or belief that buying and selling products and services is the most important or useful activity a person or society can do **2** actions to protect people from unfair prices, advertising that is not true etc.

con•sum•ing /kənˈsumɪŋ/ *adj.* [only before noun] a consuming feeling is so strong that it controls you and often has a bad effect on your life: *She was possessed by a consuming rage.* Henry's ***consuming passion*** (=something you are extremely interested in) *is birdwatching.*

struc•tur•al /ˈstrʌktʃərəl/ *adj.* relating to the structure of something: *structural damage | structural changes in the economy* —**structurally** *adv.*

PRACTICING YOUR DICTIONARY SKILLS

Use your dictionary to look up the target words in the chart below. Write the number of meanings your dictionary gives for each word. Find the forms that make up each word's family. Write those forms in the correct column in the chart below. One has been done for you.

Target Word	Number of meanings	Verbs	Nouns	Adjectives	Adverbs
complex					
concept					
contact					
element	10	X	element	1. elemental 2. elementary	X
maintain					
negative					
structure					

Now compare your chart with a partner's. Discuss any differences you find.

USING WORD ROOTS

Many words in English are built up from roots that have a meaning. For example, the word *psychology* contains the roots *psych* ("mind") and *logy* ("study of"). Below are some common word roots and their meanings. Learning the meaning of common word roots will help you figure out the meaning of unfamiliar academic words.

Root	Meaning
auto	self
equ	equal
bene	good, well
meter	measure
com	together, with
spec, spect	to look
dict	to speak
vert, verse	to change, to turn

Use the word roots above to match the following academic words with their meanings. The first one has been done for you.

__d__ **1.** automate

a. a set of limits that control the way something should be done

____ **2.** beneficial

b. to say the opposite of something

____ **3.** contradict

c. producing results that bring advantages

____ **4.** equate

d. to change to a system in which machines can do jobs by themselves

____ **5.** parameters

e. to change from one form, system, or purpose to a different one, or to make something do this

____ **6.** perspective

f. to consider that one thing is the same, or equal to, something else

____ **7.** convert

g. the way you look at things, which is influenced by the kind of person you are or by your experiences

USING AFFIXES

As you know from your word family study, English words can change their form when you add or remove word parts. A *prefix* is a word part added to the beginning of a word. A *suffix* is a word part added to the end of a word. Together, prefixes and suffixes are referred to as *affixes*.

Some affixes change a word's part of speech as shown in the examples below:

verb + *-tion* = noun   **communicate** (verb) ➔ communica*tion* (noun)

noun + *-ic* = adjective   **economy** (noun) ➔ econom*ic* (adjective)

adjective + *-ly* = adverb   **functional** (adjective) ➔ functional*ly*

When identifying and building word families, you must recognize the affixes that change a word's part of speech. The following exercises contain forms of the Unit 1 target words; the chapter numbers are given in parentheses ( ). Review how the target words were used in the readings. Then complete the exercises. Use a dictionary if you need to. An example has been done for you.

Verb		Noun	Suffix
dominate (2)	→	*dominance*	*-ance*

Identify the suffixes that are used to change the following verbs into nouns. Write the noun form and the suffix.

Verb		Noun	Suffix
evolve (1)	→	_____	_____
conform (2)	→	_____	_____
cooperate (3)	→	_____	_____
assist (3)	→	_____	_____

Identify the suffixes that are used to change the following verbs into adjectives. Write the adjective form and the suffix.

Verb		Adjective	Suffix
interact (1)	→	_____	_____
vary (2)	→	_____	_____
cooperate (3)	→	_____	_____
isolate (3)	→	_____	_____

WORD KNOWLEDGE—Making Associations

Successfully learning new vocabulary depends on finding ways to remember these new words. One way of doing this is by linking new words to words and ideas that you already know. These links are called *associations*. The more you think about and use new words, the stronger these links will become. A simple way to practice associations is by making *word maps* like those below.

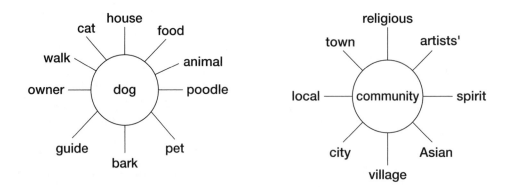

These networks are sometimes called *mind maps*, because they are made by writing down the first words that come into your mind when you see a target word. They are also called *word maps* because they show links in meaning between words.

Choose a few of the target words from Unit 1 and make your own mind maps. Then compare your maps with a partner's.

UNIT 2

Consumer Behavior and Marketing

5

Influencing the Consumer

GETTING STARTED

Discuss the following questions with your classmates.

▶ Look around at items that you or your friends own. Why did you purchase the particular pair of shoes you are wearing? What influenced your choice of book bag or backpack? What toothpaste or shampoo did you use this morning? Why?

▶ How much does the brand name of a product affect your decision to buy it?

TARGET WORDS—Assessing Your Vocabulary Knowledge

Look at each of the target words in the box. Use the scale to give yourself a score for each word. After you finish the chapter, score yourself again to check your improvement.

1 I don't know this word.

2 I have seen this word before, but I am not sure of the meaning.

3 I understand the word when I see it or hear it in a sentence, but I don't know how to use it in my own speaking and writing.

4 I know this word and can use it in my own speaking and writing.

TARGET WORDS

_____accompany	_____design	_____image	_____revenue
_____acknowledge	_____distribute	_____impact	_____strategies
_____appreciate	_____dynamics	_____issues	_____underlying
_____attachment	_____emphasis	_____policy	_____via
_____bond	_____features	_____primary	_____visible
_____controversial	_____fundamental	_____principle	_____whereby

The following passage is adapted from an introductory textbook on marketing. It describes and explains factors affecting consumer behavior. As you read, pay special attention to the target vocabulary words in **bold**.

MARKETING'S IMPACT ON CONSUMERS

1   For better or worse, we live in a world that is significantly influenced by marketers. We are surrounded by marketing stimuli in the form of advertisements, shops, and products competing for our attention and our cash. Much of what we learn about the world is controlled by marketers, whether through conspicuous consumption shown in glamorous magazine advertising or **via** the roles played by family members in TV commercials. Ads show us how we ought to act with regard to many diverse issues, including recycling, what we eat and drink, and even the types of house or car we desire. In many ways, we are "at the mercy" of marketers, since we rely on them to sell us products that are safe and that perform as promised, to tell us the truth about what they are selling, and to price and **distribute** these products fairly.

POPULAR CULTURE

2   Popular culture—the music, films, sports, books, and other forms of entertainment consumed by the mass market—is both a marketing product and an inspiration for marketers. Marketing affects our lives in very **fundamental** ways, ranging from how we **acknowledge** key social events such as marriage, death, or holidays to how we view societal **issues** such as addiction and air pollution.

3   The role marketing plays in the creation and communication of popular culture is hard to ignore. However, many people fail to **appreciate** how much their view of the world—their film and music icons, the latest fashions in clothing, food, and interior **design**, and even the physical **features** that they find attractive in another person—is influenced by the marketing system. Product placement, **whereby** products and brands are used in popular movies or TV programs, or sponsorships of various events such as rock concerts or the Olympics, is an example of how companies command our attention.

A busy shopping area at night

4   Consider the product characters that marketers use to create a personality for their products. From the Michelin Man to Ronald McDonald, popular culture is peopled with fictional heroes. In fact, many consumers are more likely to recognize characters such as these than to be able to identify former presidents, heads of corporations, or world leaders. Although these product characters may not actually exist, many of us feel that we "know" them, and they certainly are effective "spokes-characters" for the products they promote.

THE MEANING OF CONSUMPTION

5   One of the **fundamental principles** of consumer behavior is that people often buy products not for what the products do, but for what they *mean*. This **principle** does not mean that a product's **primary** function is unimportant, but rather that the roles products play and the meanings that they have in our lives go well beyond the tasks they perform. The deeper meanings of a product may help it

stand out from other similar goods and services—all things being equal, a person will choose the brand that has an **image** (or even a personality!) that matches his or her **underlying** ideas.

6   For example, although most people probably can't run faster or jump higher because they are wearing Nikes versus Reeboks, many consumers make it a **policy** to be loyal to their favorite brand. Rival brands like Nike and Reebok are marketed in terms of their **images**, which have been carefully crafted with the help of rock stars and athletes, slickly produced commercials—and many millions of dollars. So, when you buy a Nike "swoosh," you may be doing more than choosing footwear—you may also be making a lifestyle statement about the type of person you are or want to be. For a relatively simple article made of leather and laces, that's quite amazing!

MARKETING AND THE CUSTOMER

7   The key characteristic of marketing **strategies** today is an **emphasis** on building relationships with customers. The nature of these relationships can vary, and these **bonds** help us to understand some of the possible meanings products have for us. Here are some of the types of relationships a person may have with a product.

- *Self-concept* **attachment**—the product helps to create the user's identity.

- *Nostalgic* **attachment**—the product serves as a link with a past self.

The Volkswagen Beetle has nostalgic appeal.

- *Interdependence*—the product is a part of the user's daily routine.

- *Love*—the product brings out feelings of warmth, passion, or other strong emotion.

THE GLOBAL CONSUMER

8   One highly **visible**—and **controversial**—result of sophisticated marketing **strategies** is the movement toward a *global consumer culture*, in which people are united by their common loyalty to brand-name consumer goods, film stars, and rock stars. Some products in particular have become so associated with a particular lifestyle that they are prized possessions around the world.

Jeans are an "image" of America throughout the world.

9   On the other hand, popular culture continues to evolve as products and styles from different cultures mix and combine in new and interesting ways. For example, although superstars from the United States and the United Kingdom dominate the worldwide music industry, a movement is taking place to include more diverse styles and performers. In Europe, local music acts are grabbing a larger share of the market and overtaking the popularity of international (that is, English-speaking) acts. **Revenue** from Spanish-language music has quadrupled in five years. In Asia, new songs are being written to **accompany** promotions for American movies. For example, in Hong Kong the movie *Lethal Weapon 4* was promoted with a song by a local heavy metal band called "Beyond." Shots from the movie were mixed with clips of band members, even though the band does not appear in the film and the song is not included on the soundtrack.

10   Marketing activities have a major **impact** on our lives. They influence our personal and group identities and are used to promote both social ideas and commercial products. Therefore, a greater awareness of consumer behavior is important to our understanding of both social **issues** and the **dynamics** of popular culture.

_____
Adapted from Solomon, M., Bamossy, G., and Askegaard, S. (2002). *Consumer Behaviour: A European Perspective*, 2nd ed. New York: Prentice Hall Europe, pp. 13–17.

UNDERSTANDING THE READING

Respond to the following in writing. Base your responses on the reading and your own personal experiences.

1. What are three ways that marketing affects popular culture or individual behavior? Give examples of each.
2. List the spokes-characters mentioned in the reading and any other spokes-characters you know about. What product or cause is each character associated with?
3. Describe two ways that globalization has affected marketing in your country.

FOCUSING ON VOCABULARY

WORD MEANING

Match the words with their definitions. If you are unsure about a word's meaning, try to figure it out from the context by rereading the passage on pp. 38–39. Then check your dictionary.

Set 1

_____1. visible

_____2. accompany

_____3. controversial

_____4. design

_____5. whereby

_____6. features

_____7. issues

a. able to be seen

b. noticeable parts or characteristics of something

c. by means of which or according to which

d. causing a lot of disagreement

e. subjects or problems that people are thinking or talking about

f. be or go with

g. the way something has been planned or made

Set 2

_____1. dynamics

_____2. image

_____3. underlying

_____4. strategies

_____5. principle

_____6. revenue

_____7. via

a. by way of or by use of

b. money that a business, government, or organization receives

c. a well-planned series of actions for achieving a goal

d. very basic or important, but not easily noticed

e. a belief or idea on which a set of ideas, laws, or a system is based

f. a picture of what something or someone is like or looks like

g. the ways in which things or people behave, react, and affect each other

Read the row of words and phrases below each numbered word. One word or phrase in each list is *not* a synonym for the numbered word. Cross it out.

1. **primary**

   key   plan   major   main

2. **bond**

   tie   ideal   connection   relationship

3. **appreciate**

   be aware   realize   understand   stop

4. **fundamental**

   money   basic   original   elementary

5. **impact**

   influence   improvement   impression   effect

6. **acknowledge**

   accept   allow   recognize   deny

7. **emphasis**

   feeling   importance   stress   weight

8. **policy**

   plan   rule   government   guideline

9. **distribute**

   hand out   share   let out   give out

10. **attachment**

    connection   friendship   link   separation

WORD FAMILIES

The table below contains word families for some of the target words in the reading. Complete the table. An *X* indicates that there is no form or that the form is not common. Sometimes there may be more than one form possible. If you are unsure about a form, check your dictionary.

Verb	Noun	Adjective	Adverb
accompany	accompaniment		X
acknowledge		1. acknowledged 2. acknowledging	X
appreciate	appreciation		X
	attachment	attached	X
X	controversy	controversial	
distribute	distribution	distributional	X
	emphasis	emphasized	X
	strategy	strategic	
	X	underlying	X
X		visible	visibly

Choose the correct form of the word in **bold** in sentence **a** to complete sentence **b**.
Use the word families table you just completed as a guide.

1. **a.** One method of direct marketing is to **distribute** advertising materials by hand on city streets or at special events.

   b. The _____ of products for a multinational company is likely to be complex.

2. **a.** Good advice for healthy living places equal **emphasis** on diet and exercise.
   b. Guidebooks for businesspeople working abroad tend to

   _____ differences in foreign business or cultural practices.

3. **a.** Students must take care to **acknowledge** all of their sources when writing an essay; otherwise they risk being accused of plagiarism.
   b. Companies may award a year-end bonus to employees in

   _____ of outstanding work done throughout the year.

4. **a.** Using animals to test for the side effects of beauty products is **controversial**; in fact, many people think that such testing is morally wrong.

   b. The teenage years can often be a time of _____ for families as young people begin to break away from their parents' control.

5. **a.** When sending a résumé or a job application form, it is normal to include an **accompanying** letter that highlights one's special qualities.
   b. To see a movie rated PG13, children under the age of thirteen must be

   _____ by a parent.

6. **a.** The marketing department was eager to develop a new **strategy** for targeting young families.
   b. The board of directors produced a _____ plan to guide the company's development.

7. **a.** After three months of training, his performance improved **visibly**.
   b. Product placement in popular TV programs greatly increases those

   products' _____ .

8. **a.** Visitors to the Grand Canyon often develop a new **appreciation** of nature's power.
   b. Many politicians fail to _____ the relationship between poverty, lack of education, and crime.

9. **a.** Children commonly develop deep emotional **attachments** to dolls or other toys.
   b. Students of foreign language or literature can become _____ to a culture without ever having visited the country itself.

10. **a.** New medical research allows doctors to better understand the **underlying** causes of many illnesses.
    b. A theme of hope for the future of humankind _____ many science fiction movies and novels.

COLLOCATION

Each item below contains three sentences with the same collocation. Write a fourth sentence of your own using the same word partners.

1. **a.** Closing streets during construction projects can have an **adverse impact** on local businesses.
   b. Mass consumerism has had an **adverse impact** on credit card debt.
   c. Tax cuts often benefit the rich but have an **adverse impact** on lower-income groups because the government has less money to fund special programs.

   d. _____

2. **a.** The model's most **striking feature** is her long red hair.
   b. A **striking feature** of the presentation was the speaker's well-selected use of graphics to emphasize key points.
   c. The glass elevator is the hotel's most **striking feature**.

   d. _____

3. **a.** To **fully appreciate** the beauty of a garden, it is best to visit when the flowers are in full bloom.
   b. When employers do not **fully appreciate** their employees' talents, staff motivation goes down.
   c. Although the principal **fully appreciated** the teacher's position, he refused to remove the problem student from the class.

   d. _____

4. **a.** The company used the results of consumer surveys to **formulate** its new marketing **policy**.
   b. The management **formulated** a new **policy** about the use of cell phones at work.
   c. The university called together professors and academic support staff to **formulate** a new **policy** on plagiarism.

   d. _____

5. **a.** The university hoped that ticket sales for football games would help to **generate revenue** for the whole sports program.
   b. Governments normally view tax increases as a quick way of **generating revenue**.
   c. Unlike commercial television and radio stations, public television and radio cannot rely on advertising to **generate revenue**.

   d. _____

6. **a.** The planet Venus is **plainly visible** in the night sky and is sometimes wrongly referred to as the morning or evening star.
   b. The eagerness of the students is **plainly visible** despite the poor conditions in which they are forced to study.
   c. It is important that road signs be **plainly visible** during the day and at night.

   d. _____

7. a. Programs that bring young children and elderly people together can foster the development of **emotional bonds** between the young and the old.

b. Many fans develop an **emotional bond** with a favorite sports team.

c. Marketing experts are finding that creating **emotional bonds** between product and consumer may be more effective than pricing strategies.

d. _____

8. a. The discipline of child psychology places **particular emphasis** on human development and learning.

b. Some language teachers place **particular emphasis** on accuracy while others focus on communication strategies and fluency.

c. Today, many medical personnel place **particular emphasis** on disease prevention.

d. _____

EXPANSION

Read the statements below and indicate whether you agree **(A)** or disagree **(D)**. Then discuss your opinions and reasoning with a partner.

_____ **1.** Being **image**-conscious is a greater **issue** for teenagers than for other age groups.

_____ **2.** The **bond** formed between a parent and child is the most important relationship in a person's life.

_____ **3.** The **principle** of equal access to education is violated when students are allowed to enter college **via** programs that give preferential treatment to people of a particular race, gender, or social background.

_____ **4.** Capitalism is an economic system **whereby** the rich get richer and the poor get poorer.

_____ **5.** The invention of television has had a **primarily** positive effect on the world.

_____ **6.** The essential **dynamics** of family life are similar worldwide despite differing family structures.

_____ **7.** It is impossible to develop an **attachment** to a new culture without weakening the links to one's own culture.

_____ **8.** When companies market a product in a variety of countries, cultural differences may require **fundamental** changes in product **design**.

 Paragraph 7 of "Marketing's Impact on Consumers" identifies four types of relationships that a consumer may have with a product: self-concept attachment, nostalgic attachment, interdependence, and love. Write a personal essay in which you reflect on the types of relationships you have with two or three products that you own or regularly use.

Who Buys What?
The Family's Influence

GETTING STARTED

Discuss the following questions with your classmates.

▶ Think back to when you were younger and you went shopping with your parents. Who in the family decided what to buy? What products did your parents buy for you? What products did you ask them to buy?

▶ Do you buy the same brands of products now as your family did then? Why or why not?

TARGET WORDS—Assessing Your Vocabulary Knowledge

Look at each of the target words in the box. Use the scale to give yourself a score for each word. After you finish the chapter, score yourself again to check your improvement.

1 I don't know this word.

2 I have seen this word before, but I am not sure of the meaning.

3 I understand the word when I see it or hear it in a sentence, but I don't know how to use it in my own speaking and writing.

4 I know this word and can use it in my own speaking and writing.

TARGET WORDS

_____acquire	_____device	_____insight	_____occupational
_____adjustment	_____dispose	_____involve	_____ongoing
_____appropriate	_____factor	_____mode	_____reinforce
_____assume	_____foundation	_____modify	_____selection
_____category	_____illustration	_____norm	_____sole
_____constantly	_____initiate	_____obtain	_____transfer

The following passage is adapted from an introductory textbook on marketing and discusses the role the family plays in building consumer habits. As you read, pay special attention to the target vocabulary words in **bold**.

CONSUMER SOCIALIZATION OF FAMILY MEMBERS

1   The *socialization of family members*, ranging from young children to adults, is a central family function. Today that function includes developing children into consumers. This is why marketers frequently target parents who are looking for assistance in the process of socializing their children. Marketers know that the socialization of young children provides an opportunity to establish a **foundation** on which later experiences continue to build throughout life. These experiences are **reinforced** and **modified** as children grow into adolescence and, in time, into adulthood.

2   In the case of young children, parents typically are responsible for teaching and **reinforcing** the basic values and **modes** of behavior of the culture. Parents usually teach their children about moral and religious principles, interpersonal skills, dress and grooming standards, **appropriate** manners and speech, and the **selection** of suitable educational and **occupational** goals. Such parental responsibilities, in turn, affect parents' consumer behavior. Take, as an **illustration**, the many parents today who are increasingly anxious to see that their young children possess adequate computer skills, almost before the children are able to talk or walk. Because of this interest, hardware and software developers are rapidly creating products targeted at parents seeking to buy such items for their very young children.

CONSUMER SOCIALIZATION OF CHILDREN

3   Sociologists define *consumer socialization* as "the process by which children **acquire** the skills, knowledge, and attitudes necessary to function as consumers." A variety of studies have focused on how children develop consumer skills. Many pre-adolescent children **acquire** their consumer behavior **norms** by observing their parents and older siblings, who function as role models for basic consumption learning. In contrast, teenagers are likely to look to their friends for models of acceptable consumption behavior.

Parents helping to develop their child's computer skills

4   Consumer socialization also serves as a tool by which parents influence other aspects of the socialization process. For example, parents frequently use the promise or reward of material goods as a **device** to **modify** or control a child's behavior. A mother may reward her child with a gift when the child does something to please her, or she may remove it when the child disobeys.

ADULT CONSUMER SOCIALIZATION

5   Consumer socialization is not limited to childhood; it is an **ongoing** process that extends throughout a person's entire life. For example, when a newly married couple establishes a separate household, their **adjustment** to living and consuming together is part of this continuing process. Similarly, the **adjustments** a retired couple make when deciding to move to a warmer climate are also part of the **ongoing** process. Even a family that is welcoming a pet into its home will inevitably change its consumer habits to some degree as a result of this addition.

INTERGENERATIONAL SOCIALIZATION

6   It is quite common for **selected** product loyalty or brand preferences to be **transferred** from one generation to the next, maybe for even three or four generations within the same family. This passing on of preferences is known as "intergenerational brand **transfer**." For example, preferences for specific brands in certain **categories** of food, such as peanut butter, ketchup, coffee, and canned soup, are frequently passed on from one generation to another. The following quotes from research with college-aged consumers reveal how they feel about product usage from generation to generation:

My mother still buys almost every brand that her mother did. She is scared to try anything else, for it will not meet the standards, and [she] would feel bad not buying something that has been with her so long.
(Respondent is an Italian-American male in his early twenties.)

I find it hard to break away from the things I've been using since I was little; like Vaseline products, Ivory soap, Lipton tea, and cornflakes. I live on campus so I have to do my own shopping, and when I do I see a lot of my mother in myself. I buy things I'm accustomed to using . . . products my mother buys for the house.
(Respondent is a West Indian-American female.)

Consumer preferences are passed on from one generation to the next.

It is important to note, however, that socialization is in reality a two-way street, in which children of all ages also influence the opinions and behavior of their parents.

FAMILY DECISION MAKING AND KEY CONSUMPTION-RELATED ROLES

7   Although many marketers recognize the family as the basic decision-making unit, they most frequently examine the attitudes and behaviors of the one family member who is believed to be the major decision maker. In some cases, marketers also examine the attitudes and behavior of the person most likely to be the primary user of the product or service. For example, in the case of children's clothing, which is normally purchased by mothers for their sons and daughters, it is customary to seek the views of both the children who wear the clothes and the mothers who buy them. By considering both the likely user and the likely purchaser, the marketer **obtains** a richer picture of the consumption process and key consumption-related roles. In a dynamic society, family-related duties are **constantly** changing. For example, men have **assumed** many more household tasks in recent years. Despite such changes, we can identify eight distinct roles in the family decision-making process. A look at these roles provides further **insight** into how family members interact in their various consumption-related roles.

Role	Description
Influencers	Family members who provide information to other members about a product or service
Gatekeepers	Family members who control the flow of information about a product or service into the family
Deciders	Family members with the power to determine independently or jointly whether to shop for, purchase, use, consume, or **dispose** of a specific product or service
Buyers	Family members who make the actual purchase of a particular product or service
Preparers	Family members who transform the product into a suitable form for consumption by other family members (e.g., those who fix meals)

(Continued)

Role	Description
Users	Family members who use or consume a particular product or service
Maintainers	Family members who service or repair the product so that it will continue to provide satisfaction
Disposers	Family members who **initiate** or carry out the **disposal** or discontinuation of a particular product or service

Family member using a consumer product

8   The number and identity of family members who fill these roles vary from family to family and from product to product. In some cases, a single family member will independently **assume** a number of roles; in other cases, a single role will be performed jointly by two or more family members. In still other cases, one or more of these basic roles may not be required. For example, a family member may be walking down the snack food aisle at a local supermarket when he picks out an interesting new chocolate candy. His **selection** does not directly **involve** the influence of other family members. He is the decider, the buyer, and in a sense the gatekeeper, but he may not be the **sole** consumer (or user). Products may be consumed by individual family members (after-shave, lipstick), consumed or used directly by two or more family members (vegetables, shampoo), or consumed indirectly by the entire family (central air-conditioning or a home security alarm system). In the end, a family's decision-making style often is influenced by many diverse **factors**, such as its lifestyle, members' personalities and roles, and the family's cultural background.

Adapted from Schiffman, L. G. and Lazar Kanuk, L. (2000). *Consumer Behavior*, 7th ed. Upper Saddle River, NJ: Prentice Hall, pp. 277–279 and 282–283.

UNDERSTANDING THE READING

Respond to the following in writing. Base your responses on the reading and your own personal experiences.

1. How do parents use consumer goods to influence their children's behavior? Describe examples from your own childhood.
2. What is intergenerational socialization? Are there any brands from your childhood that you still buy? If so, describe them and your reasons for buying them.
3. Think of two different consumer products (e.g., bread and a computer) that you and your family use. Who is or was involved in the decision making for that product? Look back at the table on pages 47–48. Which of the roles did the members of your family assume?

WORD MEANING

Each of the following target words appears in the reading on pages 46–48. Use the paragraph number in parentheses to locate each word in context. Read the dictionary definitions below. Write the letter of the definition that reflects how the word is used in the reading.

_____**1. foundation** (1)
  a. an organization that gives or collects money for special purposes, especially charity or research
  b. a basic principle, idea, or belief that something develops from

_____**2. reinforce** (1)
  a. to make a building, structure, or object stronger by adding materials to it
  b. to strengthen or give support to a feeling, idea, opinion, or habit

_____**3. modify** (1)
  a. to make small changes to something in order to improve it
  b. to describe or limit the meaning of a word

_____**4. mode** (2)
  a. a particular way or style of behaving, living, or doing something
  b. a particular way in which a machine operates when doing a specific job

_____**5. selection** (2)
  a. a collection of things of a particular type, especially of things that are for sale
  b. the careful choice of a particular person or thing from among a group of similar people or things

_____**6. acquire** (3)
  a. to get something by buying, taking, or being given it
  b. to gain knowledge or skill by learning

_____**7. device** (4)
  a. a way of achieving a particular purpose; in some cases, a trick
  b. a machine or small object that has been made for a particular purpose

_____**8. transfer** (6)
  a. the process by which someone or something moves or is moved from one place, situation, job, etc. to another
  b. a ticket that allows a passenger to change from one bus or train to another without paying more money.

_____**9. assume** (7)
  a. to think that something is true, although you have no proof of it
  b. to start to do a job, especially an important one

_____**10. dispose** (7)
  a. to defeat an opponent
  b. to get rid of something; throw out

_____ **11. initiate** (7)

    a. to arrange for something to begin

    b. to admit someone into membership within a group, usually with a special ceremony

_____ **12. factor** (8)

    a. one of several things that influence or cause something to happen

    b. a number that divides evenly into another number

Each sentence below contains a paraphrase or set of synonyms for a target word. Read each sentence and select the matching target word from the box.

adjustments	constantly	involves	occupations
appropriate	illustration	norms	ongoing
categories	insight	obtain	sole

1. The arrival of an unexpected guest requires the host to make some

    _____ to the seating plan.
      (changes, alterations)

2. A society's _____ gradually change from generation
          (customs, rules)
    to generation.

3. The counselors at the career placement office advise students on how to best

    match their study experiences to appropriate _____.
                           (jobs, professions)

4. Until the Panama Canal was built, the _____
                                  (only, single)
    westerly shipping route from Europe to Asia was around Cape Horn.

5. Success in college _____ a lot of hard work.
             (requires, necessitates)

6. Good customer service is _____; it does not stop
                 (continuing, long lasting)
    once the customer has left the store.

7. The wide-ranging success of rap and hip-hop music is a good

    _____ of how music can help bridge cultural divides.
      (example, demonstration)

8. Studying the historical context of a work of art can provide valuable

    _____ into what influenced an artist.
    (understanding, comprehension)

9. Marketers sort people into age, income, and lifestyle

    _____ so that they can target products more
       (groups, types)
    specifically.

10. A children's librarian can assist parents in choosing books that are

    _____ for their child's age group.
      (suitable, fitting)

11. Internet users can _____ a wide range of
               (get, gain)
    information that is not readily available through other sources.

12. Consumers are _____ surrounded by advertisements
           (regularly, continually)
    encouraging them to spend more money.

▶ One feature of academic language is that multi-word verbs are used less frequently than they are in conversation or fiction. In academic writing, single-word verbs replace multi-word verbs with similar meaning:

get hold of ➔ *acquire*   *start up* ➔ *initiate*

WORD FAMILIES

Most of the target words introduced in this chapter are part of a word family. Study the members of the word families in the table below. Look for spelling patterns for the verb, noun, adjective, and adverb forms of the words. Complete the table. List the patterns in the spaces.

Verb	Noun	Adjective	Adverb
adjust	adjustment	1. adjusted 2. adjustable	X
X	appropriateness	appropriate	appropriately
assume	assumption	X	X
X	constant	constant	constantly
dispose	disposal	disposable	X
illustrate	illustration	illustrative	X
initiate	initiation	X	X
modify	modification	modified	X
reinforce	reinforcement	reinforced	X
transfer	transfer	transferable	X
Spelling patterns			

Read each sentence and identify the part of speech of the missing word. Write an appropriate form of the target word in the blank. Use the word families table above to help you.

1. The _____ (**dispose**) of garbage is one of the critical issues facing modern cities.

2. The use of genetically- _____ (**modify**) food continues to be controversial.

3. It is important to review new vocabulary relatively soon after studying it in order to _____ (**reinforcement**) learning.

4. As key role models, teachers are expected to dress and behave _____ (**appropriate**) in front of their students.

5. One way to overcome shyness is to force yourself to _____ (**initiation**) a conversation with a stranger every other day.

NAPIER UNIVERSITY LIBRARY

6. The introduction of _____ (**adjust**) seats and steering wheels has made cars much more comfortable.

7. When she first _____ (**assumption**) the new position, she underestimated how difficult it would be.

8. In addition to subject knowledge, many universities also attempt to teach learning strategies and skills that are _____ (**transfer**) to life beyond the classroom.

9. The fact that Americans generally use the name *Kleenex* in place of the word *tissue* is a good _____ (**illustrate**) of the power of a brand name.

10. With the world _____ (**constant**) changing, the only certainty is change itself.

COLLOCATION

Each item below contains three example sentences with the same target word. In each sentence, the target word is paired with a different word and forms a different collocation. In the fourth sentence, the collocation has been left blank. Choose the collocation from the examples that best fits the last sentence and write it in the blank. You may need to change the form of one of the words to fit the sentence.

1. **a.** Often consumers follow their emotions instead of using objective **selection criteria** when choosing between two products.
   b. Members of the project team will be chosen by a **selection committee** made up of departmental managers.
   c. The presidential **selection process** in the United States takes longer than it does in many other democratic countries.
   d. The school board decided to simplify one phase of the
   _____ for new teachers by removing psychological tests.

2. **a.** Omega-3 fatty acids are a **special category** of fats that protect the heart.
   b. When discussing the women's movement, you must be aware that the term *feminist* covers a **broad category** of people.
   c. Children who get into trouble with the law do not fall into a **single** family **category**; they come from a variety of backgrounds.
   d. The term *hero* covers a _____ of people because it includes sports, film, and music stars as well as artists, scientists, and political leaders.

3. **a.** The image of teaching as a **safe occupation** has been destroyed by the increase in school-related violence.
   b. Air traffic control is a very **demanding occupation** because of the concentration required.
   c. Many people find nursing a **rewarding occupation**, despite the long hours and low pay.
   d. Employers are finding that workers in _____ have a greater risk of suffering from stress-related illnesses.

4. a. Newton's theory of gravity was informed by a **flash of insight** when he saw an apple fall from a tree.

 b. The photographs of homeless families provide **unpleasant insights** into the lives of the poor.

 c. The author's new history of the political and social movements of the 1960s gave **valuable insights** into the thinking of civil rights leaders.

 d. It is said that Archimedes shouted "Eureka" when he had a(n)

 _____ about how to measure the purity of gold.

5. a. Some countries use lotteries as a **clever device** to raise money without increasing taxes.

 b. Some linguists believe that hesitations in speech are a **stylistic device** used by speakers to let their listeners know that they are uncertain about what to say.

 c. Disclaimers are a **simple device** used by sellers to avoid legal action should future problems arise with a product.

 d. Flashbacks are a common _____ used by fiction writers to introduce background information about the characters.

6. a. Financial advice that would have been very expensive in the past can now be **freely obtained** on the Internet.

 b. The local newspaper reported that the funds for the new sports center had been **fraudulently obtained** through tax evasion.

 c. Some medicines that have not been approved in the United States can be **legally obtained** in Europe.

 d. The report on the effects of the oil spill can be

 _____ from the Environmental Protection Agency.

7. a. Two new **modes of communication** were introduced to the general public in the 1990s—e-mail and text messaging.

 b. Ocean liners declined in popularity as a **mode of travel** with the arrival of transatlantic passenger flights.

 c. Distances between factories and local differences in **modes of operation** make managing multinational companies very complex.

 d. Cars have different _____—forward, neutral, and reverse.

8. a. Aerobic exercise is one important part of an **ongoing maintenance** program for people who have recently lost weight.

 b. Since the election, the four major parties have been involved in **ongoing negotiations** to form a new coalition government.

 c. Researchers at Georgia State University are conducting an **ongoing investigation** into the ability of apes to use language.

 d. Some consumers prefer to pay for the _____ associated with an older car rather than buy a new car.

Complete the passage by filling in the blanks with the target words in the box. Use each word only once.

acquisition	foundation	norm	sole
factors	involved	selecting	transferring

DIFFERENT VIEWS ON PURCHASING BEHAVIOR

1 Consumer theorists disagree about just how carefully consumers consider a product or service before they purchase it. Some theorists argue that active consumer decision making is the (1) _____ of consumer choice. Others think that deliberate decision making is *not* the (2) _____ approach, nor is it even the (3) _____. Even when consumers are purchasing something for the first time, other (4) _____ such as a consumer's past experience and habits come into play and may circumvent careful decision making. More often than not, consumers will decide out of habit to stick with a brand name they know instead of (5) _____ to a new brand.

2 Here is a scale researchers use to rate the level of decision making consumers go through when initiating a purchase.

EPS   LPS   HDM

According to this scale, consumers typically engage in *extended problem solving (EPS)* when they make an important purchase for the first time, such as buying a new washing machine or computer. EPS includes researching available choices to obtain product information, evaluating the choice of products, (6) _____ the product, and post-(7) _____ activities, such as recommending the product to others. However, even when consumers are purchasing new items for the first time, they often do not have the time, resources, or motivation to become deeply (8) _____ in EPS. Instead, they engage in *limited problem solving (LPS)*, which omits some of the stages of EPS. For repeat purchases, consumers often rely on *habitual decision making (HDM)*. They choose to buy a product because they are loyal to the brand or because they don't want to bother to change brands when the product they are used to meets their needs.

Based on East, R. (1997). *Consumer Behaviour: Advances and Applications in Marketing*. New York: Prentice Hall Europe, pp. 8–13.

EXPLORING THE TOPIC

Think about what you have read about consumption in this chapter. Identify a purchase you have made that was important to you. Ask yourself the following questions:

- Did I know what choices were available and how to evaluate them?
- Did I have a clear idea of what I wanted?
- How much investigation did I do before the purchase and how much afterwards?
- Did I consider one choice and move on to others if it was unsuitable, or did I compare a selection of items?
- Did I make the right choice? Why or why not?

Discuss your purchase with a partner.

 Write an essay in which you consider your own purchasing behavior. Consider which types of decision-making processes (EPS, LPS, HDM) you engage in. Give examples of the types of products related to your use of EPS, LPS, or HDM. Describe any relationships you see between the type of product and the process of decision making that you followed.

CHAPTER 7

How We See Ourselves

GETTING STARTED

Discuss the following questions with your classmates.

- ▶ Make a list of adjectives that you would use to describe yourself. How many of these words relate to you personally, and how many are generally true of people in your family or culture?

- ▶ If you could change one thing about yourself, what would it be?

- ▶ Do you have a hero or a role model? What are the qualities in that person that you admire?

TARGET WORDS — Assessing Your Vocabulary Knowledge

Look at each of the target words in the box. Use the scale to give yourself a score for each word. After you finish the chapter, score yourself again to check your improvement.

1 I don't know this word.

2 I have seen this word before, but I am not sure of the meaning.

3 I understand the word when I see it or hear it in a sentence, but I don't know how to use it in my own speaking and writing.

4 I know this word and can use it in my own speaking and writing.

TARGET WORDS

____accuracy	____demonstrate	____instance	____perspective
____achieve	____deny	____intensity	____prior
____alter	____derive	____mental	____rejection
____attribute	____dimension	____motivate	____stability
____challenge	____emerge	____participants	____trigger
____consistent	____expose	____perceive	____vision

The following passage is adapted from an introductory textbook on marketing and focuses on self-image and consumer behavior. As you read, pay special attention to the target vocabulary words in **bold**.

How PERSPECTIVES ON THE SELF INFLUENCE CONSUMER BEHAVIOR

1   Many people feel that their self-image and possessions affect their value as a person. Products, from cars to aftershave, are often bought because a person is trying either to show off or to **deny** some aspect of his or her self. How consumers feel about themselves shapes their consumption habits, particularly as they try to fulfill social expectations about how a male or female should look and act.

Self-image and consumer behavior are connected.

DOES THE SELF EXIST?

2   The 1980s were called the "Me Decade" because for many this time was marked by a fascination with the self. The idea that each person has a self may seem natural to us, but this concept is actually quite new. The idea that each human life is unique developed in late medieval times (between the eleventh and fifteenth centuries in Europe). **Prior** to that time, individuals were considered in relation to a group, and even today, many Eastern cultures place more emphasis on the importance of a collective self than on a unique, independent self.

3   Both Eastern and Western cultures see the self as divided into an inner, private self and an outer, public self. But where they differ is in terms of which part is seen as the "real you." Western culture tends to promote the idea of individuality—a self that is separated from other selves. In contrast, many Eastern cultures focus on an interdependent self that **derives** its identity in large part from interrelationships with others.

4   For example, a Confucian **perspective** stresses the importance of "face"—other people's perceptions of the self and maintaining one's desired status in their eyes. In the past, some Asian cultures developed clear rules about the specific clothes and even colors that people in certain social classes and occupations were allowed to display, and these live on today in Japanese style manuals. This style of dress is at odds with such Western practices as "casual Fridays," which encourage employees to dress informally and express their unique selves.

SELF-CONCEPT

5   To understand the many factors that affect a person's sense of self, sociologists look at a person's *self-concept*. The term *self-concept* refers to the beliefs a person holds about his or her **attributes**, and how he or she evaluates these qualities. While a person's overall self-concept may be positive, there are certainly parts of the self that tend to be evaluated more positively than others. For **instance**, a young man may **derive** more confidence from his identity as an employee of a large company than he does as the father of a new baby.

COMPONENTS OF THE SELF

6   A person's self-concept is a very complex structure, with many **attributes.** To evaluate a person's self-concept, it is necessary to consider the following **dimensions** of the overall self:

Content—what the self-concept is based on (e.g., is it based on a trait like facial attractiveness or **mental** ability?)
Positivity or negativity—whether it reflects a high or low degree of self-confidence
Intensity—whether it is strong or weak
Stability—whether it remains consistent over time
Accuracy—whether it corresponds to reality

As we'll see later, consumers' self-assessments can be quite inaccurate, especially when it comes to physical appearance.

SELF-ESTEEM

7   Self-esteem is a reflection of how positive or negative a person's self-concept is. People with low self-esteem do not expect that they will perform very well, and they will try to avoid embarrassment, failure, or **rejection**. In contrast, people with high self-esteem expect to be successful, will take more risks, and are more willing to be the center of attention. Self-esteem is often related to being accepted by others. For example, teenagers who are members of high status groups have higher self-esteem than their excluded classmates.

8   Marketing communications can influence a consumer's level of self-esteem. **Exposure** to advertisements can **trigger** a process of *social comparison*, in which a person tries to evaluate his or her self by comparing it to the people shown in advertising images. This form of comparison appears to be a basic human **motive**. Many marketers have tapped into this need by supplying idealized images of happy, attractive people who are using their products in order to **motivate** people to buy the products.

9   A recent study illustrates how this social comparison process works. The study showed that female college students tend to compare their physical appearance with advertising models. Study **participants** were **exposed** to beautiful women in advertisements. Afterwards the **participants** expressed lowered satisfaction with their own appearance as compared with other **participants** who were not **exposed** to the advertisements. Another study **demonstrated** that young women's **perceptions** of their own body shapes and sizes were **altered** after the women had viewed as little as thirty minutes of television programming.

10   *Self-esteem advertising* attempts to change people's product attitudes by stimulating positive feelings about the self. One strategy is to **challenge** the consumer's self-esteem and then show a product or service that will provide a remedy. For example, an advertisement for Zest soap says, "You're not fully clean until you're Zestfully clean."

11   When consumers compare their actual **attributes** to their ideal image of themselves, their self-esteem often suffers. Consumers might ask themselves questions such as, "Am I as attractive as I would like to be?" "Do I make as much money as I should?" The *ideal self*—a person's conception of how he or she would like to be—and the *actual self*—a more realistic self-evaluation of the qualities one has or lacks—are often in conflict.

12   The ideal self is partly shaped by elements of the consumer's culture, such as heroes or people shown in advertising images who serve as models of **achievement** or appearance. Consumers may purchase a product because they hope it will help them **achieve** the kind of goals or look shown in an advertisement. Consumers may also choose products that they **perceive** to be **consistent** with their actual self, or products that they believe will help them reach their ideal self.

FANTASY: BRIDGING THE GAP BETWEEN THE SELVES

13   While most people experience an **inconsistency** between their real and ideal selves, for some consumers this gap is larger than for others. These people are especially good targets for marketing communications that employ *fantasy* to attract consumer attention. The marketing strategies allow consumers to create a **vision** of themselves by placing them in unfamiliar, exciting situations or by permitting them to try interesting or challenging roles. With today's technology—for

instance, online makeovers or virtual previews of sunglasses or clothing—consumers can even experiment with different looks before actually buying products and services in the real world.

MULTIPLE SELVES

14   As we have seen, the self is complex. In addition, most people really have a variety of selves, or *role identities*. This means that in a way, any one person is a number of different people; for example, your mother probably would not recognize the "you" that **emerges** while you're on vacation with a group of friends! People have as many selves as they do different social roles (e.g., husband, boss, student). Depending on the situation, individuals act differently and use different products and services. A person may require a different set of products to play a desired role: a man may choose a blue pin-striped suit when he is being his professional self, but wear chinos and a Hawaiian shirt when he goes out on Saturday night. Like actors on a stage, consumers play different roles, and each role has its own script, props, and costumes. These roles and other factors have a strong influence on consumer behavior.

———
Adapted from Solomon, M., Bamossy, G., and Askegaard, S. (2002). *Consumer Behaviour: A European Perspective*, 2nd ed. New York: Prentice Hall Europe, pp. 189–191.

UNDERSTANDING THE READING

Respond to the following in writing. Base your responses on the reading and your own personal experiences.

1. Give an example of how self-concept might influence someone's self-esteem.
2. What is "self-esteem advertising"? Describe an example of how it works.
3. What are your different social roles? Do you require different products to play those roles? If yes, give some examples.

FOCUSING ON VOCABULARY

WORD MEANING

Read the sentences below and circle the letter of the word or phrase that best matches the meaning of the target word in **bold**. Use context clues in the sentences to determine the correct meaning. Check your dictionary if you are not sure of the answer.

1. In order to **achieve** good grades in college, students must manage their study time and social life carefully.
   a. be in charge of
   b. succeed in doing something
   c. fail to finish

2. First-class athletes require physical **attributes** such as strength and speed as well as mental **attributes** such as concentration and willpower.
   a. feelings
   b. issues
   c. qualities or features

3. When children move from adolescence to adulthood, they often go through a stage in which they **challenge** the authority of their parents.
   a. change
   b. question
   c. agree with

4. People who regularly **deny** that they are good looking or talented may have a problem with their self-image.
   a. refuse to admit
   b. expect
   c. agree

5. Parents often try to include an educational **dimension** in family vacations.
   a. an interest or thought
   b. an aspect; one part of a situation
   c. a demand or requirement

6. Thunderstorms of high **intensity** can sometimes produce tornados.
   a. strength
   b. protection
   c. damage

7. Some companies use the promise of a promotion to **motivate** their employees.
   a. move
   b. encourage
   c. fight

8. For some buyers, a luxury car is **perceived** as a sign of success.
   a. misunderstood by someone
   b. thought of in a particular way
   c. explained in a particular way

9. **Prior** to beginning college or a career, many young people take a year off to travel around the world.
   a. before or earlier
   b. secret
   c. after or later

10. Many parents find their children's **rejection** of family values or beliefs very upsetting.
    a. acceptance
    b. avoidance
    c. refusal to accept

11. If your **vision** of marriage is limited to planning the perfect wedding, you may experience problems adjusting to the ordinariness of everyday married life.
    a. a colorful view
    b. a bold discovery
    c. an idea or mental image

Read the sentences below and use context to figure out the meaning of the target words in **bold**. Look for a core meaning that provides a general understanding of each target word. Write the meaning in your own words.

1. **a.** Because of the presence of some small mistakes, the committee questioned the **accuracy** of the whole report.
   b. Despite the **accuracy** of computer calculations, they still need to be double-checked by human beings.

   accuracy _____

2. **a.** The organizers **altered** the program of events because of the band's late cancellation.

   b. The U.S. Surgeon General's office has been successful in **altering** public opinion about the dangers of cigarette smoking.

   alter _____

3. **a.** Although the basketball player was very talented, his level of playing lacked **consistency** from week to week.

   b. Parents have changeable moods, but they should be **consistent** in how they handle their children's behavior.

   consistent _____

4. **a.** The historical map **demonstrated** the different routes enslaved people took when they headed north to freedom on the Underground Railroad.

   b. The inventor **demonstrated** the functions of his new machine to a group of investors.

   demonstrate _____

5. **a.** The English word *bankrupt* is **derived** from the Italian phrase *banca rotta*, which means "broken bench."

   b. Medicines are often **derived** from plants.

   derive _____

6. **a.** The sun **emerged** from behind the clouds.

   b. Often young people feel that their true identities do not **emerge** until after they leave home and are no longer under the direct control of their parents.

   emerge _____

7. **a.** When **exposed** to highly contagious diseases, people are likely to become ill.

   b. Children who are **exposed** to books at an early age often learn to read more easily.

   exposed _____

8. **a.** People suffering from stress need both physical and **mental** relaxation.

   b. Learning a foreign language requires a great deal of **mental** effort.

   mental _____

9. **a.** Each of the **participants** in the television debate represented a different political party.

   b. **Participants** in the study were not allowed to eat meat during the experiment.

   participant _____

10. **a.** The American Civil War was followed by a long period of political and economic **stability**.

    b. Environmentalists believe that the **stability** of the earth's many ecosystems is at risk because of the actions of humans.

    stability _____

11. **a.** Hearing a familiar song can **trigger** a string of memories about old times, friends, and places.

    b. Stress, sunlight, loud noises, and certain foods can **trigger** migraine headaches.

    trigger _____

12. **a.** Poets and scientists often have very different **perspectives** on the natural world.
   b. Companies should consider cultural as well as economic **perspectives** when evaluating the success or failure of an overseas business project.

   perspective _____

WORD TIP

▶ The most common meaning of the word *instance* is "an example of a particular kind of situation."

   Instances of fighting among spectators at sports events have increased.

▶ The most frequent use of the word *instance*, however, is in the phrase *for instance*. The phrase *for instance* is used as a marker to introduce an example or a set of examples.

   Most nations and cultures have both historical and fictional heroes. Japan, *for instance*, has Tokugawa Ieyasu and Momotaro—the Peach Boy; the United States has Abe Lincoln and Paul Bunyan; and England has Lord Nelson and Robin Hood.

WORD FAMILIES

Read the sentences below. Some of the target words have been used correctly, but in six sentences a wrong word form has been used. If the wrong form has been used, cross it out and write the correct form. If the form is correct, put a checkmark (✓).

1. The **perceive** of the fans was that the referee favored the opposing team.

   _____

2. Critics called the biography **derivative** because the author had relied too much on the works of previous writers. _____

3. The **intensity** pain indicated that her injuries might be serious.

   _____

4. Management's **motivation** for introducing a new policy on working hours was to cut absenteeism. _____

5. The reporter followed the **emerging** story of a scandal involving a top movie director. _____

6. The suspect's repeated **deny** of the evidence made it difficult for the police to take the investigation forward. _____

7. Teachers believe that the **participant** of parents is essential to the success of a child's schooling. _____

8. The arguments put forward for nonapproval of the new medicine were not **consistently** with the scientific research tests. _____

9. The city government felt that the official federal figures for the local population could not be **accurate** because their own records gave a much larger number. _____

10. A major factor in job satisfaction is whether or not people find the work they do **challenged**. _____

COLLOCATION

Match each target word in the box with the group of words that regularly occur with it. In all cases, the target word comes after the word in the list.

alter	demonstrate	participant	stability
challenge	expose	rejection	vision

1._____
emotional
threaten
achieve
political

2._____
active
eager
willing
regular

3._____
cope with
fear of
overwhelming
feeling of

4._____
accept a
serious
face a
overcome a

5._____
realistic
optimistic
realize a
shared

6._____
radically
significantly
permanently
fundamentally

7._____
inadvertently
needlessly
publicly
cruelly

8._____
clearly
vividly
convincingly
conclusively

EXPANSION

Read the first paragraph about self-esteem. Follow the directions and complete the self-esteem questionnaire on your own.

Self-Esteem

1   Self-esteem is one of the key **attributes** of a healthy and happy life. Thus, it is an important component of **mental** health, and receives a great deal of attention in both popular and scientific publications. There are numerous self-report questionnaires available that claim to give an indication of a person's self-esteem, however they vary widely in quality. Self-esteem questionnaires in popular magazines may be written by authors with no psychological background and are meant to be merely entertaining. On the other end of the scale, questionnaires in scientific studies have been very carefully constructed so that they provide reliable data.

On the next page is a self-esteem questionnaire with items collected from a variety of sources. Complete the questionnaire, and then answer the questions that follow.

SELF-ESTEEM QUESTIONNAIRE

Read the statements and circle the answer that best describes your feeling about yourself.

SA = Strongly Agree
A   = Agree
D   = Disagree
SD = Strongly Disagree

1. I have a happy, **stable** life.	SA A D SD
2. I am afraid of being **rejected** by the people I know.	SA A D SD
3. I grew up in a family that helped me to **achieve** my goals.	SA A D SD
4. I feel uncomfortable trying out activities when I have no **prior** experience doing them.	SA A D SD
5. I share the same **perspectives** on life as my friends and colleagues.	SA A D SD
6. I often get sick, for **instance**, with colds, stomachaches, and other minor illnesses.	SA A D SD
7. Socializing is an important **dimension** of my life.	SA A D SD
8. When I fail at something, it **triggers** feelings of depression.	SA A D SD

Now read paragraph 2 and discuss the questions with a partner.

2   The questionnaire generally indicates positive self-esteem if you agreed with odd-numbered items and disagreed with even-numbered items. Do the results from the questionnaire correspond with your own feelings about your self-esteem? How valid do you think the questions are in determining self-esteem?

Do some research on self-esteem advertising. Look at a range of television or print advertising (e.g., in magazines and newspapers) to find five or six examples of self-esteem advertisements. Identify the product or service being advertised and the target audience. What kind of feelings about the self does each advertisement aim to stimulate? Write a report on your findings. Include copies of the advertisements wherever possible.

8

Strategy Practice

USING YOUR DICTIONARY—Abbreviations, Labels, and Codes

Your dictionary provides a lot of information about each entry word in a very small space. To do this, dictionaries use abbreviations, labels, and codes.

CRACKING YOUR DICTIONARY'S CODE

In order to use the dictionary quickly and efficiently, you must become familiar with the commonly used codes. Read the sample abbreviations, labels, and codes from *The Longman Advanced American Dictionary* (LAAD). Use them to answer the questions about the dictionary entries.

Short forms

adj.	adjective	*phr. v.*	phrasal verb	*sb*	someone
adv.	adverb	*prep.*	preposition	*sth*	something
n.	noun	*pron.*	pronoun	*v.*	verb

Labels

FORMAL a word that is appropriate for formal speech or writing, but would not usually be used in ordinary conversation

INFORMAL a word or phrase that is used in normal conversation, but may not be appropriate for use in more formal contexts, such as business letters or academic writing

LAW a word with a technical meaning used by lawyers, in court etc.

LITERARY a word used mainly in English literature, and not in modern speech or writing

OLD-FASHIONED a word that was used early in the twentieth century, but would sound old-fashioned today

TECHNICAL a word used by doctors, scientists, or other specialists

BRITISH British English

CANADIAN Canadian English

Grammar codes

[C] countable; shows that a noun can be counted and has a plural form: *We planted an orange* **tree**. | *Children love to climb* **trees**.

[U] uncountable; shows that a noun cannot be counted and has no plural form: *I need some* **peace** *and quiet.* | *a glass of* **milk**

[I] intransitive; shows that a verb has no direct object: *I'm sure I can* **cope**. | *Our food supplies soon* **ran out**.

[T] transitive; shows that a verb is followed by a direct object which can be either a noun phrase or a clause: *I* **like** *swimming, playing tennis, and things like that.* | *I* **hope** *I'm not disturbing you.* | *We never* **found out** *her real name.*

[I,T] intransitive or transitive; shows that a verb may be used with or without a direct object: *Bernice was* **knitting** *as she watched TV.* | *She was* **knitting** *a sweater.*

[not in progressive] shows that a verb is not used in the progressive form, i.e. the **-ing** form after **be**: *I* **hate** *housework (not "I am hating housework").* | *Who* **knows** *the answer?*

[only before noun] shows that an adjective can only be used before a noun: *the* **sheer** *size of the building* | *the* **main** *points of her speech*

mode /moʊd/ *n.* [C] **1** FORMAL a particular way or style of behaving, living or doing something: *Commercial airlines have the lowest accident rate of all transportation modes.* | *In the 21st century, we have more choices about modes of living.* **2 be in work/survival/teaching etc. mode** INFORMAL to be thinking or behaving in a particular way at a particular time: *While in cost-cutting mode, he replaced the security officer with a guard dog.* **3** TECHNICAL a particular way in which a machine operates when it is doing a particular job: *To put the VCR in record mode you press record and play simultaneously.* | *The car features an economy driving mode.* **4 be the mode** OLD-FASHIONED to be fashionable at a particular time—see also À LA MODE.

per•ceive /pə'siv/ *v.* [T not in progressive] **1** to think of something or someone in a particular way: **[perceive sb/sth as sb/sth]** *The tax system was widely perceived as unfair to ordinary workers* (=many people thought it was unfair). | **[perceive sb/sth to be sth]** *High-tech industries are perceived to be crucial to the country's economic growth.* | **[perceive that]** *Many students perceive that on-the-job training is more important than college.* **2** FORMAL to notice something, especially something that is difficult to notice: *The human eye is capable of perceiving thousands of insignificant details.* | *Emma had perceived a certain bitterness in his tone.* —see also PERCEPTION

sole¹ /soʊl/ *adj.* [only before noun] **1** the sole person, thing etc. is the only one: *The sole purpose of his trip was to attend a concert at Carnegie Hall.* | *the sole survivor of the crash* **2** a sole duty, right, responsibility etc. is one that is not shared with anyone else: *Arthur will retain sole ownership of the company.*

where•by /wɛr'baɪ/ *adv.* FORMAL by means of which or according to which: *The mall created a frequent shopper plan whereby customers earn discounts.*

1. Which entry word is an adjective? _____

2. Which entry word is an adverb? _____

3. Which entry word is used only in formal speech and writing?

   _____

4. Which entry word is followed by a direct object? _____

5. Which entry word can only be used before a noun? _____

6. Which entry word has different meanings depending on the situation in which it is used? _____

7. Which entry word cannot be used in the progressive tense? _____

PRACTICING YOUR DICTIONARY SKILLS

Work with a partner. Look at your own dictionaries. Find the page or pages in your dictionaries that explain its codes and abbreviations. (They are normally near the front or back cover.) List the code or abbreviation that tells you the following:

1. how formal a word is: _____

2. if it is a specific variety of English (e.g., British or Australian):

   _____

3. if a noun is countable or uncountable: _____

4. whether a verb is normally used in the passive: _____

5. whether a word is a preposition: _____

6. whether a verb is transitive: _____

Look up the following words. What do your dictionary's codes indicate about each word? List one or two codes or labels and explain what they mean. The first one has been done for you.

1. bond

   The abbreviations n. and v. indicate that the word can be a

   noun or a verb. Law indicates the legal meanings of the word.

2. demonstrate

   _____

   _____

3. initiate

   _____

   _____

4. obtain

   _____

   _____

STRATEGY—Word Parts That Change a Word's Meaning

Chapter 4, "Strategy Practice," (page 31) explained how some affixes change a word's part of speech:

> interact (verb) + **-tion** = interaction (noun)
> strategy (noun) + **-ic** = strategic (adjective)
> resourceful (adjective) + **-ly** = resourcefully (adverb)

Adding other affixes results in a change in the word's meaning.

> design + **-er** = designer (a person who designs)
> **re-** + adjust = readjust (to adjust again)

Read the following sentences. Note the italicized affix in each boldfaced word, and write the meaning of the affix.

1. **a.** Owning a car is an **achiev*able*** goal for most people in America.
   b. The points customers receive for flying frequently on a particular airline are usually not **transfer*able*** to another person.

   The suffix **-able** means

   _____

2. **a.** The military **strateg*ist*** read all of the available books on famous generals before planning for battle.
   b. The singer was pleased that her **accompan*ist*** played the piano so well.

   The suffix **-ist** means

   _____

3. **a.** The film in the camera was ***overexposed*** due to the bright sunlight.
   b. Research studies seem to suggest that while girls often lack confidence, boys tend to ***overestimate*** their abilities.

   The prefix ***over-*** means

   _____

4. **a.** Although ocean oil platforms seem huge, the ***substructure*** under water is many times the size of what is visible above the surface.
   b. Experts in education will generally specialize in one ***subcategory*** such as early childhood education, adult education, or special education.

   The prefix ***sub-*** means

   _____

WORD KNOWLEDGE—Comparing Academic and Everyday Vocabulary

Compare the two sentences in each pair. Circle the letter of the sentence that is more academic. Then describe how the underlined word and the **bold** word differ.

1. **a.** The earth contains many <u>different</u> kinds of life.
   b. The earth contains many **diverse** kinds of life.

   _____

2. **a.** The government collects <u>money</u> from taxes.
   b. The government collects **revenue** from taxes.

   _____

3. **a.** Modern labor-saving <u>machines</u> have created more free time for the entire family.
   b. Modern labor-saving **devices** have created more free time for the entire family.

   _____

Match the everyday words or phrases on the left with their academic counterparts on the right.

_____ **1.** shown   **a.** accompany

_____ **2.** go with   **b.** exposed to

_____ **3.** change   **c.** triggered

_____ **4.** pass on   **d.** alter

_____ **5.** caused   **e.** fundamental

_____ **6.** basic   **f.** transfer

Write a sentence for each of the academic words in the matching exercise above.

1. _____

2. _____

3. _____

4. _____

5. _____

6. _____

UNIT
3

Workplaces and Work Spaces

CHAPTER 9

How Office Space Affects Behavior

GETTING STARTED

Discuss the following questions with your classmates.

▶ Where do you work best? Do you like to study in the privacy of your own room? Or are you happier in the library with a group of friends around you?

▶ What conditions are important for you to work well? What makes your study space comfortable?

▶ How important is it for you to interact with others to complete your assignments?

TARGET WORDS—Assessing Your Vocabulary Knowledge

Look at each of the target words in the box. Use the scale to give yourself a score for each word. After you finish the chapter, score yourself again to check your improvement.

1 I don't know this word.

2 I have seen this word before, but I am not sure of the meaning.

3 I understand the word when I see it or hear it in a sentence, but I don't know how to use it in my own speaking and writing.

4 I know this word and can use it in my own speaking and writing.

TARGET WORDS

____administrative	____considerable	____exclusion	____restrict
____allocate	____cycle	____facilitate	____seek
____approach	____debate	____flexibility	____status
____assign	____decade	____maximum	____trace
____code	____eliminate	____percent	____traditional
____concentration	____enhanced	____phase	____widespread

The following passage is adapted from an introductory textbook on management. This section focuses specifically on the relationship between work space and employee behavior. As you read, pay special attention to the target vocabulary words in **bold**.

WORK SPACE DESIGN

1   Businesses large and small now realize that physical work space influences employee behavior. As a result, businesses are redesigning their buildings and workplaces with the intent of reshaping employee attitudes and behavior. As firms redesign their offices, they focus on three main factors that have a strong impact on employee behavior: how much space employees have, how the space is arranged, and how much privacy employees have.

SIZE

2   In relation to work space, *size* is defined by the number of square feet per employee. Historically, the amount of space an employee had was primarily related to the employee's **status**. The higher an individual was in the organization's hierarchy, the larger the office he or she typically got. That, however, no longer seems to be true. As organizations **seek** to develop more equality, the trends have been toward reducing space dedicated to specific employees, lessening or **eliminating** space **allocations** based on hierarchical position, and making more space available for groups or teams to meet in.

3   According to recent estimates, the amount of personal office space organizations give to **administrative** employees has shrunk by 25 to 50 **percent** over the past **decade**. This change is due in part to economics. Space costs money and reducing space cuts costs. But a lot of this reduction can be **traced** to changes in the organizations. As jobs have been redesigned and **traditional** hierarchies replaced with teamwork, the need for large offices has lessened.

4   In the past, it was not unusual for organizations, especially large ones such as IBM and General Motors, to define square footage for each level in the hierarchy. Senior executives, for instance, may have been **assigned** 800 square feet plus 300 square feet for a private secretary's office. A section manager may have

Open work spaces

gotten 400 square feet, a unit manager 120, and supervisors only 80 square feet. Today, an increasing number of organizations are replacing closed offices with cubicles, making the cubicles constant in size, and acknowledging little or no differences because of managerial rank.

5   When extra space is being **allocated**, rather than giving it to specific individuals, the trend today is toward setting it aside to create a place where people can meet and teams can work. These "public spaces" can be used for socializing, small group meetings, or as places where team members can work through problems.

ARRANGEMENT

6   While size is a measure of the amount of space per employee, the term *arrangement* refers to the distance between people and facilities. The arrangement of the workplace is important primarily because it significantly influences social interaction.

7   Research has shown that people are more likely to interact with those individuals who are physically close to them. Employees' work locations, therefore, are likely to influence the

information to which they are exposed and their inclusion or **exclusion** from various activities and events within the organization.

8   A topic that has received a **considerable** amount of attention is furniture arrangement in **traditional** offices, specifically the placement of the desk and where the employee chooses to sit. Unlike workers on the factory floor, individuals in offices typically have some **flexibility** in laying out their office furniture. And the arrangement of an office conveys nonverbal messages to visitors. For instance, a desk placed between two parties conveys formality and the power of the officeholder, while chairs set so that individuals can sit at right angles to each other conveys a more natural and informal relationship.

PRIVACY

9   Privacy is in part a function of the amount of space per person and the arrangement of that space. But it also is influenced by walls, screens, and other physical barriers. In recent years, a **widespread** work space design trend has been to **phase** out closed offices and replace them with open offices that have few, if any, walls or doors. The two very different perspectives on office space are sometimes described as the "cave versus cube" **debate**. The "cave" provides privacy while the "cube" **facilitates** open communication. In the United States alone, an estimated 40 million people, or nearly 60 **percent** of the whole country's white-collar workforce, now work in cubes.

10   Caves limit interaction. So organizations have sought to increase **flexibility** and employee collaboration by removing physical barriers such as high walls, closed offices, and doors. Yet, while the trend is clearly toward cubes, organizations are making exceptions for employees engaged in work that requires deep **concentration**. Companies such as Microsoft, Apple Computer, and Adobe Systems, for example, continue to rely primarily on private offices for software programmers. People who write **code** need to cooperate with others at times, but theirs is essentially a lonely task requiring tremendous **concentration**. This is best achieved in a closed workplace that is cut off from others.

11   A further extension of the open office concept is called "hoteling." Employees book reservations for space with the company office manager, get **assigned** a workplace, pull over a desk-on-wheels, plug the phone into a modem jack, and begin their work. The only space that employees actually call their own is typically a bin or locker where they can keep their personal belongings. Employees "check out" each day when they depart. Used by organizations in management-consulting, financial, and high-tech sectors, where employees spend a significant **percentage** of their work time outside the office or in team meetings, it provides **maximum** office space **flexibility**. However, hoteling has some serious downsides. Employees often feel rootless and complain that hoteling **restricts** the informal socializing and learning that come from having a fixed workplace location.

12   What about individual differences? There is growing evidence that the desire for privacy is a strong one for many people. Yet the trend is clearly toward less privacy at the workplace. Further research is needed to determine whether or not organizational efforts to create open work spaces are incompatible with individual preferences for privacy and result in lower employee performance and satisfaction.

A private office

WORK SPACE DESIGN AND PRODUCTIVITY

13   How does a redesigned work space positively affect employee productivity? Studies suggest that work space, by itself, doesn't have a

substantial motivational impact on people; rather, it makes certain behaviors easier or harder to perform. In this way, employee effectiveness is **enhanced** or reduced. More specifically, evidence shows that work space designs that increase employee contact, comfort, and **flexibility** are likely to positively influence motivation and productivity. For instance, Amoco Corporation in Denver reported a 25 **percent** decrease in product **cycle** time (the time required to make its products), a 75 **percent** decrease in formal meeting time, an 80 **percent** reduction in duplicated files, and a 44 **percent** reduction in overall space costs after offices were redesigned to **facilitate** teamwork. Based on the evidence to date, an **approach** that matches office space to the sophistication of the work required is probably best. Jobs that are complex and require high degrees of **concentration** are likely to be made more difficult by noise and constant interruptions. Such jobs are best done in closed offices. But most jobs don't require quiet and privacy. In fact, quite the contrary, jobs today increasingly require regular interaction with others to achieve maximum productivity. This is probably best achieved in an open office setting.

———

Adapted from Robbins, S. P. (2001). *Organizational Behavior,* 9th ed. Upper Saddle River, NJ: Prentice Hall International, pp. 456–459.

UNDERSTANDING THE READING

Respond to the following in writing. Base your responses on the reading and your own personal experiences.

1. What is the traditional relationship between organizational hierarchy and the amount of space allocated to an employee? Why is that relationship changing?
2. What is hoteling? What are the benefits and limitations of this type of working arrangement?
3. What kinds of effects have recent changes in work space design had on productivity?

FOCUSING ON VOCABULARY

WORD MEANING

Match the words with their definitions. If you are unsure about a word's meaning, try to figure it out from context by rereading the passage on pp. 71–73. Then check your dictionary.

Set 1

_____ 1. eliminate

_____ 2. allocate

_____ 3. decade

_____ 4. administrative

_____ 5. percent

_____ 6. trace

_____ 7. cycle

a. a number of related events or actions that happen again and again in the same order

b. a period of ten years

c. parts equal to a particular number in every 100 parts

d. to get rid of

e. related to the work of managing or organizing a company or institution

f. to find the origins of something

g. to decide officially that a particular amount of something should be used for a particular purpose

Set 2

_____ **1.** exclusion

_____ **2.** flexibility

_____ **3.** widespread

_____ **4.** debate

_____ **5.** concentration

_____ **6.** code

_____ **7.** restrict

_____ **8.** assign

a. the ability to change or be changed easily

b. the ability to think carefully about something for a long period of time

c. to control or limit someone's actions

d. happening or existing in many places, or among many people

e. the act of not allowing someone to take part in an activity

f. to give someone money, equipment, space, etc. for their use

g. a set of instructions that tell a computer what to do

h. a discussion of an issue about which people express differing opinions

Read the row of words and phrases below each numbered word. One word or phrase in each list is *not* a synonym for the numbered word. Cross it out.

1. status			
rank	position	standing	system

2. seek			
look for	search for	use up	try to find

3. traditional			
usual	variable	accepted	customary

4. considerable			
famous	extensive	large	significant

5. maximum			
most	highest	rare	utmost

6. facilitate			
make easy	hold back	assist	make possible

7. enhance			
improve	praise	increase	add to

8. approach			
method	style	agreement	way

WORD TIP

▶ The noun **phase** generally means "one stage in a process." In this chapter, however, the word is part of the phrasal verb **phase out**. The meaning of this phrasal verb is "to gradually stop using or providing something."

Due to changes in technology, music companies **phased out** record albums and cassette tapes in favor of CDs.

WORD FAMILIES

The table below contains word families for some of the target words in the reading. Complete the rest of the table. An X indicates that there is not a form or that the form is not common. Sometimes there may be more than one form possible. If you are unsure about a form, check your dictionary.

Verb	Noun	Adjective	Adverb
administer	1. administration 2.	administrative	administratively
X	X	considerable	
cycle	cycle	1. cyclic 2.	cyclically
	enhancement	enhanced	X
eliminate		eliminated	X
	exclusion	exclusive	exclusively
facilitate	1. facility 2. facilitator		X
maximize	maximum	1. maximum 2.	
X	1. percent 2.	X	X
restrict	restriction	1. 2. restricted	restrictively

Choose the correct form of the word in **bold** in sentence **a** to complete sentence **b**. Use the word families table you just completed as a guide. For two items, more than one correct answer is possible.

1. a. The CEO's **administrative** assistant provides him with background reports on topics discussed at company meetings.

    b. The university financial aid office _____ the distribution of student grants and loans.

2. a. There is **considerable** interest in voice recognition software among people who do a lot of writing.

    b. Language experts' views on how grammar works have changed

      _____ over the last decade.

3. a. The **cycle** of the seasons brings changes in temperature and the amount of daylight.

    b. The economy is _____ in nature, so boom and bust periods are to be expected.

4. a. A key cost-saving strategy for companies is the **elimination** of waste.

    b. The goal of proofreading is to _____ spelling mistakes and typographical errors from a piece of writing.

5. **a.** Computer-generated graphics are often used to **enhance** traditional special effects in films.

   b. The town center _____ project aimed to minimize traffic in order to create pedestrian-friendly shopping areas.

6. **a.** **Exclusion** from most jobs on the basis of gender is against the law in the United States.

   b. Immigration laws can be used both to welcome and to _____ people wishing to start a new life in a new country.

7. **a.** In some cultures, teachers are givers of knowledge; in others they are **facilitators** who help students discover knowledge for themselves.

   b. A matchmaker's role is to _____ meetings between young men and women of marriageable age.

8. **a.** Chimpanzee males aim to **maximize** their reproductive success by mating with several females.

   b. The French TGV trains are able to travel at a _____ speed of 515 km/h (320 mph).

9. **a.** Women made up 18.3 **percent** of the United States labor force in 1900, 29.6 **percent** in 1950, and 46.6 **percent** in 2001.

   b. Families who prepare a household budget can work out the

   _____ of income spent on food and other basic necessities.

10. **a.** Water shortages have led to **restrictions** on the watering of lawns and parks.

   b. _____ clothing can cause health problems such as stomach trouble and backaches.

COLLOCATION

Each item below contains three sentences with the same collocation. Write a fourth sentence of your own using the same word partners.

1. **a.** Relief organizations aim to help people in developing countries **allocate** limited **resources** to long-term development projects like farming.
   b. The principal **allocated** equipment and **resources** equally between girls' and boys' sports teams.
   c. In the army, it is the job of the quartermaster to ensure that **resources** such as food and clothing are **allocated** efficiently.

   d. _____

2. **a.** The company's **practical approach** to employee training included offering workshops on new software applications.
   b. Workers must take a **practical approach** to balancing career and family life.
   c. Many hospital emergency rooms use a very **practical approach** called *triage* to ensure that the most seriously ill or injured patients are treated first.

   d. _____

3. **a.** Handling the airplane during the stormy weather required all of the pilot's **powers of concentration**.

   b. These works of philosophy ask too much of the students' **powers of concentration**.

   c. The speaker needed all of his **powers of concentration** to continue his talk after the demonstrators entered the auditorium.

   d. _____

4. **a.** An **ongoing debate** between environmentalists and traffic planners concerns whether more roads actually reduce traffic problems.

   b. Recent research into ape language has refuelled the **ongoing debate** about language being a uniquely human capability.

   c. The real reasons for global warming will continue to be the subject of **ongoing debate** by scientists for many years to come.

   d. _____

5. **a.** Digital technology has **greatly enhanced** the fields of photography, video, and broadcasting.

   b. Recipients of artificial hips normally find that their mobility is **greatly enhanced** after the operation.

   c. Lighter building materials have **greatly enhanced** the speed and capabilities of modern aircraft.

   d. _____

6. **a.** The new contracts offer employees a **degree of flexibility** in how they arrange their working hours.

   b. Newer car models give owners a greater **degree of flexibility** in how they arrange seating and storage space.

   c. Home buyers today are looking for loan repayment plans with a high **degree of flexibility**.

   d. _____

7. **a.** The size of an office and the quality of the furniture are still clear **symbols** of **status** in many companies and organizations.

   b. Expensive sports cars are classic **status symbols**.

   c. The invitations given to successful sports teams and athletes to visit the White House are a **symbol** of the high **status** granted to athletic ability in the United States.

   d. _____

8. **a.** There is **widespread support** among the general public in the United States for a more equitable health care system.

   b. Attempts to limit the use of English words in the French language have not received **widespread support** from the French public.

   c. European women have expressed **widespread support** for increased paternity rights for men.

   d. _____

Read the statements below and indicate whether you agree **(A)** or disagree **(D)**. Then discuss your opinions and reasoning with a partner.

_____ **1.** In order to be considered computer literate, it is necessary to be able to write **code**.

_____ **2.** Outer space will become an ordinary vacation destination within a **decade**.

_____ **3.** **Phasing** out older forms of technology, such as video and audio tapes, in favor of more advanced media, such as DVDs and CDs, is wasteful.

_____ **4.** Young people should **seek** careers in areas that benefit humanity rather than simply search for high paying jobs.

_____ **5.** Better educational opportunities would help lower-income families break the **cycle** of poverty that often leads to crime.

_____ **6.** Many adult phobias or fears can be **traced** back to childhood.

_____ **7.** When studying a foreign language, students should be **assigned** a name from that language so that they can role-play their new identity as a speaker of that language.

_____ **8.** Governments have a responsibility to defend **traditional** views of marriage and the family.

Now choose one of the topics above and write a persuasive essay that expresses your views. Be sure to provide support for your opinions.

10

The Modern Office: Symbols of Status

GETTING STARTED

Discuss the following questions with your classmates.

▶ Think about an organization you are familiar with—work, school, or a club you belong to. Does this organization have a hierarchy in which some members are clearly more important than others? Or are most members of the organization equal to one another?

▶ If someone in the organization is more important than the others, how do you know that? Does that person wear special clothes or have other markers of status? If so, describe them.

▶ Is equality always a good thing in an organization? Explain.

TARGET WORDS—Assessing Your Vocabulary Knowledge

Look at each of the target words in the box. Use the scale to give yourself a score for each word. After you finish the chapter, score yourself again to check your improvement.

1 I don't know this word.

2 I have seen this word before, but I am not sure of the meaning.

3 I understand the word when I see it or hear it in a sentence, but I don't know how to use it in my own speaking and writing.

4 I know this word and can use it in my own speaking and writing.

TARGET WORDS

_____access	_____corporate	_____indication	_____psychologist
_____authority	_____crucial	_____innovation	_____residential
_____conclusion	_____differentiate	_____methods	_____response
_____confirm	_____display	_____obviously	_____somewhat
_____contradictory	_____equipment	_____potential	_____survey
_____conventional	_____exhibition	_____presumably	_____technical

---

The following passage is adapted from a book on product design that looks specifically at the history and development of the chair. As you read, pay special attention to the target vocabulary words in **bold**.

THE MEANING OF THE CHAIR

1 In the modern office, hierarchy is the norm, and chairs play a **crucial** part in expressing and creating status. Just consider what would happen if everyone got rid of their chairs and worked standing up. This would destroy the **corporate** image that many large companies try to project because chairs are part of a network of symbols. Much like a hotel chain, **corporate** culture allows for no variation in carpeting, chairs, lighting fixtures, telephones, or desks for employees working at similar levels.

2 Ergonomicists study office **equipment** and how it affects people's ability to use it and do

An executive desk chair

their work. Researchers in ergonomics have studied many aspects of the workplace, including status, and have **concluded** that the workstation *should* be an **indication** of the worker's status in the office hierarchy. In open-plan offices, with their clearly democratic intentions and appearance, distinguishing between managers and ordinary workers is difficult, causing dissatisfaction on both sides. Managers once assumed that workers would like a more equal-looking environment and might consequently be more productive. But that did not turn out to be the case.

3 Which type of office do you work in? Can anyone visiting for the first time guess who the boss is without being told? You can probably tell by looking at differences in cubicle wall height and amount and location of work space, lighting, and color, as well as harder-to-define variables such as privacy, ability to control

access to others, and the opportunity for personalization. You might also consider very easily recognizable characteristics—quality of furniture, upholstery, number of chairs, and thickness of carpet. Researchers report that unusual or unexpected status markers, like brightly colored telephones or wastepaper baskets, have developed because employees do not have the opportunity to **display conventional** markers of status.

4 Appropriate markers contribute to satisfaction, and worker satisfaction is essential to productivity, which is why ergonomicists have come to the **conclusion** that status differences have to be maintained. However, this **conclusion** contradicts those who believe in increasing productivity in the workplace by tapping people's creative **potential** without regard to rank. Why do workers respond positively to status markers? Perhaps they feel that as long as differences in pay and **authority** exist, the environmental messages should be consistent. People like to know where they stand, and the physical environment helps to communicate this.

5 In any case, as status markers in the office, chairs are important. After **surveying** 529 office workers in three government and three business offices, **psychologists** came to certain **conclusions**. They **confirmed** that the number of chairs in a personal office (wooden chairs were preferred to metal) was a **crucial indicator** of the occupant's supervisory status. Other **indicators** were large desks, multiple work surfaces, greater storage capacity, and privacy.

6 Most of the research done to date on office environments stems from an interest in worker productivity. But which is more important to worker satisfaction—being physically comfortable or having status symbols? In a **survey** paid for by Steelcase, the world's largest manufacturer of office furniture, 80 percent of those who complained (70% of the total) said that discomfort reduced their productivity a

great deal or **somewhat**. They defined "comfort" in rank order as: good lighting, a comfortable chair, a place to concentrate, and quiet. Chairs have become so important that organizations have finally recognized that chairs should be adjusted to fit the individual users instead of being assigned to them on the basis of rank. Concern for productivity, more than concern for democratic fairness, is responsible for the trend to push for physical comfort for each worker.

7   But concern for productivity may eventually increase fairness and equality in the workplace. Numerous research and popular magazine articles remind us that creativity is not a reflection of rank or title. People at all levels show creative **potential**. Companies that want their employees to be more productive need to abandon their status-ridden ways.

8   These two **contradictory conclusions** about productivity—the need for status and the need to be free from status—may lead to a change in office culture. Until recently, all U.S. commercial furniture lines still carried "executive" and "secretary" chair models. More progressive firms now use the terms "managerial" and "task"; however, these terms still distinguish managers from workers. The use of seating to symbolize hierarchy in the office remains a back-and-forth struggle. As the organizers of a British **exhibition** on the modern chair in the 1980s put it:

A "task" chair

*In the supposedly democratic open-plan office, with its characteristic low partitions replacing full-height walls, the rhetoric is all of teamwork, and non-hierarchical working **methods**. In fact, however, office furniture, and in particular the chair, conveys the status of the occupant. Considerable ingenuity is used to suggest the status of the owner. There are ironies here. The most costly chairs are generally those that offer the most movement, but these have come to be associated in many organizations with clerical workers, which can provide undesirable connotations for the more insecure of managers. So, paradoxically, the executive chair . . . may actually be the cheapest to produce. And, rather than add directly useful or comfort-providing extra features, the high status chairs simply use a more costly covering, or are, with unsubtle **obviousness**, made flatteringly larger.*

These ironic observations are similar to the results of a 1980 **survey** of 10,000 office workers by the Buffalo Organization for Social and **Technical Innovation**, in which researchers discovered that those whose work actually required the best lighting were the least likely to have it, while managers usually had the best.

9   An important distinction in the office, still clearly maintained, is the one between bosses and secretaries, which is still mostly a difference between men and women. Not surprising, then, that marketers of the Norwegian Balance ("Balans") Chair have had to deal with the unwritten law of office status symbols, because their chair does not **differentiate** between the boss and the secretary. In the United States, the marketers of this chair were in trouble because it does not have a back, and the height of a chair's back is one of the "essential **indicators** of high social status." In **response**, a leading manufacturer of balance chairs brought out a new line with high backs.

A "Balans Variable" chair by Norwegian designer Peter Opsvik

10 One would think that the arrival of the home office would undermine the power of status in office furniture. Surely here, of all places, one could develop a way of working based on personal physiological patterns. Advertisements for **equipment** for home offices show wood grain rather than metal shelving, desk systems, potted plants, Oriental rugs, family photos, and views out of **residential** windows. The chairs, however, are the same ergonomic computer chairs being used to promote increased productivity in offices. Ironically, many furniture companies targeting those with home offices offer an executive high-back chair, as well as a leather ergonomic chair, so you can, **presumably**, continue to feel like a big shot even while working at home!

———

Adapted from Cranz, G. (1998). *The Chair: Rethinking Culture, Body, and Design.* New York: W.W. Norton & Company, pp. 54–59.

UNDERSTANDING THE READING

Respond to the following in writing. Base your responses on the reading and your own personal experiences.

1. Describe one problem that open-plan offices have created. What types of solutions have employees found to solve the problem?
2. What effects do office status symbols have on productivity and job satisfaction?
3. Should status within a company determine the type of chair an employee or manager gets? Why or why not?

FOCUSING ON VOCABULARY

WORD MEANING

Each of the following target words appears in the reading on pages 80–82. Use the paragraph number in parentheses to locate each word in context. Read the dictionary definitions below. Write the letter of the definition that reflects how the word is used in the reading.

_____ 1. **equipment** (2)
  a. the special tools, machines, etc. that are needed for a particular activity
  b. the process of providing a place or person with the necessary things

_____ 2. **access** (3)
  a. a way of entering or reaching a place
  b. the opportunity or right to use something or to see somebody or something

_____ 3. **display** (3)
  a. to clearly show a feeling, attitude, or quality by what you do and say
  b. to show an object or specially arranged group of objects to people or put them in a place where people can easily see them

_____ 4. **conclusion** (4)
  a. something you decide after considering all the information you have
  b. the end or final part of something

_____5. **potential** (4)

    a. a natural ability or quality that could develop to make a person or thing very good

    b. the difference in voltage between two points on an electrical circuit

_____6. **authority** (4)

    a. an expert on a subject

    b. power you have because of an official position or because people respect your knowledge

_____7. **confirm** (5)

    a. to show that something is definitely true, especially by providing more proof

    b. to tell someone that a possible arrangement, date, time, is now definite

_____8. **survey** (6)

    a. an examination of an area of land in order to make a map of it

    b. a set of questions that you ask a large number of people to find out about their opinions or behavior

_____9. **exhibition** (8)

    a. a public show of paintings, photographs, or other objects that people can go and see

    b. behavior that shows rudeness, jealousy, anger, etc.

_____10. **technical** (8)

    a. using special, often difficult, terms that are connected with a particular subject

    b. relating to practical knowledge, skills, or methods, especially in industrial or scientific work

_____11. **differentiate** (9)

    a. to recognize or show that two things are not the same

    b. to treat people or things in a different, especially an unfair, way

_____12. **residential** (10)

    a. relating to homes for the old and sick

    b. relating to homes, rather than stores or office buildings

Each sentence below contains a paraphrase or set of synonyms for a target word. Read each sentence and select the matching target word from the box.

contradictory	crucial	method	psychologist
conventional	indication	obviously	response
corporate	innovations	presumably	somewhat

1. The company built its _____ image through a long
                            (business, commercial)
established tradition of exceptional customer service.

2. The two drivers involved gave _____ accounts of the
                            (conflicting, differing)
accident, so the police had to rely on other witnesses to get the full story of
what happened.

3. Some schools are replacing _____ lessons with
                            (traditional, standard)
classes on life skills such as how to run a small business.

4. The runner's time improved _____ from the previous

(to some extent, slightly)

race, but not sufficiently for him to be chosen for the Olympic team.

5. The computer manufacturer was overwhelmed by the public's

_____ to its mail-order advertising campaign.

(reaction, reply)

6. Photographs taken by the Mars rovers give scientists a clearer

_____ of the landscape of the red planet.

(suggestion, clue)

7. New understandings of organizational behavior have sparked

_____ in office layout and culture.

(improvements, advances)

8. The researchers needed a precise _____ for

(way, technique)

analyzing the data from their study.

9. The natural environment of any animal will _____

(clearly, noticeably)

be altered when humans begin developing the area for their own needs.

10. The fact that most people thought the goods were overpriced is

_____ the reason why the items failed to sell.

(most likely, probably)

11. A _____ is someone who studies the human mind,

(mental health professional, analyst)

emotions, and behavior.

12. Good working relationships between staff members are

_____ to the success of any business.

(necessary, fundamental)

WORD TIP

▶ The word family tables you have been completing in this book show that in most cases, a word will exhibit minor spelling changes depending on its form or part of speech. However, in some cases, the spelling will be exactly the same even though the part of speech is different. This is the case for three of the target words in "The Meaning of the Chair." Look at the example for **access** below:

> Certain devices allow parents to limit their children's *access* to inappropriate websites.
>
> noun form

> Passengers cannot *access* the airport parking area from the main terminal building without going outside.
>
> verb form

▶ Find two more target words in the reading that have the exact same spellings for the noun and verb forms. Write them here.

1. _____   **2.** _____

WORD FAMILIES

Most of the target words introduced in this chapter are part of a word family. Study the members of the word families in the table below. Look for spelling patterns for the verb, noun, adjective, and adverb forms of the words. Complete the table. List the patterns in the spaces.

Verb	Noun	Adjective	Adverb
access	1. access 2. accessibility	accessible	X
authorize	1. authority 2. authorization	authoritative	authoritatively
confirm	confirmation	confirmed	X
contradict	contradiction	contradictory	X
X	corporation	corporate	X
X	X	crucial	crucially
differentiate	differentiation	1. differentiated 2. differentiating	X
exhibit	1. exhibition 2. exhibitor	X	X
innovate	1. innovation 2. innovator	innovative	innovatively
X	1. psychologist 2. psychology	psychological	psychologically
Spelling patterns			

Read each sentence and identify the part of speech of the missing word. Write an appropriate form of the target word in the blank. Use the word families table above to help you.

1. Many companies have begun to use _____ (**psychologist**) tests in the hiring process to find out more about applicants' personalities.

2. _____ (**authority**) from the Federal Communications Commission (FCC) is required before any new radio or television station can be set up in the United States.

3. People who are color blind may not be able to _____ (**differentiation**) between red and green.

4. In the workplace, it is good practice to have written _____ (**confirm**) of decisions made at meetings, particularly when deadlines have been discussed.

5. Companies must be prepared to provide a workstation that is wheelchair _____ (**access**) to any staff member who may need one.

6. The discovery of the structure of DNA was a _____ (**crucially**) first step in mapping the human genome.

7. The Eiffel Tower in Paris was first built for the International

_____ (**exhibitor**) celebrating the one hundredth anniversary of the French Revolution.

8. Protesters against globalization believe that multinational _____ (**corporate**) are major contributors to the destruction of local cultures.

9. The company was looking for a young, _____ (**innovation**) person to take over the marketing of new products.

10. Although adults often advise children to tell the truth, their own actions may

_____ (**contradictory**) that advice.

COLLOCATION

Each item below contains three example sentences with the same target word. In each sentence, the target word is paired with a different word and forms a different collocation. In the fourth sentence, the collocation has been left blank. Choose the collocation from the examples that best fits the last sentence and write it in the blank. You may need to change the form of one of the words to fit the sentence.

1. a. The **impressive display** of goods in the window was intended to attract customers into the store.
   b. A **public display** of emotion at funerals is not only accepted, but expected in some cultures.
   c. The museum's **permanent display** of artwork is impressive, but it is the high quality of the changing exhibits that really makes this museum special.
   d. Although a team may have internal tensions and disagreements, the

   members are expected to put on a(n) _____ of unity.

2. a. Amniocentesis is a test given during pregnancy that provides doctors with an **early indication** of genetic disorders.
   b. Memory capacity gives a **strong indication** of the ability to learn a foreign language.
   c. Rulings from earlier court cases can provide a **reliable indication** of how judges will rule in similar cases in the future.

   d. Length of day provides a more _____ of the time of year than does temperature.

3. a. Real estate agents assess the **market potential** of a house as well as the value of the building when determining prices.
   b. High-quality staff development programs are key to unlocking the **untapped potential** of employees.
   c. Marx believed that capitalism restricted **human potential** but that communism offered the opportunity for people to become well-rounded individuals.
   d. The Amazonian rain forest represents the _____ of nature, but it is in danger of being destroyed by human exploitation of its resources.

4. **a.** Many felt that the outcome of the vote was a **foregone conclusion** because public opinion polls prior to the election clearly indicated the people would vote "no."

   b. The study only offered **tentative conclusions** about the effects of poor lighting on productivity, as the number of subjects involved in the study was small.

   c. The representatives of each side of the pay dispute were responsible for bringing the negotiations to a **satisfactory conclusion**.

   d. In the absence of long-term studies, researchers can only offer

   _____ about the overall health effects of a low carbohydrate diet.

5. **a.** Large engineering projects such as the building of the Channel Tunnel commonly experience **technical difficulties** that interfere with the construction schedule.

   b. The exceptionally precise **technical requirements** for parts in jet engines increase production costs.

   c. Successful business partnerships depend on complementary skills; one partner may possess **technical expertise** while another may have sales and marketing skills.

   d. Artistic talent is a combination of creative imagination and

   _____ .

6. **a.** The university housing office's **survey** of local landlords **asks** whether students take appropriate care of rental properties.

   b. A **survey** on diet **revealed** that malnutrition is a problem in developed countries as well as developing ones.

   c. A 2004 **survey** by CNN **suggests** that college students are turned off by politics.

   d. An international passenger _____ that during periods of economic downturn, companies are less willing to pay for business class travel.

7. **a.** The laboratory experiment is one of the main **research methods** for science, but it is used much less often in social science research.

   b. Because of its research and development program, the company is at the forefront of **production methods**, design trends, and quality control.

   c. Part of the management duties of a principal include visiting classrooms, observing **teaching methods**, and reviewing instructional objectives.

   d. A psychology student beginning a project has a variety of

   _____ to choose from, including questionnaires, interviews, and controlled experiments.

8. **a.** Airplanes **obviously benefit** from travelling with, rather than against, the jet stream; that's why eastbound flights generally are faster than westbound flights.

   b. The popularity of a particular brand of bottled water may not **obviously relate** to its true level of purity.

   c. The degree to which a mother cares for her baby in its first months will **obviously influence** the mother/child relationship.

   d. Preschool children _____ from being read to at an early age.

Complete the passage by filling in the blanks with the target words in the box. Use each word only once.

access	contradictory	corporation's	methods
alternatives	conventional	crucial	potential

OFFICE DESIGNS THAT WORK

1   Considering how much time people spend in offices, it is important that work spaces be well designed. Well-designed office spaces help to create a (1) _____ image. They inspire workers, and they make an impression on people who visit and might be (2) _____, or prospective, clients. They make businesses work better, and they are integral to the corporate culture we live in.

2   As we move away from an industrial-based economy to a knowledge-based one, office designers have come up with (3) _____ to the traditional, outmoded work environments of the past. The design industry has moved away from (4) _____, static office designs and created more flexible "strategic management environments." These innovative solutions are meant to support dynamic organizational performance.

3   As employee hierarchies have flattened, or diminished, office designers have moved open-plan areas to more desirable locations within the office and created fewer formal private offices. The need for increased flexibility has also been confirmed by changes in workstation design. Offices and work spaces often are not assigned to a given person on a permanent basis. Because of changes to (5) _____ of working, new designs allow for expansion or movement of desks, storage, and other elements within the workstation. Another (6) _____ design goal is communication, which designers have improved by lowering the walls that separate workstations to increase visual as well as vocal contact. Designers have also eliminated or downsized private offices, created informal gathering places, and upgraded employees' (7) _____ to heavily trafficked areas such as copy and coffee rooms.

4   Corporate and institutional office designers often struggle to resolve a number of competing and often (8) _____ demands, including budgetary limits, employee hierarchies, and technological innovation (especially in relation to computerization). These conflicting demands must

also be balanced with the need to create interiors that in some way enhance, establish, or promote a company's image ▶ and will enable employees to function at optimal levels.

5 All these elements of office design are related and must be integrated. The most successful office designs are like a good marriage—the well-designed office and the employees that occupy it are seemingly made for each other.

Based on Henderson, J. (2000). *Workplaces and Workspaces: Office Designs That Work.* Gloucester, MA: Rockport Publishers, pp. 9–11.

EXPLORING THE TOPIC

Both readings in this chapter link office design with employee satisfaction, productivity, and creativity. Much has been written about these issues under the wider topic "employee motivation." Do some library research on this topic, and then write an essay that describes three factors that contribute to employee motivation and satisfaction.

11

Sitting Comfortably

GETTING STARTED

Discuss the following questions with your classmates.

▶ What is the correct way to sit? Do you normally sit this way when you are studying or relaxing? Why or why not?

▶ Have you ever experienced back pain or felt stiff from sitting or standing in one position too long? What could you do to prevent this discomfort?

▶ Are you comfortable in the chair you are now using? Why or why not?

TARGET WORDS—Assessing Your Vocabulary Knowledge

Look at each of the target words in the box. Use the scale to give yourself a score for each word. After you finish the chapter, score yourself again to check your improvement.

1 I don't know this word.

2 I have seen this word before, but I am not sure of the meaning.

3 I understand the word when I see it or hear it in a sentence, but I don't know how to use it in my own speaking and writing.

4 I know this word and can use it in my own speaking and writing.

TARGET WORDS

____adapt	____establish	____overall	____stressful
____analytic	____hence	____overlap	____sufficient
____approximately	____incorporate	____parallel	____theory
____assess	____injured	____period	____transmit
____contracted	____internal	____preceding	____undergo
____discriminating	____military	____series	____volunteer

The following passage is adapted from an introductory textbook on ergonomics. As you learned in Chapter 10, ergonomicists study how to design and arrange equipment so that people can use it effectively and safely. As you read, pay special attention to the target vocabulary words in **bold**.

THE ERGONOMICS OF SITTING

1   The modern office has **undergone** many changes in the past 150 years. Now equipped with computers, it looks nothing like the rooms in which male clerks once wrote entries in account books or penned letters. By the middle of the twentieth century, clerks had changed from standing at work to sitting, and most office employees were females. The idea, however, that "healthy sitting is sitting upright" was still dominant, and modern office furniture was designed for that body position.

In 1925, rows of office clerks make manual entries to ledgers.

SITTING AND STANDING

2   In the workplace, most employees either have to stand or sit for many hours each day. Sitting is a much less tiring posture than standing, mostly because it requires fewer muscles to be **contracted** to stabilize the seated body and keep it upright. But theories about the best way to sit vary widely.

3   In 1884, the scientist Staffel published his **theories** about proper "healthy" sitting postures. He recommended a straight posture of the trunk, neck, and head, similar to the desired back posture when standing erect. This simple concept of "healthy" sitting was accepted by doctors, teachers, parents, and the **military** and has endured for a surprisingly long time. For at least a century, people have believed that standing and sitting with a straight back is physically desirable and socially proper for pupils and adults alike. Of course, there is nothing wrong with **voluntarily** sitting or standing upright, but it is unreasonable to require that a straight back be maintained for long **periods** of time, such as while sitting in the office at work. This is because the human body is **adapted** to change—to moving around—but not to standing still or sitting still. Sitting or standing still for extended **periods** is uncomfortable and leads to many problems, such as poor blood circulation and too much fluid build-up in the lower legs.

PRESSURE IN THE BACK WHILE SITTING

4   Scientists have performed many experiments to learn about how pressure in the spine varies according to different sitting and standing positions. When the **volunteers** they studied were standing at ease (see Figure 11.1 on the following page), the forces in the spine were in the neighborhood of 330 newtons. (The newton [N] is a unit used to measure force.) The force increased by about 100 N when the subjects sat on a seat with their arms supported, but without a backrest. Sitting relaxed, but letting the arms hang down, increased the **internal** force to nearly 500 N. Thus sitting down produced an increase in the force on the lower part of the spine compared with standing, but the differences among sitting postures were not quite as pronounced. However, this changed if the chair had a backrest (see Figure 11.2. on the following page). Leaning back over a small backrest and letting the arms hang down reduced the **internal** compression forces to **approximately** 400 N. This type of **analytic** study indicates the importance of supporting the back by leaning it on a rearward-declined

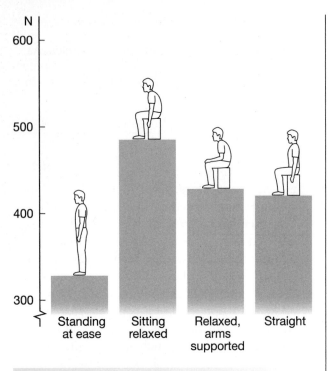

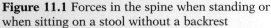

Figure 11.1 Forces in the spine when standing or when sitting on a stool without a backrest

backrest and by maintaining the natural shape of the spine. Leaning the backrest past the vertical (a line pointing straight up and down) brings about decreases in **internal** force, because part of the upper body weight is now

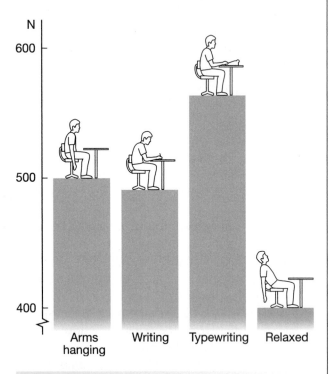

Figure 11.2 Forces in the spine when sitting on an office chair with a small lumbar backrest

transmitted to the backrest and **hence** does not rest on the spine. One summary of the available research concluded that relaxed leaning back against a rearward-declined backrest is the least **stressful** sitting posture and this position is often used by office workers if the shapes of their chairs permit it.

THERE IS NO ONE HEALTHY POSTURE

5   Neither **theories** nor practical experiences support the idea of a single healthy, comfortable, efficient sitting posture. Thus, the traditional assumption that everybody should sit upright and that furniture should be designed to that end is mistaken. Instead, there is general agreement that many postures may be comfortable (healthy, suitable, efficient, etc.) for short **periods**, depending on one's body type, physical preferences, and work activities. Consequently, furniture should allow for body movements and various postures. For example, workers should be able to make adjustments to seat height and angle, backrest position, and other key design features of their chairs. Motion, change, variation, and adjustment to fit the individual are central to a person's well-being while sitting.

COMFORT VS. DISCOMFORT

6   The concept of *comfort*, as related to sitting, was hard to grasp as long as it was defined, simply and conveniently, but falsely, as the absence of *discomfort*. In a 1997 study of chairs, researchers Helander and Zhang showed that, in reality, *comfort* and *discomfort* are not two extremes in a single scale. Instead, there are two scales, one for comfort and the other for discomfort. These scales are not **parallel**, but they do partly **overlap**. Discomfort is expressed in such terms as feeling stiff, tired, restless, sore, and in pain. Chair users can rather easily describe design features that result in feelings of discomfort, such as chairs in wrong sizes, those that are too high or too low, or those with hard surfaces or edges; but avoiding these design flaws does not by itself make a chair comfortable.

7   Comfort when sitting is associated with feelings of well-being—support, safety, pleasure, relaxation, rest, warmth, softness, and spaciousness. However, exactly what feels comfortable depends very much on the person, individual habits, the environment and the task, and the passage of time.

8   Helander and Zhang characterized discomfort and comfort separately with respect to sitting in a chair. Participants were given a **series** of statements expressing feelings or impressions about both the chair and its effects on the body or mind. For each statement below, they were asked to rate their discomfort and comfort on a scale from 1 to 9, 1 being "not at all" and 9 being "extremely."

Discomfort	Comfort
1. I have sore muscles.	**1.** I feel relaxed.
2. I have heavy legs.	**2.** I feel refreshed.
3. I feel uneven pressure.	**3.** The chair feels soft.
4. I feel stiff.	**4.** The chair is spacious.
5. I feel restless.	**5.** The chair looks nice.
6. I feel tired.	**6.** I like the chair.
7. I feel uncomfortable.	**7.** I feel comfortable.

9   Unless a chair was truly unsuitable, Helander and Zhang found it difficult to rank the chair by attributes of discomfort because the body is surprisingly **adaptive** (except when the sitter has a bad, or **injured**, back). By contrast, the ways in which comfort was described proved sensitive and **discriminating** for ranking chairs in terms of preference. Helander and Zhang's subjects found it easier to rank chairs in terms of their **overall** comfort or discomfort when provided with the **preceding** detailed descriptive statements. The rankings of chairs were **established** early during the trials and did not change much with the length of time the subject sat. Still it is not clear whether a few minutes of sitting in chairs is **sufficient** to **assess** their comfort or discomfort or whether it takes longer trial **periods**.

10   An ergonomically-designed office workstation depends on many factors, such as furniture, computer equipment, and the environment. All of these factors must "fit" the person. Because our bodies must be allowed to move and assume various postures, modern design models for furniture need to **incorporate** the full range of body sizes and working postures among humans. Only then will we be able to work in comfort.

_____

Adapted from Kroemer, K.H.E., Kroemer, H. B., and Kroemer-Elbert, E. (2001). *Ergonomics: How to Design for Ease and Efficiency,* 2nd ed. Upper Saddle River, NJ: Prentice Hall, pp. 350, 404–406, 409–411, 413, 415–416.

UNDERSTANDING THE READING

Respond to the following in writing. Base your responses on the reading and your own personal experiences.

1. According to Staffel, what is the correct and healthy way to sit? Do you normally sit that way? Why or why not?
2. What is a key difference between sitting and standing?
3. Why is it so difficult to design comfortable chairs? What kind of chair do you find most comfortable for work? Why?

FOCUSING ON VOCABULARY

WORD MEANING

Read the sentences below and circle the letter of the word or phrase that best matches the meaning of the target word in **bold**. Use context clues in the sentences to determine the correct meaning. Check your dictionary if you are not sure of the answer.

1. Companies that set up offices in foreign countries often need to **adapt** traditional working practices to suit local customs and conditions.
   a. make something start working
   b. change to suit a new situation or need
   c. change something for the worse

2. No one actually counted the number of people at the political rally, but some newspapers reported that **approximately** 1,200 people had attended.
   a. false but seeming to be right or true
   b. correct or right for a particular time
   c. a little more or less than an exact amount

3. About 4.5 million years ago, a large cloud of gas slowly **contracted** under gravity into the glowing ball that became the sun.
   a. became smaller, narrower, tighter
   b. became breakable
   c. became different from one another

4. Researchers have **established** a clear link between smoking and cancer.
   a. forced something to grow
   b. found out facts that will prove that something is true
   c. continued to experience

5. Courses that prepare students for careers in the sciences normally **incorporate** a lot of mathematics.
   a. develop something gradually
   b. include something as part of a plan or system
   c. give something more energy

6. Everyone hoped that the problems between the two countries could be solved by talks between their leaders rather than by **military** means.
   a. relating to a secret political organization
   b. relating to a group of political protesters
   c. relating to the army, navy, etc.

7. Although the number of robberies has risen in the last year, the **overall** crime rate for the city has gone down.
   a. including or considering everything
   b. a type of clothing worn over other clothes to protect them
   c. containing too many people or things

8. During the 1950s' space race, scientists in both the United States and the Soviet Union were carrying out **parallel** research programs in the area of rocket science.
   a. similar and happening at the same time
   b. having qualities that attract each other
   c. concentrated in one time and place

9. In order to understand the origins of World War II, you must know something about the peace treaties for the **preceding** war.
   a. preventing something from happening in a particular way
   b. representing facts through a group of numbers
   c. happening or coming before the time, place, or part mentioned

10. The companies' recruitment procedures have **undergone** a number of changes that will be tested at the university careers fair.
    a. created something that did not exist before
    b. happened or been done to someone or something
    c. given strength or support to someone or something

11. The final exams period can be very **stressful** for students, so to avoid getting sick, they should eat well and get plenty of exercise and sleep.
    a. physically relaxing
    b. involving a lot of pressure
    c. mentally relaxing

12. Einstein's **theory** of relativity describes the relationship between time, space, and movement.
    a. the way an action changes something
    b. an idea that is intended to explain something about life or the world
    c. a piece of information that is known to be true

Read the sentences below and use context to figure out the meaning of the target words in **bold**. Look for a core meaning that provides a general understanding of each target word. Write the meaning in your own words.

1. a. Police officers and detectives must take an **analytic** approach to solving crime; they must consider every detail, no matter how small.
   b. Higher education aims to develop **analytic** thought by encouraging students to examine and question in detail the accepted ideas of everyday life and culture.

   analytic _____

2. a. The magazine *Consumer Reports* **assesses** products such as fitness equipment on the basis of price, usability, ergonomics, and construction.
   b. The program used three types of tests to **assess** students' language proficiency.

   assess _____

3. a. Improved labelling of the ingredients and nutritional values of food products has enabled consumers to become more **discriminating** about their food purchases.
   b. A **discriminating** collector of art will attend only the best sales in hopes of purchasing high-quality paintings.

   discriminating _____

4. a. The marathon runner was not able to continue because of her **injured** ankle.
   b. In the tropics, even superficial **injuries** need to be treated promptly to avoid infection.

   injured _____

5. a. When remodelling the office, several **internal** walls were removed to create an open-plan space.
   b. The **internal** ear is the innermost part that includes the ear canal, vestibule, and cochlea.

   internal _____

6. a. Because much of the content of history and politics **overlaps**, students majoring in these subjects often share several classes.
   b. The tiles on a roof must **overlap** in order to prevent water and wind from getting through cracks.

   overlap _____

7. **a.** The contract gave the buyers a thirty-day **period** during which they could change their minds and receive a full refund on the purchase price.

   b. A cicada is an insect that takes a **period** ranging from four to seventeen years to develop to adulthood. In contrast, its adult lifespan lasts only a few weeks.

   period _____

8. **a.** Most research findings are based on information assembled from a **series** of studies rather than from one single piece of research.

   b. The students were required to write a **series** of essays, each one longer and more complex than the one before.

   series _____

9. **a.** Fresh water supplies that were **sufficient** to sustain the global population in 1950 were only enough for one-third of the population in 1995.

   b. The lack of **sufficient** jobs is a major reason for urban poverty in developing countries.

   sufficient _____

10. **a.** The telegraph, invented in the 1820s, was the first instrument used to **transmit** messages by electric current.

    b. Although humans communicate many of their emotions through words, we also **transmit** our feelings through facial expressions and gestures.

    transmit _____

11. **a.** The school relied on **volunteers** to assist with serving school lunches as it could not afford to pay for lunchroom staff.

    b. Many charities use **volunteers** to run their operations so that money received from donations is not spent on staff salaries.

    volunteer _____

WORD TIP

▶ The word **hence** is found at the start of a sentence, clause, or phrase, and is used to show a cause-and-effect relationship between the first and second pieces of information.

The site of the restaurant is a crossroads where five roads meet, **hence** its name, "Five Ways."

The school had very strict rules about lateness, **hence** the teacher's anger when the students arrived fifteen minutes after the beginning of class.

WORD FAMILIES

Read the sentences below. Some of the target words have been used correctly, but in six sentences a wrong word form has been used. If the wrong form has been used, cross it out and write the correct form. If the form is correct, put a checkmark (✓).

1. Many "new" products in the marketplace are really only traditional products

   to which minor **adaptables** have been made. _____

2. An accountant's job is to keep a record of a company's accounts, while a financial **analytic's** job is to examine these records for business trends.

   _____

3. It is important to do warm-up exercises before beginning heavy exercise because cold muscles may **contract**, leading to greater risk of injury.

_____

4. Product styling often makes it difficult to **discrimination** between good and poor quality furniture design. _____

5. Because U.S. law is based on the principle of "innocent until proven guilty," prosecuting attorneys must **establish** a defendant's guilt in the courtroom.

_____

6. When developing **internal** policies for the hiring and firing of employees, companies must take into account state and national employment laws.

_____

7. It is important to make **period** checks of your smoke and fire detectors to ensure that the batteries are functioning. _____

8. There are more than 12 million motor vehicle accidents in the United States annually that result in approximately 2 million disabling **injure**.

_____

9. Researchers **theory** that differences in the occurrence of heart disease between racial groups may be explained by differences in genetics, diet, and socioeconomic status. _____

10. When selecting candidates, many universities and employers consider whether applicants have participated in **volunteer** activities.

_____

COLLOCATION

Match each target word in the box with the group of words that regularly occur with it. In all cases, the target word comes before the word in the list.

approximately	overall	stressful	transmit
military	preceding	sufficient	undergo

1._____	2._____	3._____	4._____
treatment	impact	one-third	job
examination	performance	forty percent	lifestyle
change	usefulness	ten minutes	conditions
surgery	reliability	sixty dollars	events

5._____	6._____	7._____	8._____
junta	section	signals	evidence
attaché	year	data	time
coup	generation	images	merit
regime	remarks	information	funds

Read the following checklist which summarizes some of the crucial points from the book *Office Ergonomics* (K.H.E. Kroemer and A.D. Kroemer, 2001, London: Taylor and Francis). As you go through the list, **assess** how ergonomically sound your work space is. Think about what aspects you can improve.

1. When your shoulders are relaxed, is your keyboard at **approximately** elbow height?

2. Do you have soft pads to help support your wrists when using your keyboard and mouse, thus avoiding potential wrist problems? If you do have wrist problems, have you considered **incorporating** voice-recognition software into your method of working?

3. Does your chair have armrests? They can be useful for relieving **stress** on your arms, but only if they are well padded, with no sharp edges or corners.

4. Do you have ample room to stretch your legs while sitting? Furniture sold for residential use may lack some of the ergonomic **adaptations** found in commercial office furniture, and sometimes computer desks lack **sufficient** space for full leg extension.

5. Is some of your office equipment and storage space, such as the printer and filing cabinet, out of easy reach? This requires you to get up from your chair and walk over to them. The human body prefers movement to being stationary for long **periods** of time, so this method of enforcing movement can be an important part of a healthy work/study environment.

6. Is there an acceptable level of noise in your space? Are there distracting noises? Do keep in mind that if you find complete silence uncomfortable, pleasant background sounds, e.g., soft music, can help to create a positive **overall** atmosphere.

7. Is the temperature comfortable for you? For most people, this means **internal** temperatures of between 21°–27°C (70°–80°F) in summer (or a warm climate) and between 18°–24°C (64°–75°F) in winter (or a cool climate). The most comfortable humidity is usually around 40–50 percent. In general, if you are aware of the temperature, it is an indication that it needs to be adjusted.

8. Do you take a short break at least every thirty minutes? Since the body is made for movement, this is perhaps the best ergonomic tip. Although it may seem contradictory, **establishing** a work pattern that allows you to move your muscles and change your posture frequently will do as much as anything else to increase your comfort while sitting.

 Recently, more and more office workers are suffering from repetitive strain injuries that cost their companies a considerable amount of money because of lost work time. Investigate and write an essay on one type of stress injury. Describe the causes and effects of this injury and identify specific ergonomic ways to prevent it.

Strategy Practice

USING YOUR DICTIONARY — Grammar Information

Dictionaries written especially for English language learners provide more than just information about word meaning. As you learned in Chapter 8, "Strategy Practice," a good dictionary can also play the role of a grammar guide.

USING A DICTIONARY TO FIX GRAMMATICAL MISTAKES

Look at the entry for the noun **potential**. Then read the numbered explanations for certain parts of the entry. Notice how the dictionary grammar information can help you correct sentence errors.

①

potential² *n.* [U] **1** the possibility that something will develop in a certain way, or have a particular effect: [+ **for**] *Consult a doctor to minimize the potential for health risks.* **2** a natural ability or quality that could develop to make a person or thing very good: *This room* **has potential**. | *In his third year Stokes is finally* **showing** *his great* **potential**. | **achieve/reach/realize your (full) potential** (=succeed in doing as well as you possibly can) **3** TECHNICAL the difference in VOLTAGE between two points on an electrical CIRCUIT

③

②

① The symbol [U] indicates that the word **potential** is uncountable, which enables you to select the correct noun below.

* The question now is whether Greece has the ~~potentials~~ potential to make tourism profitable.

② The entry shows possible collocations and how they should be used in a sentence. This helps you replace an incorrect collocation with the right one.

* I believe that if someone is in danger of failing his course, he should muster his courage to ~~bring the~~ realize his full **potential**.

③ Example sentences in the entry show you that a possessive pronoun such as *his* can precede the word **potential**. Therefore, *my* is the correct pronoun to use in the following sentence.

* The film showed me how to bring ~~the~~ my **potential** into full play.

PRACTICING YOUR DICTIONARY SKILLS

Read the dictionary entries for the three words below. Use the grammar information in each entry to identify and correct the errors in the sentences that follow. All of the sentences have been written by learners of English.

in•di•ca•tion /ˌɪndəˈkeɪʃən/ *n.* [C,U] a sign that something is probably happening or that something is probably true: [+ **of**] *Dark green leaves are a good indication of healthy roots.* | [**indication that**] *Police said there was no indication that the two robberies were related.* | *Collier* **gave every indication** (=gave very clear signs) *that he was ready to compromise.*

seek /sik/ *v. past tense and past participle* **sought** [T] **1** FORMAL to try to achieve or get something: *Do you think the President will seek re-election?* | [**seek to do sth**] *Local schools are seeking to reduce the dropout rate.* | **attention-seeking/publicity-seeking** (=trying to get people's attention) **2 seek (sb's) advice/help/assistance etc.** FORMAL to ask someone for advice or help: *Brenda was encouraged to seek counseling for her depression.* **3** FORMAL to look for something you need: *The number of needy Americans seeking emergency food and shelter increased by 7% last year.* **4 seek your fortune** LITERARY to go to another place hoping to gain success and wealth: *Coles came to the Yukon in the 1970s to seek his fortune.* **5** to move naturally toward something or into a particular position: *Water seeks its own level.* —see also HEAT-SEEKING, SELF-SEEKING, SOUGHT-AFTER

   seek sb/sth ↔ **out** *phr. v.* [T] to look very hard for someone or something: *The Demo Derby was set up to seek out local music talent.*

un•der•go /ˌʌndɚˈgoʊ/ *v. past tense* **underwent** *past participle* **undergone** /-ˈgɔn/ [T not in passive] if you undergo a change, a bad experience etc., it happens to you or is done to you: *In March he underwent surgery for the cancer.* | *The computer industry has undergone some major changes over the past 15 years.*

1. We can think of wrinkles as a story that life has written on the body, as an **indication** the laughter and sorrow a person has experienced in life.

2. A person's pronunciation makes an **indication** of the region of the country a person comes from.

3. The expansion of the United States was led by people who **seeked** their own land and fortune.

4. Now a lot of people **seek** for democracy.

5. China has **undergo** significant changes in the development of its educational system.

6. The American population has **underwent** major changes over the last twenty years.

STRATEGY — Guessing from Context

Guessing a new word's meaning from context is an important vocabulary learning strategy. Use this step-by-step guide to help you guess more successfully.

1. Look at the unknown word and decide its part of speech—noun, verb, etc.
2. Look at words around the new word and try to find other words linked to it. For example, if the word is a noun, what adjectives describe it?
3. Pay attention to the wider context. Look for relationships like cause and effect, contrast, and summary. Sometimes such relationships between words are signalled by conjunctions like *but* and *because*. Punctuation may also provide a

clue. Semicolons (;) may be used to distinguish between similar items in a long list (e.g., *Mr. Dentz, the principal of the school; Ms. Poreba, the special education instructor; and Mrs. Couturier, the new reading specialist*). Dashes (—) may be used to signal restatement or definition (e.g., *mobile office furniture—a laptop, lightweight printer, and a table on wheels*).

4. Use the knowledge you have acquired from Steps 1–3 to guess the meaning of the word.
5. Check that your guess is appropriate:
   a. Is the part of speech of your guess the same as the part of speech of the unknown word? If it is not the same, then something is wrong with your guess.
   b. Replace the unknown word with your guess. If the sentence makes sense, your guess is probably correct.
   c. Break the unknown word into its prefix, root, and suffix, if possible. If the meanings of the prefix and root correspond to your guess, good. If not, look at your guess again.

Using this procedure, guess the meaning of the word **disparity** in the second sentence of the next paragraph.

WORD KNOWLEDGE — Frequency of Occurrence

Academic words are used less frequently than the common English words we use in everyday situations. This disparity in frequency is one of the things that make academic words "feel" more academic.

Look at the Word Frequency Table on the following page. Compare the frequency of occurrence of academic words with their more commonly used (or "general") counterparts. The table includes examples of the 3,000 most frequently occurring words in spoken **(S)** or written **(W)** English, according to the *Longman Advanced American Dictionary (LAAD)*. A number *1* in the **S** or **W** column on the chart indicates that a word is among the 1,000 most frequently occurring words in spoken or written English. A number *2* indicates that a word ranks between 1,001 and 2,000, and a number *3* shows that a word ranks between 2,001 and 3,000. Here is an example of how *LAAD* indicates a word's spoken and written frequency. The verb *study* is among the 1,000 most frequently occurring words in both spoken and written English.

Frequency marker

S	W
1	1

study[2] *v.* **studies, studied, studying 1** [I,T] to spend time reading, going to classes etc. in order to learn about a subject: *I can't study with that music playing . . .*

Academic Words	Frequency per Million Words	S	W	General Words	Frequency per Million Words	S	W
facilitate	8			help	327	1	1
preceding	9			previous	95	3	2
approximately	23			about	1789	1	1
crucial	37		3	important	301	1	1
sufficient	41		3	enough	289	1	1
display	47		2	show	251	1	1
authority	127	3	1	power	284	1	1
period	181	1	1	time	1305	1	1

The frequency of academic words varies, but academic words will almost always be less frequent than their everyday, or general, English counterparts.

The box below contains eight words from this unit. Replace the general English word in the sentences with its academic counterpart from the box. Be careful to use the correct form of the word. There are two extra words in the box. The first sentence has been done for you.

assign	~~contract~~	enhance	exhibition	restrict
conclusion	corporate	exclusion	innovation	transmit

1. Most materials _____contract_____ (get smaller) when they cool.

2. The automobile _____ (show) displayed cars from twenty countries.

3. The _____ (end) of the report contained sharp criticism of the president.

4. Malaria is _____ (spread) by mosquitoes.

5. The general _____ (gave) the dangerous mission to his best soldiers.

6. Due to the drought, the watering of gardens was _____ (limited) to ten minutes per day.

7. The expense of entertaining clients is usually charged to a _____ (business) account.

8. Some athletes illegally _____ (improve) their body strength through the use of steroids.

UNIT

4

Use and Abuse of Natural Resources

CHAPTER 13

Water for Sale

GETTING STARTED

Discuss the following questions with your classmates.

▶ What kinds of drinks are most popular with you and your friends? Is water one of them?

▶ What brands of bottled water can you name? Which are considered the best?

▶ Why do you think bottled water has become so popular recently?

TARGET WORDS—Assessing Your Vocabulary Knowledge

Look at each of the target words in the box. Use the scale to give yourself a score for each word. After you finish the chapter, score yourself again to check your improvement.

1 I don't know this word.

2 I have seen this word before, but I am not sure of the meaning.

3 I understand the word when I see it or hear it in a sentence, but I don't know how to use it in my own speaking and writing.

4 I know this word and can use it in my own speaking and writing.

TARGET WORDS

____aid	____confine	____highlight	____predominate
____alternative	____criteria	____imply	____proportion
____arbitrary	____despite	____inherent	____random
____chemical	____extract	____justify	____regulate
____complement	____federal	____label	____unique
____comprise	____guarantee	____layer	____whereas

The following passage discusses the increasing consumer demand for bottled water. As you read, pay special attention to the target vocabulary words in **bold**.

EXPLODING SALES FOR BOTTLED WATER

1   Walk down the drinks aisle at the supermarket. Look in the beverage cooler in your local convenience store. A new beverage is taking over more and more space on the shelves, and that drink is water. Bottled water sales in the United States rose to 1.7 billion gallons (6.4 billion liters) in 2000 for plastic bottles alone, compared to total sales of only 700 million gallons (2.6 billion liters) in 1980. **Whereas** bottled water was once associated only with the rich and privileged, it is now regularly drunk by people at all income levels **despite** the fact that the price of bottled water can be between 240 and 10,000 times higher per gallon than tap water. What accounts for this astounding increase in demand?

2   Traditionally, people have drunk bottled water for health reasons. The practice of "taking the waters" originated with the Romans, who believed that a person developed a healthy mind by nurturing a healthy body. Across Europe, drinking or bathing in mineral water has been associated with curative powers for ailments such as arthritis, kidney stones, and skin diseases. Health spas such as those at Evian in France and San Pellegrino in Italy began bottling water so that their patrons could continue their treatments at home. Twenty-first-century consumers are also concerned about health. However, in America, where the habit of drinking bottled water is relatively new, the concern is often more related to the purity or sterility of the water than to its mineral contents. Americans are worried about the effects of **chemical** pollution and other contaminants on the water supply. Many view bottled water as a safe **alternative** to tap water.

3   Further reasons for drinking bottled water are its usefulness as an **aid** to digestion, as a **complement** to a good meal in a restaurant, and for taste. Municipal tap water is often treated with chlorine to guard against harmful microorganisms. Chlorine, as well as metals from pipes and tanks used to distribute and store tap water, can leave behind an unpleasant taste.

4   Health and taste are not, however, the only reasons for drinking bottled water. Marketing studies have shown that the consumer most likely to use bottled water is an adult, eighteen to thirty-four years of age, who is educated, upscale, and health conscious. Even early European health spas were very fashionable places with grand hotels, casinos, and social facilities in addition to the halls for drinking the waters. Today, many bottled water brands are associated with celebrities and their glamorous lifestyles. Water bottle **labels** and the shape of the bottles themselves are in the hands of designers and marketers. Packaging emphasizes health, purity, vitality, youth, and nature. Is all the hype surrounding bottled water **justified**?

Many health-conscious consumers drink bottled water.

5   In the United States, bottled water is defined as water that is sealed in a sanitary container, is sold for human consumption, and meets all

state, **federal**, and industry standards. Bottled water that **comprises** more than 1 percent by weight of sweeteners or **chemicals** is considered to be a soft drink. Beverages with sweeteners or chemicals are not **regulated** by the government in the same way as bottled water. In France, other **criteria** must be met. One condition is that the mineral content of the water must be low enough for there to be no maximum safe daily limit on the amount of water that can be consumed. Waters with higher mineral contents can only be consumed under medical supervision at spas. Generally, bottled water can be either carbonated (sparkling) or non-carbonated (still). Consumption of carbonated water **predominates** in Germany, while in the rest of Europe and the United States, non-carbonated water is more popular.

6   Spring water in particular is associated with a type of purity many consumers want. Given the sudden growth in the number of brands of bottled water available today, consumers now want to know how they can **guarantee** that the water they are buying is really spring water. For this reason, the U.S. Food and Drug Administration (FDA) requires that a bottle's **label** clearly indicates what type of water is in the bottle.

The varieties of bottled water include the following:

- *Artesian water* is **extracted** by means of a well from a **confined** water-bearing **layer** of sand or rock known as an *aquifer*. The water is pressurized and will flow naturally once tapped.

- *Mineral water* contains a constant level and **proportion** of dissolved minerals such as calcium and magnesium. In order to be **labeled** "mineral water," it must contain no less than 250 parts per million (ppm) of these dissolved solids. The 250 ppm threshold is in reality an **arbitrary** level because many excellent European mineral waters do not meet this requirement and therefore cannot be marketed as mineral water in the United States.

- *Distilled water* has undergone a process of distillation, whereby the water is vaporized to remove dissolved minerals and then recondensed into liquid form.

- *Sparkling water* is naturally carbonated due to geothermal conditions at its source. If the natural carbonation level is diminished during processing, the carbon dioxide can be replaced up to the original level of natural occurrence.

- *Spring water* is derived from an underground rock formation from which water flows naturally to the surface. Natural springs occur **randomly** (in a variety of geological formations), and each one has **unique** properties.

- *Drinking water* has been significantly processed via treatments such as reverse osmosis, deionization, or activated carbon filtration. The source of this water need not be indicated. In the United States, more than 25 percent of bottled waters are derived from municipal water sources. Two major brands—Aquafina, bottled by Pepsi, and Dasani, bottled by Coca-Cola—fall under this category.

7   An **inherent** element in the production and marketing of any product is the packaging. Despite the clarity required by the FDA, water bottlers are promoting a market perception that bottled water is pure, safe, and good for you. A survey of the labels and websites of fifty water bottlers by the National Resources Defense Council **highlights** the widespread use of terminology that **implies** that bottled water is extraordinarily pure and derived from pristine natural sources.

Terminology	Number of Bottlers
pure	8
purest or purity	3
pristine	5
glacial	2
natural or prepared by nature	8
naturally purified or naturally occurring	3
premium	5
mountain water	7
clean	2
good health or healthy	2
for health conscious	2

8   In addition, images of mountain lakes and glaciers or flowing streams abound on **labels**, and may even be imprinted on the bottles, even though the water may be sourced from some

place as flat as Texas. Although many consumers find such labeling misleading, it is not illegal unless a company makes a direct claim that the picture represents the source of the water.

9   In summary, the leap in demand for bottled water can be attributed to the public perception, fueled by industry marketing, that bottled water is a cleaner, healthier **alternative** to tap water. While U.S. consumers can be confident that bottled water is subject to strict health and food packaging **regulations**, bottle **labels** may not yet tell them everything they wish to know.

UNDERSTANDING THE READING

Respond to the following in writing. Base your responses on the reading and your own personal experiences.

1. Why is bottled water so popular today?
2. What are some of the key differences between the different varieties of bottled water?
3. How carefully do you read the labels on the foods or beverages you buy? What kind of information are you looking for on the labels?

FOCUSING ON VOCABULARY

WORD MEANING

Match the words with their definitions. If you are unsure about a word's meaning, try to figure it out from the context by rereading the passage on pp. 105–107. Then check your dictionary.

Set 1

_____**1.** justify

_____**2.** comprise

_____**3.** guarantee

_____**4.** federal

_____**5.** criteria

a. to consist of particular parts, groups, etc.

b. the standards upon which judgments or decisions can be made

c. to make it certain that something will happen

d. to give a good and acceptable reason for something

e. concerning the central government of a country as opposed to the governments of the individual states

Set 2

_____**1.** complement

_____**2.** imply

_____**3.** layer

_____**4.** regulate

_____**5.** random

a. happening or chosen without any definite plan, aim, or pattern

b. something or someone that emphasizes the good qualities of another person or thing

c. to suggest that something is true without saying or showing it directly

d. a single amount of a substance either on top of a surface or between two other things or substances

e. to control an activity or process, especially by rules

Set 3

_____1. unique
_____2. highlight
_____3. whereas
_____4. despite

a. to make something easy to notice so that people pay attention to it

b. without being prevented or influenced by something else; even though something else exists or is true

c. although something is true of one thing, it is not true of another

d. being the only one of its kind; unusually good or special

Read the row of words and phrases below each numbered word. One word or phrase in each list is *not* a synonym for the numbered word. Cross it out.

1. **chemical**

   | substance | element | compound | weight |

2. **confine**

   | supply | restrict | limit | put in prison |

3. **label**

   | description | tag | vision | sticker |

4. **extract**

   | supplement | take out | remove | dig out |

5. **arbitrary**

   | random | deliberate | by chance | unfair |

6. **alternative**

   | option | idea | choice | substitute |

7. **inherent**

   | inborn | intrinsic | innate | intelligent |

8. **aid**

   | assistance | help | support | obstacle |

9. **proportion**

   | amount | part | goodness | percentage |

10. **predominant**

    | minor | main | largest | principal |

WORD TIP

▶ In most countries, the government is referred to as the "national" government. However, in the United States, when people refer to the national government, they usually use the term *federal*, e.g., the Federal Communications Commission or the Federal Reserve Bank.

▶ A system in which powers are divided between a central government and local governments is called a "*federal* system." In the United States, government powers are divided between the national government in Washington, D.C., and each of the fifty states. Other countries with *federal* systems of government include Canada and Germany.

WORD FAMILIES

The table below contains word families for some of the target words in the reading. Complete the rest of the table. An *X* indicates that there is no form or that the form is not common. Sometimes there may be more than one form possible. If you are unsure about a form, check your dictionary.

Verb	Noun	Adjective	Adverb
X	1. chemical 2. chemist 3.	chemical	chemically
complement	complement		X
confine	confinement		X
federate	1. federation 2.	federal	federally
guarantee		guaranteed	X
justify	justification	1. justifiable 2. justified	
	layer	layered	X
	proportion	1. proportional 2. proportionate	1. proportionally 2. proportionately
regulate	1. regulation 2. regulator		X
X	uniqueness	unique	

Choose the correct form of the word in **bold** in sentence **a** to complete sentence **b**. Use the word family table you just completed as a guide.

1. **a.** The water in many cities is **chemically** treated with fluoride to help prevent tooth decay.

   b. _____ is one of the core science subjects in school, along with biology and physics.

2. **a.** Although the striker did not score a goal, his overall performance in the game clearly **justified** his selection for the soccer team.

   b. The _____ given for most divorces is "irreconcilable differences."

3. **a.** The **regulatory** body in charge of air safety in the United States is the Federal Aviation Authority (FAA).

   b. Safety _____ require the use of protective helmets and goggles at all building sites.

4. **a.** The **guaranteed** monthly payout from the pension upon retirement was 0.4 percent of the final monthly salary.

   b. Most car manufacturers _____ their vehicles for three years or 30,000 miles, although some warranties are for as long as ten years.

5. a. In imperial Rome, there was **proportionally** much more public space and much less private space than in modern cities.

   b. Stefan's Law states that the sun's brightness is _____ to the fourth power of its temperature.

6. a. Sparkling water is often served as a **complement** to fine food because it can aid digestion.

   b. To build an effective team for sports or work, it is important to select members whose skills _____ those of other team members.

7. a. The pain in her arm was **confined** to a point just above her elbow.

   b. Prisoners causing problems with other inmates are sometimes put in solitary _____ as punishment.

8. a. The traditional Japanese wedding kimono is a multi**layered** gown made of fine silk of various colors.

   b. The deterioration of the ozone _____ in the atmosphere means that skin cancer rates are likely to rise in the future.

9. a. The artist was successful in developing a style that was **uniquely** hers.

   b. Teachers must always be aware of the _____ of each student, each with his or her own individual learning preferences.

10. a. Although city and state governments finance many American universities, there are **federally** funded programs that help ensure equal access to all universities.

   b. On several occasions, the province of Quebec has threatened to separate from the Canadian _____.

COLLOCATION

Each item below contains three sentences with the same collocation. Write a fourth sentence of your own using the same word partners.

1. a. The aim of the computer simulation was to **highlight** potential **problems** in implementing the new traffic control system.

   b. The television station ran special programs to **highlight** the **problem** of runaway children.

   c. The Aral Sea can be used as an example to **highlight** the **problem** of environmental mismanagement.

   d. _____

2. a. At many universities, the **financial aid** package includes a combination of grants, loans, and work-study jobs.

   b. Because of the recent slump in airline travel, the major industry players have decided to ask the government for **financial aid**.

   c. Even when **financial aid** to farmers aims to provide security for staple food crops, it may be viewed by some as an obstacle to free trade.

   d. _____

3. **a.** The **criteria** for the **selection** of astronauts are very challenging, both in terms of intelligence and physical fitness.

   b. Prestigious universities such as Harvard and Stanford are able to set extremely high **criteria** for the **selection** of new students.

   c. The European Union has set **criteria** for **selecting** which new countries can join the association.

   d. _____

4. **a.** The stylized fight scenes were the **predominant feature** of the film.

   b. The **predominant feature** of the Atkins Diet is the emphasis on minimizing the number of calories from carbohydrates in a person's daily food intake.

   c. By the end of the American Civil War, rifles had become the **predominant feature** of the battlefield, making infantry charges obsolete.

   d. _____

5. **a.** The soldiers tried to **extract information** from the prisoner.

   b. It takes a great deal of expertise to **extract** meaningful **information** from raw financial data.

   c. Modern database software allows researchers to easily locate and **extract** the **information** they need.

   d. _____

6. **a.** Ian Fleming made an **arbitrary decision** to name his hero "James Bond" after seeing the name on the book *Birds of the West Indies*.

   b. The three candidates for the job were all equally qualified, so the employer made an **arbitrary decision** to hire the first one.

   c. Although naming the new building after a former president appeared to be an **arbitrary decision**, in fact the committee had given it a lot of thought.

   d. _____

7. **a.** To be valid, psychological research must use a **random sample** of subjects who accurately reflect the behavior and characteristics of the group to be studied.

   b. World-class athletes must submit to **random sampling** of their urine to prove that they are not taking banned substances.

   c. Companies test **random samples** of their products during the manufacturing process to ensure quality control.

   d. _____

8. **a.** Hitler decided to invade Russia **despite the fact that** he was already waging war on England.

   b. The gallery was forced to close the traveling Rembrandt exhibition on schedule **despite the fact that** there were still thousands of people who wanted to view it.

   c. Dolphins can hold their breath for five minutes or more **despite the fact that** their lungs are not particularly large.

   d. _____

Read the statements below and indicate whether you agree (**A**) or disagree (**D**). Then discuss your opinions and reasoning with a partner.

_____ 1. The advertising and **labels** on many weight-loss products are misleading.

_____ 2. Clubs that **comprise** only male or only female members should be illegal.

_____ 3. **Whereas** athletes from wealthy countries have an unfair advantage because of their access to state-of-the-art training programs, athletes from poorer countries are unfairly handicapped by the lack of such programs.

_____ 4. It is acceptable for newspapers to print stories **implying** the guilt of people suspected of a crime before their trial.

_____ 5. A government must always **justify** the reasons for going to war to its people.

_____ 6. All people are **inherently** good.

_____ 7. Having richer countries supply foreign **aid** to poorer countries is one of the best ways of promoting world peace.

_____ 8. Wind and solar power offer viable **alternatives** to conventional energy sources such as oil and coal.

In the reading "Exploding Sales for Bottled Water," the writer notes that health concerns are a major reason for the consumption of bottled water in the United States. Write an essay that investigates the health issues surrounding the consumption of water, bottled or otherwise, in a specific part of the world.

The Aral Sea—An Environmental Disaster

GETTING STARTED

Discuss the following questions with your classmates.

▶ What factors could cause a lake to die?

▶ Why might farming be more profitable than fishing?

▶ Think of ecological or environmental problems in your part of the world. Which of these are natural and which are the result of human interference with nature?

TARGET WORDS—Assessing Your Vocabulary Knowledge

Look at each of the target words in the box. Use the scale to give yourself a score for each word. After you finish the chapter, score yourself again to check your improvement.

1 I don't know this word.

2 I have seen this word before, but I am not sure of the meaning.

3 I understand the word when I see it or hear it in a sentence, but I don't know how to use it in my own speaking and writing.

4 I know this word and can use it in my own speaking and writing.

TARGET WORDS			
_____ abandon	_____ devote	_____ input	_____ prohibitive
_____ adjacent	_____ diminish	_____ minimize	_____ region
_____ annual	_____ duration	_____ nevertheless	_____ terminate
_____ benefit	_____ expansion	_____ occur	_____ ultimate
_____ cite	_____ expert	_____ outcome	_____ virtually
_____ conduct	_____ inevitable	_____ predict	_____ volume

The following passage is adapted from reports on the catastrophic consequences of the shrinking of the Aral Sea. As you read, pay special attention to the target vocabulary words in **bold**.

THE DYING LAKE

1   The Aral Sea, located in the deserts between Kazakhstan and Uzbekistan, is the site of one of the largest man-made environmental disasters of modern times. Poor agricultural planning has robbed the Aral of **virtually** all of its inflowing river water, which has caused it to shrink to a salty, lifeless lake. In 1960, the Aral was the world's fourth largest inland body of water, behind the Caspian Sea, Lake Superior, and Lake Victoria. It covered 68,000 km^2 with a **volume** of 1,090 km^3 and an average salt content of about 10 grams per liter.* By 1998, the sea's area had decreased to 28,687 km^2, its **volume** had **diminished** to 181 km^3, and its average salinity had risen to around 45 grams/liter. By 2010, it is estimated that it will shrink to an area of 21,058 km^2 and a **volume** of about 124 km^3 and that it will have a salt content of nearly 70 grams/liter. Some experts predict that the Aral will dry up completely by 2020.

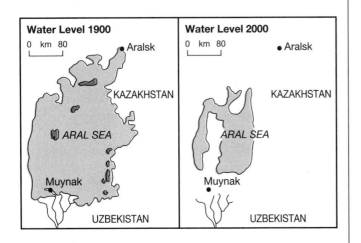

2   What caused the Aral Sea to shrink to less than half its size? Both weather and human involvement have contributed to the Aral's shrinkage. A drought in the 1970s, particularly between 1974 and 1975, lowered the amount of river water flowing into the Aral Sea by around 27 percent, compared to the average during the preceding forty-five years. The 1982-to-1986 period also had low river flows. **Nevertheless**, the main cause of the Aral's shrinkage was the massive amount of water taken from its "feeder" rivers for farming. The area around the lake is dry, and **virtually** all of the river water that once fed the Aral has been diverted to irrigate the surrounding fields of cotton and rice. The end result is that since the mid-1980s, very little river water has reached the lake. Without any **input** of new water, the lake is rapidly drying up.

3   For thousands of years, irrigation had been practiced on the Amu Darya and Syr Darya rivers that feed the Aral Sea. In the 1950s and 1960s, the amount of water diverted for irrigation greatly increased. In 1900, approximately 3 million hectares were under irrigation in the Aral Sea basin. This amount grew to 5 million by 1960, and by 1980, the irrigated area in the Aral Sea basin had grown to nearly 6.5 million hectares. When Soviet planners began this major **expansion** of irrigation in the Aral Sea basin, **conducted** in the 1950s and 1960s, it was **predicted** that increased irrigation would reduce the amount of water flowing to the sea and substantially reduce its size. At the time, a number of **experts** saw the potential shrinkage of the Aral as a worthwhile tradeoff: A cubic meter of river water used for irrigation would bring far more value than the same cubic meter delivered to the sea. This calculation was based on a simple comparison between economic gains from irrigated agriculture and economic **benefits** from the sea. Indeed, the **ultimate** shrinkage of the Aral to a relatively small, salty lake—as all its inflow was **devoted** to agriculture and other economic needs—was viewed at the time as both desirable and **inevitable**.

*Note: To convert metric measurements to U.S. equivalents, use the following: 1 km^2 = 0.3861 mile^2; 1 km^3 = 0.2399 mile^3; 1 gram/liter = 0.1335 ounce/gallon; 1 hectare = 2.4711 acres; 1 metric ton = 1.1023 tons.

4   However, the Soviet planners did not fully understand the consequences of their actions, and there have been three devastating **outcomes** as a result of the sea's shrinkage. First, much of the exposed lake bottom is salt-covered. Winds have blown this salty dust over a huge amount of the farmland supplied by the irrigation water, and this has negatively affected the farm harvests. Traces of Aral salt have been found as far away as 1,000 km to the southeast of the sea, in Georgia on the Black Sea coast, and even along the arctic shore of Russia. Soviet scientists began reporting major dust storms in the area in 1975, with up to ten major storms **occurring** per year in the period between 1975 and 1981. Observations by Soviet cosmonauts indicated that the frequency and size of the storms grew as the Aral continued to decline. Overall, an estimated 43 million metric tons of salt are carried from the sea's dried bottom **annually** and deposited over an **adjacent** area as wide as 150,000 to 200,000 km².

5   Second, changes in the Aral Sea have had adverse effects on the **region's** climate. Research has established that the Aral affects temperature and moisture conditions in surrounding lands. As the sea has contracted, its beneficial influence on climate has substantially **diminished**. The summers have become warmer, winters cooler, spring thaws later, and the fall frosts earlier. As a result, the **duration** of the crop-growing season has shortened. For example, the growing season in the Amu Darya delta just south of the sea has been reduced by an average of 10 days, forcing cotton farmers there to **terminate** cotton production and switch to growing rice.

6   Third, as the sea has shrunk and become more salty, commercial fishing has been destroyed. By the early 1980s, twenty of twenty-four native fish species had disappeared and the commercial catch (48,000 metric tons in 1957) had fallen to zero. Employment directly and indirectly related to Aral fishery, reportedly 60,000 jobs in the 1950s, has disappeared. Because of the end of commercial fishing and other harmful consequences of the sea's drying, tens of thousands of people have **abandoned** the cities and villages on the Aral's coast. For those people who remain, the drinking water is a major problem. The declining quality of the drinking water is **cited** as the main factor in the increase in respiratory ailments, cancer, and other illnesses in the **region**, particularly among children. The desert animals who used the Aral Sea as a drinking source have died or been driven away because of its greatly increased mineral content.

7   The future of the Aral Sea looks bleak. Back in the 1980s, Soviet planners spoke of diverting Siberian rivers to save the Aral Sea, but they came to the conclusion that the expense of such a project would be **prohibitive**. A 2004 U.N. report on the Aral came to the same conclusion. As Yevgenii Nadezhdin, U.N. Adviser and Project Manager for the report, said:

It is possible in principle to reestablish the Aral Sea and there [have been calculations of how much money it would cost to do this], but I think the world community does not have such an amount of money to invest. The rough estimate shows that [some $250 billion to $300 billion will be needed].

8   Today Central Asian governments of former Soviet nations have come together to establish the International Fund for Saving the Aral Sea. The most direct way of saving the Aral would be to **minimize** irrigation and allow the feeder rivers to once again flow into the sea. However, despite the shortened growing season, the economies of the **region** are still dependent on cotton exports made possible by irrigation, so a reduction in irrigation does not seem possible.

A fisherman and his boat in the dry Aral Sea

The Aral seems doomed to become ever smaller, more salty, and more lifeless. The already substantial ecological damage and economic losses will **inevitably** grow worse.

_____

Adapted from Micklin, P. P. "Desiccation of the Aral Sea: A Water Management Disaster in the Soviet Union."

In A. Goudie (ed.) (1997). *The Human Impact Reader*. Oxford, UK: Blackwell, pp. 130–142, and from Krastev, Nikola, *Central Asia: New UN Report Warns Aral Sea on the Verge of Disappearing*, Radio Free Europe, 21 June 2004, RFI/RL, Inc. Available at http://www.rferl.org (accessed July 20, 2004).

UNDERSTANDING THE READING

Respond to the following in writing. Base your responses on the reading and your own personal experiences.

1. What has happened because of the shrinkage of the Aral Sea? Describe the unexpected outcomes of the changes in the sea's size and salt content.
2. The diminishing size and volume of the Aral Sea was part of a long-term Soviet plan. What factors did the planners fail to take into account?
3. When have the effects of pollution or man-made environmental disasters been successfully reversed? Describe an ecological success story that you know about.

FOCUSING ON VOCABULARY

WORD MEANING

Each of the following target words appears in the reading on pages 114–116. Use the paragraph number in parentheses to locate each word in context. Read the dictionary definitions below. Write the letter of the definition that reflects how the word is used in the reading.

_____ **1. volume** (1)
   a. the amount of space that something contains or fills
   b. a book, particularly one that is part of a set or series

_____ **2. diminish** (1)
   a. to deliberately devalue someone
   b. to become smaller or less important

_____ **3. input** (2)
   a. something that is put in as an amount
   b. ideas, advice, money, or effort that you put into a job, meeting, etc. in order to help it succeed

_____ **4. expansion** (3)
   a. the act or process of increasing in size, number, amount, or range
   b. the act or process of making a company or business larger by opening new shops, factories, etc.

_____ **5. conduct** (3)
   a. to do something, especially in order to get information or prove facts
   b. to have the quality of transmitting light, heat, sound, or electricity

_____ **6. ultimate** (3)
   a. happening at the end of a long process
   b. better, bigger, worse, etc. than all other objects of the same kind

_____ 7. **devote** (3)
     a. to give your time, money, attention, etc. to do something or help something be successful
     b. to use a particular area, period of time, or amount of space for a specific purpose

_____ 8. **abandon** (6)
     a. to go away from a place, vehicle, etc. permanently, especially because the situation makes it impossible for you to stay
     b. to stop doing something because there are too many problems and it is impossible to continue

_____ 9. **cite** (6)
     a. to give the exact words of something that has been published in order to support an opinion or prove an idea
     b. to mention something as an example, especially one that supports, proves, or explains an idea or situation

_____ 10. **region** (6)
     a. used to describe an amount of time, money, etc. without being exact
     b. a fairly large area of a state, country, etc., usually without exact limits

_____ 11. **prohibitive** (7)
     a. too expensive to pay for
     b. preventing people from doing something by law

_____ 12. **minimize** (8)
     a. to make the degree or amount of something as small as possible
     b. to make something seem less serious or important than it really is

Each sentence below contains a paraphrase or set of synonyms for a target word. Read each sentence and select the matching target word from the box.

adjacent	duration	nevertheless	predict
annual	expert	occur	terminated
benefit	inevitable	outcome	virtually

1. Change is an _____ fact of life.
   (unavoidable, inescapable)

2. Production at the factory was _____ as a result of the fire.
   (ended, concluded)

3. The new university sports center is _____ (to) the Students'
   (next, side by side with)
   Union.

4. Environmentalists _____ that global warming could cause
   (anticipate, forecast)
   the polar ice caps to melt.

5. The company's _____ report showed that profits had fallen
   (yearly, twelve-month)
   from the previous year.

6. The _____ of the election surprised voters because early
   (result, conclusion)
   reports had indicated that the losing candidate was ahead.

7. The patient was advised to avoid caffeine while taking the medicine in order
   to derive the maximum _____ from the drugs.
   (gain, advantage)

8. Buffalo had _____ disappeared from the Great Plains before
<u>(almost, nearly)</u>
the American Bison Society was organized in 1905 to save them.

9. The rules stated that sports could not be played indoors;

_____ , students regularly played soccer in the corridors.
<u>(yet, even so)</u>

10. The floods that regularly _____ in India and Bangladesh are
<u>(happen, take place)</u>
the long-term result of the removal of trees from the slopes of the Himalayas.

11. The form and size of a volcano will be affected by its overall age and the

_____ of the volcanic eruption.
<u>(length, period)</u>

12. The charity sent an agricultural _____ to provide information
<u>(specialist, professional)</u>
about irrigation techniques.

WORD TIP

▶ **_Nevertheless_** is synonymous with the everyday spoken English expression
"but . . . anyway." It is an adverb that is used primarily as a transitional word to
signal an unexpected result. **_Nevertheless_** is often used to link two sentences.
He had no qualifications; **_nevertheless_**, he got the job.

The new drug was expensive. **_Nevertheless_**, it was not very effective.

WORD FAMILIES

Study the members of the word families in the table below. Look for spelling patterns
for the verb, noun, adjective, and adverb forms of the words. Complete the table. List
the patterns in the spaces.

Verb	Noun	Adjective	Adverb
abandon	abandonment	abandoned	X
X	X	annual	annually
benefit	benefit	beneficial	beneficially
conduct	conduct	X	X
expand	expansion	1. expandable 2. expansive	X
X	1. expert 2. expertise	expert	expertly
input	input	X	X
minimize	minimum	1. minimum 2. minimal	minimally
occur	occurrence	X	X
X	volume	voluminous	X
Spelling patterns			

Read each sentence and identify the part of speech of the missing word. Write an appropriate form of the target word in the blank. Use the word families table on page 118 to help you.

1. The United Nations sends observers to monitor elections in countries where there is a risk of the election being _____ (**conduct**) undemocratically.

2. The first _____ (**occur**) of many words in English is in Shakespeare's plays.

3. Students in graduate agriculture programs take courses in crop production systems and crop protection to develop their _____ (**expert**) in crop technology.

4. One of the _____ (**benefit**) effects of sunshine on the human skin is the creation of vitamin D.

5. There has been a huge amount of research on World War II, and the literature based on it is _____ (**volume**).

6. A local group transformed the _____ (**abandon**) property into a community garden.

7. The graduate assistant was responsible for _____ (**input**) research data into the computer.

8. Early discharge of mothers and newborn babies from hospitals after birth helps to _____ (**minimal**) both parties' exposure to hospital-acquired infections.

9. If a region receives less than twenty inches of rainfall _____ (**annual**), it is difficult to grow food without the help of irrigation.

10. The computer came with 128 Mb of RAM, which has been _____ (**expansion**) to 512 Mb.

COLLOCATION

Each item below contains three example sentences with the same target word. In each sentence, the target word is paired with a different word and forms a different collocation. In the fourth sentence, the collocation has been left blank. Choose the collocation from the examples that best fits the last sentence and write it in the blank. You may need to change the form of one of the words to fit the sentence.

1. a. His willingness to **devote** all his free **time** to charity work impressed his friends.
   b. The committee recommended that the city **devote** more **resources** to its police and fire departments.
   c. Many politicians **devote** too much of their **attention** to getting reelected, and too little to being effective public servants.

   d. Unions _____ much of their _____ and energy to trying to improve the pay and work conditions of their members.

2. a. The goal of equal rights between the sexes is not to **diminish the importance** of men in relation to women, but to recognize the valuable contributions of both sexes to society.
   b. Ear plugs and other protective devices can **diminish the impact** of loud noise on the eardrums.

    c. The university attempted to **diminish the influence** of the outspoken professor by transferring him to a smaller and less prestigious department.

    d. Automobile air bags are supposed to _____ of passengers against the inside of the car and steering wheel in an accident.

3. a. The **maximum duration** of a U.S. president's time in office is two terms or eight years.

    b. Most students entering a foreign country receive a visa of **limited duration** and must apply for an extension if they wish to study for a longer period of time.

    c. Most airlines now recommend that passengers wear their seat belts for the **entire duration** of the flight.

    d. The _____ of the strike action ensured that the employers would not take the workers' demands seriously.

4. a. In most employment contracts, both the employer and the employee have the right to **terminate employment** after a notice period, typically 30–90 days.

    b. When drawing up a contract, it is common practice to include a clause outlining the conditions under which the signing parties can **terminate the contract**.

    c. The employees were instructed to **terminate** their **relationship**, as it was against company policy to date fellow employees.

    d. The manufacturer wished to _____ its annual

    _____ with the supplier because the supplier had failed to meet agreed upon shipping schedules.

5. a. The **final outcome** of a legal case may not be determined for many years, because the law allows for appeals to higher courts.

    b. The scientists tried to predict the **likely outcome** of the experiment.

    c. Democracy and prosperity in western Europe were two **successful outcomes** of the Marshall Plan.

    d. When warm, moist air rises through the atmosphere, thunderstorms are a

    _____ .

6. a. Increased worldwide usage of automobiles is an **inevitable consequence** of the economic growth of developing countries.

    b. The reduction of fishing fleets and diminished catches are an **inevitable result** of years of overfishing.

    c. The Industrial Revolution led to the **inevitable decline** of feudalism as power moved from the landowners to the owners of plants and equipment.

    d. Scientific evidence now clearly shows that smoking is connected to an

    _____ in physical health.

7. a. Linguists can **cite** the **example** of Welsh as an illustration of how one endangered language has been saved.

    b. It is not difficult to **cite** several **reasons** why the *Mona Lisa* is one of the most famous paintings in the world.

    c. One need only **cite** the **case** of Nelson Mandela to show that one person can make a difference in governmental reform.

    d. Educators can normally _____ for children's poor performance in school despite access to high-quality teaching.

8. **a.** Although no one can **predict the future** for certain, weather forecasters can be quite accurate at least three days in advance.

   b. Political polls are generally able to **predict the outcome** of elections fairly well.

   c. It is very difficult to **predict the effects** of new medicines, so a carefully planned series of studies is necessary before new drugs are approved.

   d. The range of evidence given at the trial ensured that it would be very difficult for any one to _____.

EXPANSION

Complete the passage by filling in the blanks with the target words in the box. Use each word only once.

adjacent	nevertheless	regions	virtually
beneficial	prohibitively	ultimately	volume

CREATING MORE FRESH WATER THROUGH DESALINATION

1 As fresh water becomes more and more scarce, several countries have begun to use the ocean as a source of water. *Desalination*, or the removal of salt from seawater, is a (1) _____ method of providing fresh water for business, home, and agricultural use. Today, there are more than 12,500 desalination plants in existence worldwide that annually provide about 1 percent of the world's drinking water. The majority of these plants are located in the Middle East, the Caribbean, and the Mediterranean.

2 One method of desalination is *distillation*. Salt water is boiled and the resulting water vapor is passed through a cooler, where it condenses and is collected as fresh water. This simple procedure is very efficient at purifying seawater. Distillation of seawater produces (2) _____ pure water that is about ten times fresher than bottled water. Because the taste of distilled water is rather flat, it needs to be mixed with less pure water to improve the taste. Distillation is expensive, however, because it requires large amounts of

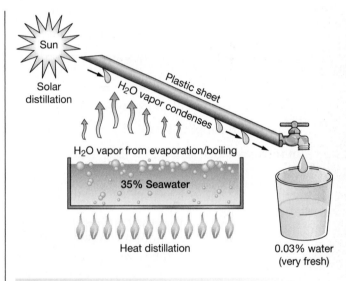

Solar distillation

Sun

Plastic sheet

H_2O vapor condenses

H_2O vapor from evaporation/boiling

35% Seawater

Heat distillation

0.03% water (very fresh)

Distillation

heat energy to boil the salt water. It takes a minimum of 540,000 calories of heat energy to make a half-liter (about one pint) bottle of distilled water; (3) _____, more than half of the world's desalination plants use the distillation process.

3 *Reverse osmosis* (*osmos* = to push) may (4) _____ have better potential for large-scale desalination. In osmosis, fresh water and salt water tanks are placed (5) _____ to one another. The

water molecules naturally pass through a thin, semi-permeable membrane from the fresh water solution to the salt water solution. In reverse osmosis, water on the salty side is highly pressurized to drive water molecules— but not salt and other impurities—through the membrane to the fresh water side. A significant problem with reverse osmosis is that the membranes are flimsy, become clogged, and must be replaced frequently. Advanced composite materials may help eliminate these problems because they are sturdier, provide better filtration, and last up to ten years. Worldwide, at least thirty countries located in arid (6) _____ are operating reverse-osmosis units. For example, Santa Barbara, California, operates a reverse-osmosis plant that produces a (7) _____ of up to 34 million liters (9 million gallons) daily, which supplies up to 60 percent of its municipal water needs.

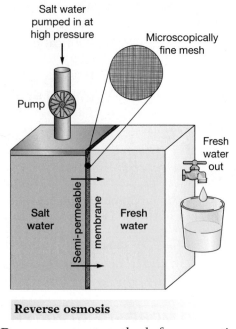

Reverse osmosis

4   Because current methods for converting seawater to fresh water remain (8) _____ expensive for many countries and regions, scientists continue to search for novel approaches to desalination.

Adapted from Thurman, H.V. and Trujillo, A.P. (2002). *Essentials of Oceanography*, 7th ed. Upper Saddle River, NJ: Prentice Hall, pp. 155–157.

EXPLORING THE TOPIC

Water is perhaps the earth's most precious resource, as human and animal life cannot be sustained without it. What's more, as the population increases, there will be a greater and greater need for more fresh water. Desalination is one method of increasing the earth's fresh water supply.

With a partner, create a list of additional ways we can create, purify, discover, or conserve fresh water. Next, compare your list with another pair and discuss the advantages and disadvantages of each method. Finally, rank your ideas according to the likelihood of them being implemented in the future.

Write a persuasive essay in which you argue in favor of a method or group of methods for using water more wisely in the future. Keep in mind that a persuasive essay is like a debate on paper. As you write, think back to your group discussion and any counterarguments that were made to the methods you have chosen to promote. Be sure to address these different viewpoints in your essay.

15 International Conflict over Natural Resources

GETTING STARTED

Discuss the following questions with your classmates.

▶ What are some of the most important natural resources a country can have?

▶ Natural resources are not evenly distributed across the world. How has access to resources made a difference in the economic development of "resource rich" and "resource poor" countries?

▶ Water is scarce in many parts of the world. In what places might competition over water cause friction between two or more countries?

TARGET WORDS—Assessing Your Vocabulary Knowledge

Look at each of the target words in the box. Use the scale to give yourself a score for each word. After you finish the chapter, score yourself again to check your improvement.

1 I don't know this word.

2 I have seen this word before, but I am not sure of the meaning.

3 I understand the word when I see it or hear it in a sentence, but I don't know how to use it in my own speaking and writing.

4 I know this word and can use it in my own speaking and writing.

TARGET WORDS			
_____adequate	_____commodity	_____fluctuate	_____secure
_____anticipate	_____discrete	_____insert	_____site
_____attain	_____enable	_____mutually	_____supplement
_____aware	_____ensure	_____nonetheless	_____sustain
_____capable	_____exploit	_____precise	_____transport
_____clarify	_____export	_____sector	_____utilize

The following passage is adapted from an article on water politics that appeared on the International Red Cross website. As you read, pay special attention to the words in **bold**.

Water Politics in the Middle East and North Africa

1   Conflicts between nations can arise from numerous issues, such as disputes over territory. But nations will also go to war over natural resources. In the Middle East and North Africa, oil is the most valuable natural resource. Nevertheless, water is also of obvious importance to the individual economies of that region. In contrast to oil, however, water is of little economic significance on a global scale. It is not a surplus resource to be imported and **exported**. It certainly does not attract the interest of the global community—along with its international corporations—in the way that oil does. These global players are only **aware** of water in the Middle East and North Africa because disputes over scarce water would **insert** an additional source of political instability into a region already partially destabilized by political and religious conflicts.

TRANSBOUNDARY WATER

2   Water and oil are natural resources that differ significantly in another important way. Most oil **sites** in the Middle East, North Africa, and other parts of the world are located within the borders of a particular country. This makes it relatively easy to establish the national ownership and control of oil resources. Conversely, over 90 percent of the water in the Middle East and North Africa crosses international borders as surface flows such as rivers; this type of shared water is known as *transboundary water*. For example, over 95 percent of Egypt's water resources is transboundary water that flows from other countries. Shared surface water is critical to national economies, especially where there is little water below the ground that could be **utilized** by pumping. Any downstream country fears that its neighbor upstream will **exploit** increasing amounts of water, leaving less to share. Egypt is very anxious in this regard, although it has only suffered a diminishment that it **mutually** agreed to with its immediate neighbor, the Sudan, in the 1959 Nile Waters

Fellucas—traditional sailing vessels—on the Nile

Agreement. Other countries have not been so lucky. Syria and Iraq have actually endured a dramatic reduction of almost 50 percent in the average flow of the Euphrates since the 1970s. They are **anticipating** additional reductions in the flow of the Tigris.

3   Fortunately, since the 1990s, agreements over water have been made, such as the Jordan-Israel Agreement of 1994 and the PLO-Israel Interim Agreement of 1995. These agreements do not define true ownership; **nonetheless** they do provide **adequate** arrangements for naturally **fluctuating** water resources. The agreements provide guidelines about how water should be allocated and managed within **discrete** territories. The agreements help to satisfy national honor, and they **ensure** the **secure** and **sustainable** growth of the region's economies.

THE GLOBAL DEMAND FOR VIRTUAL WATER

4   As useful as such water agreements are, it is impossible to define ownership of water **precisely**, which means that stressful water

politics in the Middle East and North Africa are inevitable. Water politics will remain stressful until all the economies of the region have **attained** advanced levels of socio-economic development. In such diverse economies, water resources are only one of many minor factors of production rather than the major economic input. When water is a major economic factor in food production, for example in agriculture, its role in the livelihoods of a majority of a country's people is direct and obvious. The significance of that water in terms of international relations makes water scarcity an easy focus for national and community anxiety. In the region of the Middle East and North Africa, there is sufficient water to **enable** countries to meet their industrial and domestic needs, but not enough to meet their food production needs.

5   One way around the region's water deficiency is to import the **commodities** that require large amounts of water to produce. For example, about 1,000 tons of water are required to produce a ton of wheat. When an economy imports a ton of wheat, it is in effect importing 1,000 tons of "virtual" water. (Here the word *virtual* means "something equivalent to something else.") In the Middle East and North Africa, about 40 million tons of grain and flour were being imported annually by the end of the 1990s as a **supplement** to domestic production. About 40 billion tons of water would be required to produce this volume of grain. Such a volume reflects about 20 percent of the region's annual water use,

and it is equivalent to the water used each year by Egypt in its agricultural **sector**. Engineers could not consider **transporting** so much water, but those involved in the international grain trade are **capable** of accepting the challenge. Water, food, and trade are intricately connected, and this interconnectedness is of major strategic significance to grain-importing economies in arid and semiarid regions. Virtual water has, since the early 1970s, **ensured** the economic stability of this major arid region in the world. Future economic stability here will depend on the region's capacity to **sustain** this trade in virtual water.

6   Importing water-intensive **commodities** is so effective that the substantial lack of water is not particularly noticeable to the 300 million people living in the Middle East and North Africa. It is not a political issue at the domestic level or the international level, except where governments choose to make it one. With political stress over water being so easily managed at the level of the whole economy, it should not be surprising that there has been so little armed conflict over water since the early 1960s. If the region enters into further water agreements, **clarifies** existing agreements, and continues to trade in virtual water, there is reason to hope that nations can continue to avoid conflicts over water in the future.

Adapted from Allan, J. A. *Avoiding War Over Natural Resources*, 11 January 1998, ICRC. Available at http://www.icrc.org (accessed November 21, 2003).

UNDERSTANDING THE READING

Respond to the following in writing. Base your responses on the reading and your own personal experiences.

1. What are two fundamental differences between oil and water in relation to trade?
2. What is virtual water? How can it help countries in the Middle East and North Africa?
3. Identify some advantages and disadvantages of thinking in terms of virtual natural resources.

WORD MEANING

Read the sentences below and circle the letter of the word or phrase that best matches the meaning of the target word in **bold**. Use context clues in the sentences to determine the correct meaning. Check your dictionary if you are not sure of the answer.

1. Gold, sugar, and petroleum are some of the **commodities** commonly traded on the open market.
   a. something that you work hard to attain
   b. a product that is bought and sold
   c. the best example of something

2. Most modern coal-fired boilers **utilize** coal that has been ground down to fine particle sizes.
   a. use something for a particular purpose
   b. refuse to do something
   c. abandon something or someone

3. The prime minister was **aware** of the decline in his popularity.
   a. realizing that something exists
   b. denying a situation
   c. uninformed

4. Contracts are normally written in **precise** legal terminology to avoid any uncertainty about the responsibilities of the parties signing the agreement.
   a. unknown
   b. approximate
   c. exact

5. The priority of the hotel staff was to **ensure** that the guests had an enjoyable stay.
   a. delay
   b. make sure something will happen
   c. ask that something be done

6. The speaker could see that the audience did not understand her statement, so she was forced to go back and **clarify** the point.
   a. call out
   b. forget
   c. make clear

7. To make the writing process easier, the teacher broke it down into a series of **discrete** steps and set clear deadlines for the completion of each one.
   a. clearly separate
   b. difficult
   c. serious in nature

8. The height of ocean tides **fluctuates** according to the positions of the sun and the moon.
   a. changes often, e.g., from high to low levels and back
   b. destroys something completely
   c. understands something completely

9. The cost of **transporting** produce to market must be added to the final cost that consumers pay.
   a. the process of taking something from one place to another
   b. the process of treating something in a bad manner
   c. the process of making something shine brightly

10. The manual included directions on how to **insert** additional memory cards onto the computer motherboard.
    a. keep out of
    b. stay away from
    c. put in

11. Diamonds, copper, nickel, and beef are the major commodities that Botswana **exports** to other countries.
    a. sells goods to another country
    b. buys goods from another country
    c. exchanges goods with another country

12. The decline in the manufacturing **sector** has been offset by the growth of the service sector.
    a. a specific kind of business
    b. an area of activity, especially of business or trade
    c. the process of getting better

Read the sentences below and use context to figure out the meaning of the target words in bold. Look for a core meaning that provides a general understanding of each target word. Write the meaning in your own words.

1. a. Closed circuit TV cameras have been installed in many downtown areas to provide a more **secure** environment for the general public.
   b. Data encryption provides a **secure** way of transmitting data over the Internet.

   secure _____

2. a. Sand dunes in the Egyptian Sand Sea can **attain** a height of 100 meters (330 feet).
   b. An internal combustion engine must **attain** a high rate of revolution (RPM) in order to produce maximum power output.

   attain _____

3. a. The negotiations started positively, but the momentum was difficult to **sustain** and the talks broke down within a week.
   b. Good managers aim to provide their employees with good working conditions and levels of pay high enough to **sustain** their motivation.

   sustain _____

4. a. The owner left the company in the **capable** hands of his son when he retired.
   b. Pigeons are **capable** of finding their way home even if released 100 miles away.

   capable _____

5. a. After a long period of disagreement, the two parties were able to work out a **mutually** beneficial solution to their problem.
   b. Coaches communicate with their players, spectators, and colleagues via **mutually** agreed upon signals.

mutually _____

6. a. Lillehammer, Norway, was the **site** of the 1994 Winter Olympics.
   b. In 1997, a new Globe Theatre was opened on the **site** of the original theater where Shakespeare's plays were first performed.

site _____

7. a. Although suntan lotions can help prevent the skin from burning, most do not provide **adequate** protection from ultraviolet radiation.
   b. Many people feel that the Warren Commission failed to provide an **adequate** explanation of the assassination of John F. Kennedy.

adequate _____

8. a. Western petroleum companies are working with local companies to **exploit** the opportunities for oil production around the Caspian Sea.
   b. Developing countries need to find ways to **exploit** their natural resources for the good of their own people.

exploit _____

9. a. One key to good management is **anticipating** potential problems before they occur.
   b. If investors **anticipate** a decline in the stock market, they will sell stocks and invest in bonds.

anticipate _____

10. a. In hunting and gathering societies, plants were only intended to be a **supplement** to a meat-based diet.
   b. Social security is intended to be a **supplement** to the savings of retirees, rather than their sole source of income.

supplement _____

11. a. Infrared satellite photography from space **enables** scientists to track changes to the earth's environment, such as the destruction of the rainforests.
   b. Antibiotics **enable** the body to resist disease and infection.

enable _____

> *Nonetheless* and *nevertheless* are both adverbs that mean "in spite of what you have just mentioned." Usually synonyms have some distinguishing features, but *nonetheless* and *nevertheless* both have a formal tone and are used interchangeably. The only difference is that *nevertheless* appears to be used three times more frequently than *nonetheless*.

WORD FAMILIES

Read the sentences below. Some of the target words have been used correctly, but in six sentences a wrong word form has been used. If the wrong form has been used, cross it out and write the correct form. If the form is correct, put a checkmark (✓).

1. Homeowners can improve the **secure** in their own areas by participating in Neighborhood Watch programs. _____

2. After the phenomenal success of the first Harry Potter book, readers looked forward to subsequent books in the series with great **anticipate**.

    _____

3. The two main languages of Belgium are **discrete** as they stem from separate ethnic backgrounds—Walloon and Flemish. _____

4. During the height of the Cold War, both the United States and the Soviet Union had the **capable** of destroying each other. _____

5. Neil Armstrong was forced to identify a new safe landing place for his lunar lander when the original landing **site** proved to be filled with large rocks.

    _____

6. Second language learners have the advantage of already knowing their first language; thus they have some **aware** of how languages work in general.

    _____

7. Cloning is achieved by the **insert** of parent DNA into a host cell.

    _____

8. Air traffic controllers must ensure **adequate** separation between the aircraft flying in a particular airspace. _____

9. Careful conservation and **utilize** of water must be a key part of any water management plan. _____

10. A sustained rally of prices in the financial **sector** led to a 100-point rise in the Dow Jones stock market index. _____

COLLOCATION

Match each target word in the box with the group of words that regularly occur with it. In all cases, the target words come before the word in the list.

clarify	ensure	fluctuating	precise
commodity	exploit	mutual	supplementary

1. _____
prices
production
market
exchange

2. _____
a position
a point
a situation
an issue

3. _____
safety
success
compliance
standards

4. _____
opportunities
resources
technology
potential

5. _____
fund
respect
support
friend

6. _____
nature
moment
details
location

7. _____
budget
material
information
income

8. _____
levels
patterns
rates
fortunes

EXPANSION

The use of natural resources always has consequences, often in terms of environmental cost. Sometimes these consequences affect other nations, and this may lead to international conflict.

Read the scenarios that follow. Each involves a conflict over natural resources. Decide how likely each scenario is to cause serious armed conflict between the countries and put a checkmark (✓) in the appropriate box.

Scenario	Likelihood of leading to armed conflict		
	Very likely	**Somewhat possible**	**Very unlikely**
1. A country builds a dam and does not allow an **adequate** amount of river water to flow to a downstream neighbor.			
2. Diamonds smuggled from one country to another are used to finance a revolutionary army in the second country. The first country is **aware** of the smuggling and **capable** of stopping it, but does nothing.			

Scenario	Likelihood of leading to armed conflict		
	Very likely	Somewhat possible	Very unlikely
3. One country relies heavily on coffee for its **export** income, and the adjacent country makes a big push to increase its own coffee production and **exports**.			
4. A petroleum reserve is discovered across the shared border of two countries. One country immediately begins to **exploit** this resource and may nearly pump the reserve dry before the other can begin production.			
5. A country **attains** prosperity by **utilizing** its large coal resources to produce inexpensive electricity. However, the pollution from its power plants poisons a neighboring country's lakes and rivers.			
6. A country builds a dam across a large river, but this disrupts fish returning to an upstream country whose non-industrial **sector** relies heavily on fishing.			
7. The harvest of wood in a high mountainous country results in rain flowing directly down the rivers to a lower country, which **sustains** heavy losses through persistent flooding.			
8. Poor farming practices in an upstream country **enable** sediment to flow down rivers to a downstream country, where it clogs ports and harbors, crippling its **transportation** system.			

With a classmate, choose one or two of the situations from the chart on pages 130–131 and discuss how you would try to negotiate an agreement between the countries involved. What are some of the key issues? What compromises would you suggest to the countries?

 Identify a genuine international conflict over natural resources. Write an essay in which you describe the development of that conflict.

Strategy Practice

USING YOUR DICTIONARY—Pronunciation

The English language has a history of borrowing words from other languages, most notably French, Latin, and Greek. In addition, modern English evolved from Old English, which included words from Scandinavian and Germanic languages (e.g., *man, woman*, and *field*). English continues to borrow new words from other languages and to invent new words based on the patterns of existing words. This is why it is often hard to figure out the pronunciation of new words on your own.

USING PHONETIC SPELLINGS AND THE PRONUNCIATION KEY

Your dictionary can help you determine how to pronounce new words. To figure out a word's pronunciation, use both the phonetic spelling that accompanies each entry and your dictionary's pronunciation key.

All dictionaries provide phonetic spellings next to each word entry.

> **ar•bi•trar•y** /ˈɑrbəˌtrɛri/ *adj.* decided or arranged without any reason or plan, often unfairly: *The government has carried out numerous executions and arbitrary arrests.* —**arbitrariness** *n.* [U] —**arbitrarily** *adv.*

A dictionary will also include a guide to its pronunciation symbols in the introduction or an appendix. This guide will explain the dictionary's phonetic alphabet. Look at the pronunciation table from the *Longman Advanced American Dictionary (LAAD)* on the following page. Using the phonetic spelling in the entry above and the table, you can determine how to say the word *arbitrary*. For example, the pronunciation symbols let you know that the final *y* in *arbitrary* stands for the long *e* sound.

Pronunciation table

Vowels

Symbol	Keyword
i	beat, feed
ɪ	bit, did
eɪ	date, paid
ɛ	bet, bed
æ	bat, bad
ɑ	box, odd, father
ɔ	bought, dog
oʊ	boat, road
ʊ	book, good
u	boot, food, student
ʌ	but, mud, mother
ə	banana, among
ɚ	shirt, murder
aɪ	bite, cry, buy, eye
aʊ	about, how
ɔɪ	voice, boy
ɪr	beer
ɛr	bare
ɑr	bar
ɔr	door
ʊr	tour

/t/	means that /t/ may be dropped
/d/	means that /d/ may be dropped
/ˈ/	shows main stress
/ˌ/	shows secondary stress
/◄/	shows stress shift

Consonants

Symbol	Keyword
p	pack, happy
b	back, rubber
t	tie
d	die
k	came, key, quick
g	game, guest
tʃ	church, nature, watch
dʒ	judge, general, major
f	fan, photograph
v	van
θ	thing, breath
ð	then, breathe
s	sip, city, psychology
z	zip, please, goes
ʃ	ship, machine, station, special, discussion
ʒ	measure, vision
h	hot, who
m	men, some
n	sun, know, pneumonia
ŋ	sung, ringing
w	wet, white
l	light, long
r	right, wrong
y	yes, use, music
t̪	butter, bottle
tˀ	button

Each dictionary is slightly different. *LAAD* uses the International Phonetic Alphabet, but another dictionary might use a different set of symbols. Becoming familiar with your dictionary's pronunciation symbols will enable you to pronounce new words correctly.

PRACTICING YOUR DICTIONARY SKILLS

Match the words below with their phonetic spellings.

_____ **1.** adequate   **a.** /saɪt/

_____ **2.** adjacent   **b.** /ˈrɛgyəˌleɪt/

_____ **3.** chemical   **c.** /proʊˈhɪbət̬ɪv, prə-/

_____ **4.** cite   **d.** /ˈflʌktʃuˌeɪt/

_____ **5.** federal   **e.** /ˈkɛmɪkəl/

_____ **6.** fluctuate   **f.** /ˈridʒən/

_____ **7.** prohibitive   **g.** /əˈdʒeɪsənt/

_____ **8.** proportion   **h.** /ˈfɛdərəl/

_____ **9.** region   **i.** /ˈædəkwɪt/

_____**10.** regulate   **j.** /prəˈpɔrʃən/

STRATEGY—Using Prefixes as Clues to Word Meaning

Study the following words with the prefixes *e-*, *es-*, *ex-*; *im-*, *in-*; *inter-*; and *trans-*:

emission, escape, exit, except
import, implant, include, induction
international, interact, interdisciplinary, interrelationship
transaction, translate, transplant, transpose

Match the prefixes with their meanings.

_____**1.** *e- / es- / ex-*   **a.** between or among

_____**2.** *im- / in-*   **b.** across

_____**3.** *inter-*   **c.** out of

_____**4.** *trans-*   **d.** in, into

The academic words in the box below contain the prefixes above. Match each word with its definition. The first one has been done for you.

emerge	incorporate	internal	~~intervene~~	transmit
expose	insert	interval	transfer	transport

1. to come between two or more parties in a conflict _____*intervene*_____

2. to appear or come out from somewhere _____

3. to make someone move from one place, job, etc. to another _____

4. the period of time between two events, activities, etc. _____

5. inside something rather than outside _____

6. to carry passengers or goods from one place to another _____

7. to include something as part of a group, system, plan, etc. _____

8. to show something; bring something out that had been hidden _____

9. to put something inside or into something else _____

10. to send electronic signals, e.g., by wire or radio _____

In the collocation sections of this book, you have seen how words often form regular partnerships. Collocation does not, however, apply only to pairs of words. Often academic words are part of longer phrases that express particular meanings.

Look at the phrases in the following sentences. The academic word is in **bold** and the longer phrase is in italics:

- A good way *to **minimize** the risk of* catching a cold is to wash your hands often.
- The cut in interest rates may not be enough to ***sustain*** *economic growth*.
- Having talent is *no **guarantee** of success* in the music business; one must also have a good manager.
- The increase in food poisoning cases ***highlights*** *the need for* closer supervision of food processing facilities.

The following box contains phrases that form around academic words from Unit 4. Read the sentences and write the appropriate phrase from the box in the blanks. The first one has been done for you.

are not mutually exclusive	the precise nature of
forced to abandon its plan	the ultimate goal of
the inevitable consequence of	to secure the future of

1. Given the lack of funds, the university was ___forced to abandon its plan___
    _____ to build a new sports hall.

2. The increase in housing prices was _____
    _____ the shortage of available homes.

3. Getting people back to work is _____
    _____ any welfare system.

4. The development of durable lightweight fabrics for backpacking equipment
    has proven that strength and light weight _____
    _____.

5. The Apollo lunar landings allowed scientists to determine _____
    _____ the moon's surface.

6. The government tried _____
    the country's aerospace industry by contracting to buy 200 of the new aircraft.

UNIT

5

We Are What We Eat

Food Roots and Foodways

GETTING STARTED

Discuss the following questions with your classmates.

▶ What foods do you associate with your cultural or regional background?

▶ Are these foods served in other parts of the world, for example, in ethnic restaurants representing a particular culture or place? If so, why? If not, why not?

▶ What is the strangest food you have ever eaten? What was exotic about it?

TARGET WORDS—Assessing Your Vocabulary Knowledge

Look at each of the target words in the box. Use the scale to give yourself a score for each word. After you finish the chapter, score yourself again to check your improvement.

1 I don't know this word.

2 I have seen this word before, but I am not sure of the meaning.

3 I understand the word when I see it or hear it in a sentence, but I don't know how to use it in my own speaking and writing.

4 I know this word and can use it in my own speaking and writing.

TARGET WORDS			
_____assemble	_____denote	_____inclination	_____quote
_____assure	_____domain	_____investment	_____reluctance
_____collapse	_____explicit	_____license	_____specify
_____constraint	_____framework	_____mature	_____subordinate
_____constructed	_____immigrate	_____notion	_____subsidy
_____core	_____implication	_____oddness	_____validity

The following passage is adapted from a textbook on the economic, cultural, and geographical aspects of food. It focuses on regional and cultural influences on food customs and beliefs. As you read, pay special attention to the target vocabulary words in **bold**.

FOOD HABITS AND BELIEFS

1   Although **specific** food habits and food systems may not be confined to a particular place or cultural **domain**, place and space do play an important role in regional geographies of food production, food marketing, and food preparation. Because of their comparative advantages of climate and soil, coupled with historical traditions based upon particular skills or trade patterns, certain regions of the world are **assured** of having market dominance for their products. In studying the geography of food, we find that certain foods, habits, and customs, including specific food taboos, are associated with particular places and/or cultures.

VARIOUS TYPES OF FOOD-PLACE ASSOCIATIONS

2   The association of food with a particular place has many variations. We have divided them into four categories for the purposes of this discussion. The first type of food-place category includes food items that come from highly specialized production regions. For example, cranberries are specially cultivated in the United States in Wisconsin, as are grapevines in the Barossa Valley in Australia. Some of these regional specialties are of relatively recent origin; they are a result of intensive capital **investment** and/or a government **subsidy**. For this category of foods, the association between food and place is weak or nonexistent in the mind of the consumer.

3   The second kind of food-place category includes foods that may have originated with a traditional recipe in a particular place, but which over time have become generic food products. New England clam chowder, Black Forest cake, and Yorkshire pudding are examples of such foods. They were once associated with a region, but now are universally known and manufactured without **explicit** production links to their places of origin other than in their names.

A poultry market in Western Asia

4   In the third food-place category, we might include foods that have maintained strong links with particular regions in terms of production, quality control, and identity. One thinks here of Parma ham, Florida orange juice, and many types of Continental cheeses. Some of the strongest links are maintained by the legal **framework** of Apellations Controllées in France, which over decades has protected and **licensed** individual varieties of wine.

5   Our fourth food-place category is the regional cuisine that depends upon its distinctive ingredients, the style and skill of

cooking, and the high quality and superb taste of the resulting dishes. These foods include various kinds of haute cuisine and other lesser regional traditions recognized around the world. When cooks **immigrate** to a new country, they bring their cooking traditions with them. The haute cuisine of places like Mexico, France, and southern China has migrated far from its origin as **immigrant** restaurant cooks **assemble** regional dishes into a representative selection from their countries. Sometimes these regional cuisines have come to symbolize, or **denote**, an entire nation's cuisine even though they, in fact, only represent dishes from a specific area. This seems to be the case with much of the world-renowned "Italian" dishes of pasta and pizza, which are heavily reliant upon the cuisines of southern Italy, **specifically** Napoli.

THE CULTURAL GEOGRAPHY OF FOOD

6   There has been a tradition of seeing human behaviors (e.g., food habits) as within the **domain** of regional cultures. An example of this is the traditional dishes of the Alsace-Lorraine region. It seems that certain foods characterize the French- and German-speaking peoples to the west and east respectively of the linguistic frontier. In the French-speaking region, red cabbage is used in salad, soup is consumed in the evening, and a regional cheese (cancoillotte) is typical; in German Alsace, red cabbage is cooked as a vegetable, soup is a midday item, and typical foods are naveline (turnips fermented like sauerkraut) and onion tart. The **implication** is that culinary preferences reflect more than individual taste—they reflect a wider culture as well.

7   Some food habits and foodways are culturally **specific**. Food is the focus of many cultural festivals, both regularly occurring events such as those **denoting** yearly religious and cultural celebrations, and occasional events such as weddings and funerals. A festival may only be an annual event, such as the American celebration of Thanksgiving with its roast turkey, dressing, and pumpkin pies, but it is culturally important, and even people who find themselves halfway around the world have a strong **inclination** to continue observing these social traditions.

8   Most cultures and places have time-honored food habits and meal patterns, but some of these are starting to **collapse** under the pressure of modern life. Time has become such a **constraint** for busy people that the leisured cooking of complex recipes is now less of an option than it was only a few decades ago, and meals of a predictable composition served at set times have also declined. Moreover, there have been powerful shifts in family structure, with the growth in single-person households undermining traditional collective meals. As a result, it seems that both the family and the family meal have been **subordinated** to other interests, with one survey finding that two-thirds of evening meals in Britain are now consumed in front of the television.

FOOD AVOIDANCES AND TABOOS: THE "YUK" FACTOR

9   *Neophobia* is a dislike of the new, and in the case of food, this newness or **oddness** may be manifested in its taste, odor, or appearance. Young children are especially prone to the rejection of food for this reason, but adults may also show a **reluctance** to try novel foods or dishes that seem to lie beyond the limits of their socially **constructed** taste. But it is not only new foods that are avoided.

10   In its raw state, much of the food that we eat is highly perishable and potentially dangerous if it is allowed to become contaminated or to decay. Even the most delicious food is only a few hours or days away from becoming rotten, unhealthy matter. As a result, disgust is never too far away from the enjoyment of food and eating. Scholars suggest that such revulsion may be classified into "**core** disgust" (from very bitter tastes or toward certain animals and insects) and "animal nature disgust" (from poor hygiene or contact with death). But they also find that there are remarkable degrees of cultural variation in disgust responses. This is because our behavior is affected by our conception of the polluting power of "unclean" foods, which may originate from a religious taboo or from a disgust generated by custom. Many Britons may abhor the **notion** of eating horseflesh, snails, or dog meat, but some of their traditional foods, such as black pudding (dried

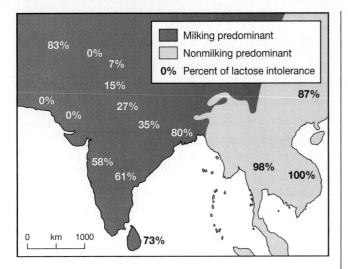

Figure 17.1 Lactose intolerance and the milking and nonmilking regions of Asia

blood), tripe (cow's stomach), and **mature** cheese veined with blue mold, are equally nauseating for other peoples.

11 Simoons (1994) wrote a classic scholarly text on food avoidance. He **reconstructed** the spatial extent of taboos on the consumption of foods like pork, beef, chicken, horseflesh, camel, dog, and fish. He was also able to **specify** how long-standing economic or cultural practices can influence human genetics. When Simoons studied the correlation between dairying and lactose tolerance, he found that nonmilking areas of the Old World coincide with higher percentages of lactose intolerance (the inability to absorb milk sugar, or lactose). (See Figure 17.1.) The **implication** of this study is that people in milking regions gradually adapted genetically to the nutritional dairy products that their female livestock supplied.

12 Anthropologists and sociologists have taught us a great deal about regional food habits and beliefs. The origins and evolution of taste are complex and have a big impact on cultures and regions. Food behavior research appears to confirm the **validity** of the following **quote** from George Orwell: "It could plausibly be argued that changes of diet are more important than changes of dynasty or religion."

_____
Adapted from Atkins, P. and Bowler, I. (2001). *Food in Society*. London, UK: Arnold Press, pp. 274–280, 297–298, 301–304.

UNDERSTANDING THE READING

Respond to the following in writing. Base your responses on the reading and your own personal experiences.

1. Describe the four types of food-place associations. Give an example of each.
2. How is food linked to important cultural events in your country or region? How is it linked to more common everyday cultural practices?
3. What is the "yuk" factor? What are two explanations for its existence?

FOCUSING ON VOCABULARY

WORD MEANING

Match the words with their definitions. If you are unsure about a word's meaning, try to figure it out from context by rereading the passage on pp. 139–141. Then check your dictionary.

Set 1

_____**1.** subordinate   **a.** to enter a country in order to live there permanently

_____**2.** reluctance   **b.** the desire to do something

_____**3.** immigrate   **c.** the state of being real, true, or based on facts

_____**4.** inclination   **d.** to put something or someone in a less important position

_____**5.** validity   **e.** unwillingness or slowness

Set 2

_____**1.** quote

_____**2.** license

_____**3.** notion

_____**4.** mature

_____**5.** implication

a. to give official permission for someone to do something or for an activity to take place

b. an idea, belief, or opinion about something, especially one that you think is wrong

c. words from a book or speech that you repeat exactly in your own speech or piece or writing

d. something that is not directly said or shown but that is suggested or understood

e. having a good strong taste developed over a long period of time

Set 3

_____**1.** oddness

_____**2.** specify

_____**3.** domain

_____**4.** investment

a. to state something in an exact and detailed way

b. the range of things that are included in a particular subject, type of art, or activity

c. the money that people or organizations have put into a company or business in order to get a profit

d. strangeness or difference from what is expected

Read the row of words and phrases below each numbered word. One word or phrase in each list is *not* a synonym for the numbered word. Cross it out.

1. **collapse**
   fall down | cave in | split | give way

2. **core**
   main | primary | central | principle

3. **framework**
   skeleton | structure | contract | support

4. **constraint**
   limitation | puzzle | restraint | restriction

5. **explicit**
   unconscious | precise | definite | specific

6. **denote**
   stand for | reject | represent | symbolize

7. **assure**
   prevent | guarantee | make certain | ensure

8. **subsidy**
   funding | grant | assistance | colleague

9. **assemble**
   assist | bring together | collect | accumulate

10. **constructed**
    formed | created | limited | built

WORD FAMILIES

The table below contains word families for some of the target words in the reading. Complete the rest of the table. An *X* indicates that there is no form or that the form is not common. Sometimes there may be more than one form possible. If you are unsure about a form, check your dictionary.

Verb	Noun	Adjective	Adverb
assemble		assembled	X
assure	assurance		assuredly
construct	1. construct 2.	constructed	X
X	explicitness	explicit	
	inclination	inclined	X
	1. maturity 2. maturation	mature	X
X	1. oddity 2. oddness		
quote	1. quote 2. quotation		X
subordinate	1. subordination 2.	subordinate	X
	1. validity 2. validation	valid	validly

Choose the correct form of the word in **bold** in sentence **a** to complete sentence **b**. Use the word families table you just completed as a guide.

1. a. The ability to **assemble** and inspire effective teams is a more important quality for managers than technical knowledge.
    b. The principal presented the awards for outstanding scholarship at the weekly school _____.

2. a. The long jumper had an **assured** place on the Olympic team, so he did not need to compete in the indoor tournament.
    b. Any quality _____ program for schools should make certain that money is spent effectively on learning goals.

3. a. The poorly designed and **constructed** apartment blocks are a danger to residents.
    b. The psychologist Piaget believed that children must _____ the universe of objects through experience.

4. a. Speech is often accompanied by gestures and words like *this* and *that*, whereas writing normally requires greater linguistic **explicitness**.
    b. Many widely supported objectives for schooling, such as personal and social skills, are not _____ recognized in assessment procedures.

5. a. The referee showed little **inclination** to penalize players for minor fouls.

   b. Scandinavian citizens are more _____ to pay high taxes for comprehensive social services than Americans are.

6. a. The meat of a young chicken is tender and juicy, but it may lack the flavor of **mature** poultry.

   b. High-quality Manchego cheese from Spain must _____ for over a year to develop its full nutty flavor.

7. a. In the 1960s and 1970s an imported car was something of an **oddity**, but by the 1990s one-quarter of all cars sold in the United States were imports.

   b. Some might say that Matisse's paintings include an _____ mixture of color and perspective.

8. a. The average **quote** from a presidential candidate on network television lasted forty-three seconds in 1968.

   b. John F. Kennedy's most famous _____ is engraved on his memorial in Virginia's Arlington National Cemetery.

9. a. In ape societies, **subordinate** males must defer to the one dominant male in the group.

   b. The _____ of strategic planning to day-to-day decision making can lead to poor organizational performance.

10. a. Although the **validity** of crime statistics is often questioned, such figures provide an important basis for people's beliefs about crime.

   b. One of the best ways to _____ the results of a scientific study is to repeat the study again and see if the second set of results matches the first.

COLLOCATION

Each item below contains three sentences with the same collocation. Write a fourth sentence of your own using the same word partners.

1. a. Scientists now understand the mechanics that cause earthquakes, but they still cannot **specify precisely** when one will occur.

   b. Typically, the terms of a grant to support research will **specify precisely** how the money can be spent.

   c. Global Positioning Satellite (GPS) navigation systems can now **specify precisely** where an airplane, ship, or car is located.

   d. _____

2. a. Medical developments in fertility treatments are forcing societies to reexamine their **core beliefs** about the family.

   b. The **core beliefs** of Republicans and Democrats differ when it comes to the issues of taxation, welfare, and government regulation.

   c. The performance of a company depends on its building up a set of **core beliefs** that will guide decision making, especially in times of change or difficulty.

   d. _____

3. **a.** Software falls into four categories: freeware, shareware, **public domain**, and commercial.
   b. Some public figures support privacy laws that would prevent newspapers and magazines from releasing details of their personal lives into the **public domain**.
   c. One role of investigative journalism is to bring into the **public domain** subjects that have previously been hidden from view.

   d. _____

4. **a.** The International Space Station aims to **establish** a **framework** for cooperative exploration of space.
   b. The goal of the meeting was to **establish** a **framework** upon which future cooperation between the two institutions could be built.
   c. The report will summarize past research into the development of adult literacy and **establish** a **framework** for further research in this area.

   d. _____

5. **a.** Any government money spent on the education and welfare of children is a **sound investment** in a country's future.
   b. Companies that spend time on thorough market research are making a **sound investment** in the future success of their products.
   c. Young people just starting out in the workplace who are looking for a **sound investment** for their savings should consider beginning a retirement fund.

   d. _____

6. **a.** The country hovered on the **brink of collapse** for two decades because of ethnic infighting.
   b. The company managers were laboring under a mountain of debt and the company's stock prices were on the **brink of collapse**.
   c. The negotiations between the unions and employers were again on the **brink of collapse**.

   d. _____

7. **a.** Overcrowding at the world's major airports **imposes constraints** on growth in the airline industry.
   b. Peer pressure **imposes constraints** on an individual's freedom of choice.
   c. Inheritance tax laws **impose constraints** on how parents can distribute their belongings to their children in their wills.

   d. _____

8. **a.** Police are often **reluctant to get involved** in disputes between family members.
   b. New employees may be **reluctant to get involved** in arguments over working conditions for fear of being branded troublemakers.
   c. The company was **reluctant to get involved** in the new business venture until further market research had been carried out.

   d. _____

EXPANSION

Read the statements below and indicate whether you agree **(A)** or disagree **(D)**. Then discuss your opinions and reasoning with a partner.

_____ 1. Lack of **investment** in the arts is the reason for the poor quality of television programming.

_____ 2. Free and open **immigration** to a country should not be **constrained** by quotas that restrict the number of new immigrants.

_____ 3. Young people should not be able to apply for a driver's **license** until they have reached at least eighteen years of age.

_____ 4. The government should fully **subsidize** college education so that students do not have to pay tuition fees.

_____ 5. Food producers should not use labels that **denote** false places of origin for their products.

_____ 6. The whole **notion** of democracy must be questioned when fewer than 50 percent of the citizens of a "democratic" nation fail to participate in elections.

_____ 7. The **implication** behind falling birth rates in developed countries is that economic development leads to a less family-oriented lifestyle.

_____ 8. Local dialects and accents are as **valid** a means of communication as so-called standard versions of a language, e.g., standard English.

Now choose one of the topics above and write a short essay that expresses your views. Be sure to provide support for your opinions.

18

Getting Back to Nature

GETTING STARTED

Discuss the following questions with your classmates.

▶ Have you ever been on or worked on a farm? If so, how did your experiences affect your perspective on the foods you buy and eat?

▶ What is the difference between organic food and other foods you might buy in a store?

▶ Do you buy any organic food? Why or why not?

TARGET WORDS — Assessing Your Vocabulary Knowledge

Look at each of the target words in the box. Use the scale to give yourself a score for each word. After you finish the chapter, score yourself again to check your improvement.

1 I don't know this word.

2 I have seen this word before, but I am not sure of the meaning.

3 I understand the word when I see it or hear it in a sentence, but I don't know how to use it in my own speaking and writing.

4 I know this word and can use it in my own speaking and writing.

TARGET WORDS			
_____ advocate	_____ ethics	_____ legislation	_____ philosophy
_____ bias	_____ external	_____ levy	_____ portion
_____ bulk	_____ finite	_____ margin	_____ practitioner
_____ coincide	_____ forthcoming	_____ ministry	_____ priority
_____ compatible	_____ infrastructure	_____ orient	_____ qualitatively
_____ contrary	_____ integration	_____ output	_____ refine

The following passage is adapted from a book on organic farming that argues in favor of organic farming practices. As you read, pay special attention to the target vocabulary words in **bold**.

ORGANIC FARMING VERSUS TRADITIONAL FARMING METHODS

1   Agriculture today is finding itself in increasing difficulties. It is being assailed on so many sides that it hardly knows which way to turn. The environmental lobby complains about pollution from pesticides, fertilizers, and livestock waste and about the destruction of the countryside; the health-conscious are worried about the residues of harmful substances in their diet and about the tastelessness of food; and the anti-marketeers point accusingly at the surpluses arising from current agricultural policy. All this **coincides** with current perceptions that the great technological advances of recent years are causing, rather than alleviating, the terrible famines of the Third World. Farmers are desperate because their profit **margins** are squeezed and the policies that they are told to follow are continually being reversed.

2   Where is the way out of this predicament? Will any of the suggestions **advocated** by the authorities ever get to the root of the problem? Taxes and **levies** on the use of certain substances (e.g., the nitrogen used in fertilizers); crop quotas; more pesticide **legislation**; provisions in the farm subsidy framework for environmentally sound practices—however beneficial these proposals may be in themselves, they merely tackle the symptoms of the problems.

3   There is, however, one solution that is **qualitatively** different. It addresses all of the problems currently facing agriculture, and so far it is performing well. That solution is organic agriculture.

4   Farming is a way of life. But organic agriculture is more than that; it is also a **philosophy** of life. In order to appreciate the tenets of organic agriculture, you have to look behind its practical principles to this **philosophy**. Some people call it a "holistic" **philosophy**, as it places **priority** on the wholeness and interconnectedness of life. The **ethics** of organic agriculture stem from this, and the practices follow naturally. An organic approach to farming is therefore something that extends far beyond the farm gate, just as the effects of our actions do.

5   Organic agriculture aims to be in harmony, rather than in conflict, with natural systems. This idea pervades all aspects of an organic farm, from how pests and diseases are controlled, through the treatment of livestock and the **integration** of the farm with the natural environment, to marketing, labor relations, and health. The powers of nature are harnessed and developed to their fullest extent, rather than dominated.

6   **Practitioners** of organic agriculture adopt an approach that minimizes the use of nonrenewable sources of energy. Chemical fertilizers and pesticides are either synthesized from oil or require large amounts of oil to extract and process them. It seems extraordinary that food production, a method of actually producing energy, or rather of tapping the sun's abundant

An organic farmer mowing weeds instead of using pesticides

energy, has itself developed into a **bulk** user of energy sources. It is even more extraordinary that one suggested solution to the problem of overproduction is to produce crops that can be turned into energy such as ethanol.

7   Organic food aims to be of optimum nutritional value. Varieties and methods of production are geared to this end. So too is processing, for having produced such quality food, no organic farmer wants to see it degraded, **refined,** or processed like white bread that needs additives to replace what is removed during processing. The modern food industry is **oriented** toward its own interests— a food's storage life, impact on consumers, and profitability—not to those of the consumer— nutritional value, health, and safety.

8   The organic world strives to be localized. Local markets and decentralized distribution and processing **infrastructures** are sought. An old and much respected organic farmer tells the story of one time when he was visiting his local agricultural college. He got stuck in its rather narrow driveway behind a truck bringing potatoes to the college kitchens. It had met and could not pass another truck, coming the other way, which was taking potatoes from the college farm to market! The present system may be profitable for some, but it cannot be said to be efficient in a wider context.

9   Organic agriculture does not use artificial fertilizers or chemical pesticides; it is not, however, a low-input system. **Contrary** to popular opinion, these two statements are not at variance with each other. Organic may be a low "**external**" input system, but, more importantly, it is also an optimum "internal" input system. It may not be the most efficient in terms of **output** per acre or per person, but it is certainly the most efficient in terms of **output** per unit of input. With **finite** resources, this is important. In Paraná and Santa Catarina in southern Brazil, over 200,000 farmers use green manures recycled from their own farms and cover crops of legumes instead of artificial fertilizers and chemical pesticides. Even so, they have been successful in increasing their crop yields of maize and wheat from about 2–3 to 4–5 ton/hectare.

10   Organic agriculture does not pollute the environment. Residual poisons that stay in circulation to the detriment of other living things, including humans, are not used. The waste products of conventional agriculture, which are such a problem in the current farming world, are actually **compatible** with organic agriculture. In fact, they are the foundation upon which sound agricultural practices are based, for they return to the soil that which has been taken out.

11   There is a research **bias** in favor of conventional farming, with very little research being carried out on organic farming. The United Nations Food and Agricultural Organization reports that 63 percent of sub-Saharan African farmers and 73 percent of North American organic farmers cite a lack of knowledge as the greatest barrier to wider adoption of organic farming methods. Nevertheless, organic agriculture is emerging as a credible and entirely possible way of farming. Imagine what could be achieved if government **ministries** funded even a **portion** of the research and development on organic farming that conventional agriculture currently receives. At least organic farming is beginning to be formally recognized. In Europe, a European Union (EU) regulation officially defines organic agriculture and the control procedures required for food to be sold as organic. The European Union (EU) has also specified organic farming as eligible for funding within its Agri-environment Program. In the United States, the U.S. Department of Agriculture (USDA) outlined its policy on quality standards in the Organic Foods Production Act of 1990. We can be sure that additional **legislation** on other aspects of organic farming will be **forthcoming** as well. Thus, the foundations for organic farming to start making a significant contribution to solving the current agricultural crisis are beginning to emerge.

Adapted from Blake, F. (1990). *Organic Farming and Growing*. Wiltshire, UK: The Crowood Press, pp. 9–12.

Respond to the ▶ following in writing. Base your responses on the reading and your own personal experiences.

1. What are some of the pressures agriculture is under today?
2. What is the point of the story told by the old organic farmer in paragraph 8?
3. Organically grown food is more expensive and not necessarily better tasting than conventionally farmed food. Are you willing to spend more money on food in order to preserve the environment? Why or why not?

FOCUSING ON VOCABULARY

WORD MEANING

Each of the following target words appears in the reading on pages 148–149. Use the paragraph number in parentheses to locate each word in context. Read the dictionary definitions below. Write the letter of the definition that reflects how the word is used in the reading.

_____ 1. **margin** (1)
   a. the difference in the number of votes or points between winners and losers
   b. the difference between what a business pays for something and what it sells it for

_____ 2. **philosophy** (4)
   a. the study of what it means to exist, what good and evil are, what knowledge is, etc.
   b. a set of beliefs that someone has about how they live their life, do their job, etc.

_____ 3. **integration** (5)
   a. the combination of two or more things so that they work together effectively
   b. the acceptance of someone or something into a group or society

_____ 4. **practitioner** (6)
   a. someone who does a particular job
   b. someone who follows the rules of a particular religion or philosophy

_____ 5. **refined** (7)
   a. made pure through an industrial process
   b. well made and of high quality

_____ 6. **orient** (7)
   a. to have as its main purpose or area of interest
   b. to position something in a particular direction

_____ 7. **contrary** (9)
   a. being the opposite of what is believed or expected
   b. deliberately doing things differently from the way other people do them

_____ 8. **external** (9)
   a. coming from outside something such as an organization, group, or business
   b. relating to foreign countries, e.g., *external affairs*

_____ **9. bias** (11)

    a. an opinion about whether a person, group, or idea is good or bad

    b. an interest or a natural skill in one particular area

_____ **10. ministry** (11)

    a. the profession of being a church leader, especially of the Protestant church

    b. a government department in some countries, such as the *Ministry of Agriculture*

_____ **11. portion** (11)

    a. a part of something larger

    b. a standard amount of food for one person, especially when served in a restaurant

Each sentence below contains a paraphrase or set of synonyms for a target word. Read each sentence and then select the matching target word from the box.

advocated	compatible	infrastructure	output
bulk	ethics	legislation	priority
coincided	finite	levy	qualitatively

1. The Natural Foods store received a _____
(being large in quantity)
shipment of organic soy products.

2. The government placed a pollution _____ on the
(tax, additional charge)
purchase of all new sport-utility vehicles.

3. The 1960s were a time of political and social unrest; protests against the

Vietnam War _____ with actions in support of the
(happened at the same time, overlapped)
civil rights movement.

4. Doctors must follow a medical code of _____ .
(principles, beliefs)

5. Newspaper editors can give _____ to one story
(main concern, most importance)
over another simply by making changes to the size of the headline or to

where the article is placed in the newspaper.

6. Dr. Martin Luther King Jr. and Mahatma Gandhi both were leaders who

_____ nonviolence as a means of social change.
(supported, promoted)

7. The politician changed parties because his views on key issues such as health

care and defense spending were no longer _____
(well-matched, consistent)
with the mainstream of the party.

8. The country lost its bid to host the Olympics because the International

Olympic Committee felt that the nation's transportation

_____ was not up to standards.
(basic system, organization)

9. OPEC (the Organization of Petroleum Exporting Countries) manages the

_____ and sale of much of the world's oil.
(production, yield)

10. The ancient Chinese believed that human beings are born with a

_____ amount of chi, or energy.
(fixed, limited)

11. The government introduced new _____ reducing
(laws, statutes)

speed limits in residential areas and raising the level of fines for speeding.

12. The reunification of East and West Germany has resulted in a(n)

_____ better standard of living for many citizens.
(distinctively, essentially)

WORD TIP

▶ Although there are some exceptions, the word **forthcoming** typically has three
meanings, depending on its position in a sentence.

1. *before a noun*: "happening or coming soon"—She has a part in a **forthcoming**
movie.

2. *not before a noun*: "given or offered when needed"—If more *money* is not
forthcoming, the theater will have to close.

3. *not before a noun*: "be willing to give information about something" [+ *about*]—
The *charity* has been very **forthcoming** *about* its finances.

WORD FAMILIES

Study the members of the word families in the table below. Look for spelling patterns for
the verb, noun, adjective, and adverb forms of the words. Complete the table. List the
patterns in the spaces.

Verb	Noun	Adjective	Adverb
advocate	1. advocate 2. advocacy	X	X
X	compatibility	compatible	X
X	ethics	ethical	ethically
externalize	X	external	externally
minister	1. ministry 2. minister	ministerial	ministerially
orient	orientation	oriented	X
philosophize	1. philosophy 2. philosopher	philosophical	philosophically
prioritize	priority	priority	X
X	X	qualitative	qualitatively
refine	refinement	refined	X
Spelling patterns			

Read each sentence and identify the part of speech of the missing word. Write an appropriate form for the target word in the blank. Use the ▶ word families table on page 152 to help you.

1. Although William Morris is now best known as a designer of home furnishings, he was also an important _____ (**advocate**) of socialism.

2. Some colleges in the United States are using computer-based matching systems that are very similar to popular dating websites to help incoming freshmen find _____ (**compatibility**) roommates.

3. In a company's management structure, the position and authority of employees must be clear, both internally to staff members and _____ (**external**) to clients.

4. The unlocking of the human genome has lead to moral, _____ (**ethics**), and social dilemmas regarding the extent to which that knowledge should be applied.

5. In a parliamentary system of government, _____ (**ministry**) duties are assumed by select members of parliament who also form the prime minister's cabinet.

6. The adult education program has a practical _____ (**orient**) because it concentrates on job skills.

7. There are both _____ (**philosophy**) and ethical arguments surrounding the care of the mentally ill and who is responsible for them.

8. Jobs that involve caretaking tend to attract people who place a high _____ (**prioritize**) on relationships.

9. The professor gathered _____ (**qualitatively**) data on the participants in the study by interviewing them individually and eliciting their personal opinions.

10. The United Nations is a relatively successful _____ (**refine**) of the previously unsuccessful League of Nations.

COLLOCATION

Each item below contains three example sentences with the same target word. In each sentence, the target word is paired with a different word and forms a different collocation. In the fourth sentence, the collocation has been left blank. Choose the collocation from the examples that best fits the last sentence and write it in the blank. You may need to change the form of one of the words to fit the sentence.

1. **a.** Because of allegations of **gender bias** against the interview panel, the whole interview process had to be repeated.
   b. **Class bias** is considered to be a much bigger problem in Britain than in the United States, however there is plenty of evidence that it exists on both sides of the Atlantic.

c. The perceived **political bias** of the news media does not prevent readers from rating newspapers and television as useful.

d. When designing a test of ability, it is important to avoid

_____ by ensuring that the questions do not favor either males or females.

2. a. Now that the restaurant was part of a larger chain, it was able to benefit from the **bulk discounts** available to those buying in large quantities.

b. The National Library of Scotland provides a **bulk supply** of maps to local and school libraries for use in their resource centers.

c. The supermarket promoted the new laundry detergent by setting up a **bulk display** at the end of one aisle.

d. Customers who buy more than thirty computers at a time may request a

_____ on their purchase.

3. a. A hospital's **finite resources** may be overly stretched during the flu season.

b. The earth offers only a **finite space** for both human civilization and animal habitats.

c. Increased stress is one result of workers being asked to complete more and more tasks within a **finite amount** of time.

d. Pensions only provide a _____ of income during the retirement years, so it is important to consider additional ways of saving for the future.

4. a. The club newsletter publishes a list of **forthcoming events** on the last page.

b. The leader of the Green Party announced that he would not run in the **forthcoming elections**.

c. The secretary of state's **forthcoming tour** of South America is not expected to be met with the same number of protests as his recent tour of Europe.

d. An opinion poll carried out by a national newspaper indicates that the prime minister's party will have difficulty retaining a majority in the

_____ .

5. a. The European Economic Community (EEC) was originally formed to enhance **economic integration** across the continent of Europe; the current European Union (EU) is much more politically oriented.

b. When moving to a new city, parents often find that the family's **social integration** into the new community is facilitated by their children.

c. One method of quieting dissent in countries suffering from internal unrest is for the governing parties to work toward the **political integration** of their opponents.

d. Many schools have successfully managed both the educational and

_____ of disabled students.

6. **a.** Prior to the American Civil War, several Northern states **enacted legislation** that prohibited ownership of slaves, while Southern states passed laws prohibiting anti-slavery debates.
    b. Although the president of the United States can **veto legislation**, Congress can override that veto.
    c. The president intends to **introduce legislation** that allows workers to take time off in exchange for overtime pay and gives them additional unpaid leave.
    d. There is no way for the American people to require Congress and the president to _____ to cut spending or raise taxes in order to balance the national budget.

7. **a.** In 1990, the Securities Exchange Commission received permission from Congress to **levy fines** on companies that violate civil securities laws.
    b. Individual school districts decide whether to **levy charges** for participation in extracurricular activities.
    c. Not only do tax rates vary from country to country, the income, goods, and services on which governments choose to **levy taxes** also vary considerably.
    d. The British decision to _____ on tea imported to the American colonies resulted in the Boston Tea Party.

8. **a.** **General practitioners** treat a wide range of medical conditions, but often refer their patients to specialists when those patients need advanced care.
    b. A **family practitioner** is able to handle the day-to-day medical needs of all members of a family.
    c. Studying for a doctoral degree involves doing research under the guidance of a supervisor who is already a **skilled practitioner** with a particular area of expertise.
    d. A _____ of massage can treat conditions such as insomnia and hypertension.

EXPANSION

Complete the passage by filling in the blanks with the target words in the box. Use each word only once.

advocates	incompatible	output	portion
coincident	infrastructure	philosophy	priority

GENETICALLY MODIFIED FOODS

1   There are many (1) _____ of genetic engineering of food as a means of increasing the world's food supply while at the same time minimizing the use of chemicals. Supporters of genetically modified (GM) food point out that the world requires an ever-increasing (2) _____ of food annually. (3) _____ with this is the increasing occurrence of droughts and flooding, which regularly cripple food production in some parts of the world. Not surprisingly, many supporters of GM food feel that (4) _____ must be given to the increased production of all kinds of foodstuffs.

2   Many others hold a contrary view. They are afraid that GM food may be
(5) _____ with environmental safety, and these people suggest
limiting or abandoning GM research. They believe that if we exploit the
advantages of GM foods, undesirable effects will inevitably occur. Because GM
foods are such a new phenomenon, it is impossible to predict what those
specific effects might be. The agricultural industry does not have an
(6) _____ that can ensure that GM crops and natural crops are
kept separate both before and after harvest, so some contamination of the
environment is sure to occur. Even if the (7) _____ of GM foods
leaking into the environment is small, the consequences are unpredictable.

3   Because of this, people who are against genetic modification believe that
governments must put safety first, and should therefore orient policies toward
limiting subsidies for GM food development while legislating tighter controls
on GM food research. Opponents of GM food advise a fundamental shift in
(8) _____: Instead of investing time and money into engineering
food, they would prefer to build a culture that places more value on natural,
unrefined, organically grown food.

EXPLORING THE TOPIC

Work with a partner. Discuss the advantages and disadvantages of GM food.

- What is the worst-case scenario of the effects of GM food on both consumers
  and the environment? The best-case scenario?
- Are the advantages of GM foods worth the risks?
- Are GM foods more suitable for some parts of the world than others?
- Given that some insects are becoming resistant to current pesticides, is there
  any real alternative to GM food?

Choose one of the above questions and write an essay in which you argue your
position. Remember to counter any opposing points raised in your discussion.

19 Microorganisms: The Spice of Life?

GETTING STARTED

Discuss the following questions with your classmates.

▶ What kind of spices are regularly used in cooking in your region of the world? Why are they popular? How do they improve certain dishes?

▶ What foods are very nutritious? What qualities make these foods good for us?

▶ Are nutritious foods the ones you like to eat? Why or why not?

TARGET WORDS—Assessing Your Vocabulary Knowledge

Look at each of the target words in the box. Use the scale to give yourself a score for each word. After you finish the chapter, score yourself again to check your improvement.

1 I don't know this word.

2 I have seen this word before, but I am not sure of the meaning.

3 I understand the word when I see it or hear it in a sentence, but I don't know how to use it in my own speaking and writing.

4 I know this word and can use it in my own speaking and writing.

TARGET WORDS

_____behalf	_____empirical	_____liberal	_____statistics
_____colleague	_____equate	_____mediate	_____straightforward
_____compile	_____guideline	_____notwithstanding	_____substitute
_____compound	_____identical	_____pursue	_____summarize
_____comprehensive	_____infer	_____restrain	_____survive
_____deduce	_____journal	_____reveal	_____undertake

The following passage is adapted from an introductory textbook on microbiology. It discusses microorganisms, herbs, and spices and the roles they play in food production, flavor enhancement, and preservation. As you read, pay special attention to the target vocabulary words in **bold**.

FOOD MICROBIOLOGY

1   Most people are aware of the continuing problems we face in producing sufficient food for the world's population. However, food production is just one aspect of food supply. Food must also be preserved and stored. As agents of spoilage, microorganisms are serious competitors for the world's food supply. Louis Pasteur (1822–1895) was one of the first researchers to study food microbiology. He began by **pursuing** a career as a chemist, but his work soon became connected with microorganisms as he **undertook** to solve the problem of spoilage of wine and milk. Pasteur's studies **revealed** the microbiological nature of fermentations and led the way to using heat to prevent spoilage of vinegar, beer, wine, and milk. Soon "pasteurization" became used throughout the world. Today, it is still used to preserve beverages and control communicable diseases.

MICROORGANISMS: FOOD PRODUCERS AND ENHANCERS

2   Microorganisms play major roles in many aspects of food. **Notwithstanding** their role as agents of spoilage, microorganisms play two roles in the production of foods. First and most importantly, they modify foods through their biochemical activities. Microbial fermentation of foods results in biochemical changes that can lead to desirable flavors and textures in foods. It can also increase the nutritional quality and digestibility of foods. Second, microorganisms may be grown, harvested, and served as foods themselves. For example, marine algae have been harvested as food for centuries in Asian countries, and mushrooms are consumed throughout the world as a protein-rich food.

3   Microbial fermentation of foods has been used since ancient times. Stone tablets that have **survived** from Babylon describe beer, and Egyptian hieroglyphics and figures depict the making of fermented foods.

4   Today, microbial fermentations remain a significant part of food production. Fruits are

A model depicting the preparation of bread and beer in ancient Egypt

still fermented to produce wines, grains are fermented into beers, fermented milk becomes cheese, and fermented vegetables become a variety of delicious foods. Sometimes the choice of microorganism is **straightforward**, with fermentation relying on the bacteria naturally present on the food. Other fermented foods may be prepared by enhancing natural microbial populations with cultures grown in the laboratory, or they may be totally dependent on laboratory-grown cultures. For example, wines and beers rely on cultures of specific yeast strains maintained and tightly guarded by wineries and breweries. Cheeses are made by adding specific cultures of bacteria or fungi to milk at various stages of production. In contrast, sauerkraut production uses natural bacterial populations on cabbage, and pickles are fermented with populations of bacteria that occur naturally on cucumbers.

ANTIMICROBIAL PROPERTIES OF HERBS AND SPICES

5   Herbs and spices also play an important role in the microbiology of food. We tend to **equate** herbs and spices with flavorful foods. But herbs

Bowls of spices at a bazaar in Jerusalem

and spices do more than make foods taste better. They have been used for centuries as medicines and to preserve foods. Today, there is renewed interest in the potential medicinal value of these traditional food flavor enhancers.

6 Although the terms *herb* and *spice* are sometimes used interchangeably, they are not **identical**. An herb is generally considered to be a plant that is used as a medicine, seasoning, or flavoring, whereas a spice usually is thought of as a dried plant product used mainly as a seasoning. There is considerable **empirical** evidence that both have antimicrobial properties.

7 In 1997, Dr. Paul Sherman and Dr. Jennifer Billing **summarized** the results of their examination of forty-three herbs and spices used in more than 4,000 meat dishes from thirty-six countries. **Statistics** showed that onions, black and white pepper, garlic, lemon juice, hot peppers, and ginger were used most often. When they evaluated the antimicrobial activities of each plant product, they found that garlic, onion, allspice, and oregano killed all the different types of harmful bacteria they tested, including *Salmonella* and *Staphylococcus*. Other herbs and spices killed at least 75 percent of the test bacteria. The ten heaviest spice-using countries—Ethiopia, Greece, India, Indonesia, Iran, Kenya, Malaysia, Morocco, Nigeria, and Thailand—all have hot, tropical climates, and Sherman and Billing **deduced** that their heavy use of spices has served to **mediate**, or decrease, the effects of microorganisms in food spoilage, which is much more of a problem in the tropics than in temperate and cool climates.

8 In a 1998 paper in *The New England Journal of Medicine*, Dr. Amy Howell reported on **behalf** of her research team at Rutgers University that cranberries contain antibacterial **compounds** called *proanthocyanidins*. These **compounds** appear to work by **restraining** *Escherichia coli*, the leading cause of urinary tract infections, from colonizing in the bladder and kidneys. This study thus substantiated claims that drinking cranberry juice regularly can reduce the incidence of urinary tract infections.

9 In 1998, Dr. Daniel Y. C. Fung and his **colleagues** reported that five common spices can kill bacteria that cause food poisoning. During their experiments, they mixed twenty-three spices with beef and salami infected with bacteria. The most powerful antibacterial agents were garlic, cloves, cinnamon, oregano, and sage.

10 Research under laboratory conditions clearly indicates that herbs and spices both flavor foods and inhibit, or **restrain,** microorganisms. Although we may **infer** that herbs and spices play a similar role under natural conditions, not enough scientific data has been **compiled** to prove this. Nevertheless, the antimicrobial effects of herbs and spices are supported by cultural traditions and folklore.

11 Despite the undeniable benefits of herbs and spices, there are some cautions to be observed. The active components of herbs and spices, primarily oils, are changed through cooking and digestive processes. Heat especially will evaporate or inactivate their antimicrobial properties. Some herbs and spices also could cause illness if taken internally in large doses, and the medical community is concerned that people may get into trouble by self-medicating with **liberal** or excessive amounts of herbal remedies. Some people may also be tempted to **substitute** herbal remedies for more conventional medicines without first consulting their doctor. Additionally, although the Food and Drug Administration (FDA) offers some **guidelines** on the use of some specific herbal preparations, there are no **comprehensive** federal regulations governing the quality of herbal remedies, including those that contain potentially harmful contaminants.

12   Overall, microorganisms can be seen both as enhancers and destroyers of food. Employing beneficial microorganisms in food production and fighting harmful microorganisms through heat treatment and the careful use of herbs and spices are two ways of using microbiology to maximize the world's food resources.

_____

Adapted from Batzing, B. L. (2002). *Microbiology: An Introduction*. Pacific Grove, CA: Brooks/Cole-Thomson Learning, pp. 661–662, 672.

UNDERSTANDING THE READING

Respond to the following in writing. Base your responses on the reading and your own personal experiences.

1. What are two roles microorganisms play in food production?
2. What did Sherman and Billing **deduce** from the findings of their study of herbs and spices?
3. What cultural or regional traditions do you know of that link particular foods to health remedies? Describe some examples.

FOCUSING ON VOCABULARY

WORD MEANING

Read the sentences below and circle the letter of the word or phrase that best matches the meaning of the target word in **bold**. Use context clues in the sentences to determine the correct meaning. Check your dictionary if you are not sure of the answer.

1. The lawyer spoke on **behalf** of the parents' group that was fighting against closure of the local primary school.
   a. in contrast to another's belief
   b. in answer to someone
   c. as a representative of someone

2. The product development team relies on its **colleagues** in the marketing department to supply information on consumer wants and needs.
   a. companions
   b. coworkers
   c. enemies

3. Table salt is a **compound** made up of sodium and chloride (NaCl).
   a. a seasoning for food
   b. a substance consisting of two or more elements
   c. a large amount or quantity of something

4. The personnel manager prepared a **comprehensive** report on areas where the company was not meeting employment legislation guidelines.
   a. including everything that is necessary
   b. well-timed
   c. trying to avoid blame for something

5. Alexander Fleming **deduced** that the spores of a mold called penicillin had disease-preventing qualities when he observed that it prevented the growth of germs.
   a. took responsibility for something
   b. used information to make a judgment about something
   c. gave a reason for something

6. NASA's Mars Rovers are gathering samples that may provide **empirical** evidence that water once flowed on Mars.
   a. based on feelings and emotions
   b. based solely on theory or ideas
   c. based on scientific testing or practical experience

7. The editor of the medical association's **journal** was responsible for collecting articles, sending them out for review, and deciding which were to be published.
   a. a newspaper
   b. a serious magazine for professionals
   c. a technical book

8. The boss was so **liberal** with his praise that his employees began to question his sincerity.
   a. generous
   b. stingy
   c. admirable

9. Exercise can help to **mediate** the effects of a high calorie diet.
   a. change the effect of something to make it less negative
   b. make something do what you want
   c. tell or show openly what you are thinking

10. We must **restrain** urban growth in order to protect the countryside.
    a. help something develop
    b. avoid doing something
    c. control or limit the development of something

11. Government **statistics** show that household spending has increased steadily over the last decade.
    a. a collection of technical reports
    b. a collection of numbers representing facts
    c. a group of causes or influences

12. The literature review of an article should **summarize** the main research studies that have already been undertaken in the subject area.
    a. pay careful attention to
    b. keep an idea strong
    c. make a short statement of the main information

Read the sentences below and use context to figure out the meaning of the target words in **bold.** Look for a core meaning that provides a general understanding of each target word. Write the meaning in your own words.

1. a. When looking for a new job, one way to get started is to **compile** a list of companies in your area that might be looking for someone like you and then write to them.
   b. The environmental group monitored the variety of wildlife in the area over a period of three months and then **compiled** a report on its findings.

   compile _____

2. a. People should not necessarily **equate** high test scores with high intelligence.
   b. Larger jet engines are **equated** with increased noise, causing problems for airports located in metropolitan areas.

   equate _____

3. **a.** The referees' association issued new **guidelines** for penalizing unsportsmanlike conduct on the playing field.

   b. The manufacturer's **guidelines** recommended that children under the age of ten not use the machines without the assistance of an adult.

   guidelines _____

4. **a.** Although the twins clearly looked like sisters, their appearances were not **identical**.

   b. If we compare the DNA of chimpanzees and humans, we might infer that they are nearly **identical** species because there is a 98.6 percent overlap in their DNA.

   identical _____

5. **a.** After studying children raised in varying conditions, psychologists have **inferred** that children who receive more stimulation develop greater mental capacity.

   b. The children were able to **infer** from the facial expressions of the adults that something terrible had occurred.

   infer _____

6. **a.** Culture shock and language problems **notwithstanding**, the immigrants were successfully integrated into their adopted culture.

   b. **Notwithstanding** the overall slowdown in the airline industry, the discount airlines have had a very profitable year.

   notwithstanding _____

7. **a.** Most high school graduates have little choice but to **pursue** further education if they want to be successful in the job market.

   b. The Democratic president was forced to **pursue** a policy of cooperation with the Republican-controlled Congress in order to achieve his election goals.

   pursue _____

8. **a.** A report by the National Center for Statistics and Analysis **reveals** that seat belt use is lower in pickup trucks than in passenger cars, vans, and sport-utility vehicles.

   b. A search into the applicant's background **revealed** that he had in fact been fired from his last three jobs.

   reveal _____

9. **a.** Meeting the requirements of the assignment should be a **straightforward** task as the criteria for each section are clearly explained.

   b. Although travel across the continent was once long and tiring, greater access to air travel now means that a trip from Miami to Seattle is quite **straightforward**.

   straightforward _____

10. **a.** Many vegetarian recipes simply **substitute** a vegetable, such as eggplant or zucchini, for meat.

    b. Scientists looking for a cure for cystic fibrosis found that if they **substituted** a normal gene in the lungs of mice for a defective one, the mice recovered.

    substitute _____

11. **a.** The young football team managed to **survive** a number of close games only to be beaten in the final round of the play-offs.
    b. In the eighteenth century, there were over 500 aboriginal languages in Australia. Today, only 250 of these **survive,** and only five have more than 1,000 speakers.

survive _____

12. **a.** The building of the Channel Tunnel between Britain and France was one of the most complex tunneling projects ever **undertaken.**
    b. It is important that the Food and Drug Administration **undertake** more research to determine whether gender differences can influence the effectiveness of new drugs.

undertake _____

WORD FAMILIES

Read the sentences below. Some of the target words have been used correctly, but in six sentences a wrong word form has been used. If the wrong form has been used, cross it out and write the correct form. If the form is correct, put a checkmark (✓).

1. Authorities should **restraint** television stations from showing too much violence at prime viewing times. _____

2. The researchers **inferred** from the mortgage data that house prices were going down. _____

3. In **summarize**, people of different ages and interests can live together without disagreement if they are willing to compromise. _____

4. The two jobs offered **identical** salaries, even though one required much greater responsibility. _____

5. It is not yet known if there are any **survivals** of the factory fire.

   _____

6. The Sunday newspapers were filled with new **revelations** about the corruption scandal hitting the Department of Defense. _____

7. As a means of providing good customer service, some supermarkets will offer a **substitution** product if a sale item has been sold out. _____

8. The instructions on the tube advised that the medication be spread **liberal** on the skin around the area of infection. _____

9. Many people take antacids to **mediate** the effects of overeating on their gastrointestinal tract. _____

10. The mayor ordered a **comprehensively** report into the cause of the bridge's collapse. _____

COLLOCATION

Match each target word in the box with the group of words that regularly occur with it. If the (~) symbol appears before a word in a list, the target word comes before the word in the list. In all other cases, the target word comes after the word in the list.

(on) behalf (of)	compile	pursue	straightforward
colleague	journal	statistical	undertake

1. _____
campaign
speak
negotiate
lobby

2. _____
~analysis
~significance
~techniques
~tables

3. _____
longtime
former
senior
noted

4. _____
fairly
quite
reasonably
remarkably

5. _____
~data
~information
~lists
~statistics

6. _____
bi-monthly
weekly
quarterly
annual

7. _____
~a challenge
~research
~a responsibility
~training

8. _____
~objectives
~careers
~interests
~policies

EXPANSION

We are what we eat, so it is not difficult to **deduce** that one of the most important things a person can do to stay healthy is to eat healthful food. But how much do you know about the nutritional value of various kinds of food?

The following questions test your knowledge about food and its health benefits. Complete the quiz and then discuss the answers with a partner.

Healthful Food Quiz

Read the statements and circle the best answer.

1. As a **guideline**, which food group should you eat the most from?
   a. meat group
   b. dairy group
   c. bread and cereal group

2. A **straightforward** way to ensure that you are getting enough protein in your diet is to eat what kind of food?
   a. fruit
   b. noodles
   c. meat

3. **Notwithstanding** the amount necessary for general health, how much water do you need to drink per day to keep your skin healthy?
   a. 33–67 oz. (1–2 liters)
   b. 101–135 oz. (3–4 liters)
   c. 169–202 oz. (5–6 liters)

4. Which contains more vitamin C?
   a. white grapefruit
   b. pink grapefruit
   c. they have **identical** amounts

5. Which items **mediate** hay fever symptoms?
   a. vitamin C and garlic
   b. vitamin A and fish
   c. vitamin D and milk

6. **Empirical** evidence has shown that some types of foods help lower harmful cholesterol. Which ones are they?
   a. pork and beef
   b. salmon and tuna
   c. butter and cheese

7. In terms of caffeine levels/content, one cup of coffee can be **equated** with how many cups of tea?
   a. 1 cup
   b. 2–3 cups
   c. 4–5 cups

8. Which food or beverage does *not* contain chemical **compounds** that may trigger migraine headaches?
   a. apple juice
   b. chocolate
   c. coffee

Write an essay that outlines the steps you can take to live a more healthy lifestyle. Possible aspects could include diet, exercise, sleep, stress reduction, and relaxation.

Strategy Practice

USING YOUR DICTIONARY — Pronunciation and Stress

Words in the same family may have different pronunciations according to their part of speech. Take the words *reveal* and *revelation,* for example. The second syllable in the verb *reveal* has a long *e* sound, whereas the second syllable in *revelation* has a schwa sound. This change is caused by the addition of the suffix *-tion.* When certain suffixes are added to words, they can cause the stress to shift to the syllable immediately preceding the suffix.

Phonetic spellings within a dictionary contain specific marks to show you which syllables are stressed. You need to check your dictionary's key or explanatory notes on pronunciation to understand the particular marks it uses to indicate stress. Normally, dictionaries place a mark (such as a heavy line or an accent) before or after the syllable that receives the *main stress.* If a word has two stressed syllables, the dictionary will use a different mark to show you which one receives the *secondary stress.* Below is an example of a phonetic spelling from *LAAD (*the *Longman Advanced American Dictionary).* Notice the marks *LAAD* places before syllables to indicate the main and secondary stresses in *coincide.* Compare this method with the one in your own dictionary.

Example: **co•in•cide**   /ˌkoʊɪnˈsaɪd/   — main stress

secondary stress

PRACTICING YOUR DICTIONARY SKILLS

Complete the table below by writing the phonetic spelling of each word in the box below it. Use your dictionary to help you. Notice the pronunciation patterns you see across the word families. One row has been done for you.

	Verb	Noun	Adjective	Adverb
1.	deduce	deduction	X	X
			X	X
2.	X	empiricism	empirical	empirically
	X			
3.	incline	inclination	inclined	X
				X
4.	reveal	revelation	revealing	revealingly
	/rɪˈvil/	/ˌrɛvəˈleɪʃən/	/rɪˈvilɪŋ/	rɪˈvilɪŋli

Use a dictionary to identify the syllable that receives the main stress in each word in the table below. Underline the syllable that receives the main stress. The verb and noun columns in the first row have been done for you.

	Verb	Noun	Adjective	Adverb
1.	coin<u>cide</u>	co<u>in</u>cidence	coincidental	coincidentally
2.	conceptualize	concept	conceptual	conceptually
3.	philosophize	philosophy	philosophical	philosophically
4.	specify	specifics	specific	specifically

STRATEGY—Vocabulary Learning Strategy Questionnaire

There are many diverse vocabulary learning strategies. Here is a list of strategies you can use to increase your word knowledge. Talk with a partner and discuss the value of each strategy. Indicate whether you currently use the strategy. If you do not, discuss whether it is potentially worth trying in the future.

U = I currently *use* this strategy.
P = I don't use this strategy now, but I think it has the *potential* to help me.
X = I *don't* think this strategy is appropriate for me.

STRATEGIES FOR DISCOVERING A NEW WORD'S MEANING

	U P X
Analyzing a word's part of speech	U P X
Analyzing a word's affixes and roots	U P X
Checking whether a word is related to a word in my mother tongue	U P X
Guessing meaning from textual context	U P X
Using a bilingual dictionary	U P X
Using a monolingual dictionary	U P X
Asking your teacher for the meaning	U P X
Asking classmates for the meaning	U P X

STRATEGIES FOR CONSOLIDATING / DEEPENING KNOWLEDGE OF A WORD ONCE IT HAS BEEN ENCOUNTERED

	U P X
Making a mental image of the word's meaning	U P X
Associating the word with related words (*cat: dog, bird, horse*)	U P X
Relating the word to its synonyms and antonyms (*gigantic: huge, tiny*)	U P X
Using word maps / mind maps	U P X
Using the word in sentences	U P X
Saying the word aloud when studying it	U P X
Studying the spelling of the word	U P X

(Continued)

Paraphrasing the word's meaning	U	P	X
Using physical action when studying the word (waving your hand when studying the word *wave*)	U	P	X
Using grids to study collocation	U	P	X
Saying the word aloud many times when learning it	U	P	X
Writing the word many times when learning it	U	P	X
Using word cards	U	P	X
Listening to a tape of word lists	U	P	X
Putting English labels on physical objects (taping a *bookshelf* label on the bookshelf)	U	P	X
Keeping a vocabulary notebook	U	P	X
Using English language media (songs, movies, newscasts, etc.)	U	P	X
Testing oneself to measure progress in learning vocabulary	U	P	X
Continuing to study words over a period of time	U	P	X

WORD KNOWLEDGE—Collocation Partners

We have seen how academic words collocate with particular words. Many words collocate with more than one academic word. In the sentences below, all of the academic words in bold collocate with the word *business*:

> Their *business* **investment** proved to be very profitable.

> The city required a *business* **license** before the new store could open.

> The *business* **ethics** of the salesman were called into question when he knowingly sold defective merchandise.

> My *business* **colleague** was just awarded the Manager of the Year award.

The grid below includes four verbs and four nouns that are regularly used to discuss or report research. Although every combination is possible, some of these words form common collocation partnerships, while others do not. Work with a partner. Combine your knowledge of these words to identify the word pairs that form common collocation partnerships. In the grid below, write a (+) sign for the common collocation pairs. The first word *assemble* has been done for you.

	information	data	a report	figures
assemble	+	+		
compile				
quote				
reveal				

Now check your answers. Make a note of any collocation pairs that are new for you.

UNIT
6

Encounters with Music and Sound

21

Music as Social Conscience

GETTING STARTED

Discuss the following questions with your classmates.

▶ What kind of music do you like to listen to? What are the subjects of the song lyrics?

▶ Do you know any songs that highlight social issues, such as "We Shall Overcome" or "Give Peace a Chance"? List them.

▶ Have the singers and songwriters of those socially conscious songs caused you to think more deeply about any of the issues they highlight? Explain how.

TARGET WORDS—Assessing Your Vocabulary Knowledge

Look at each of the target words in the box. Use the scale to give yourself a score for each word. After you finish the chapter, score yourself again to check your improvement.

1 I don't know this word.

2 I have seen this word before, but I am not sure of the meaning.

3 I understand the word when I see it or hear it in a sentence, but I don't know how to use it in my own speaking and writing.

4 I know this word and can use it in my own speaking and writing.

TARGET WORDS

_____ author	_____ constitute	_____ induce	_____ radical
_____ cease	_____ exceed	_____ interpret	_____ revolution
_____ civil	_____ format	_____ interval	_____ subsequent
_____ classical	_____ grant	_____ objective	_____ theme
_____ commentary	_____ ideological	_____ principal	_____ vehicle
_____ compute	_____ implicit	_____ proceed	_____ violation

The following passage is adapted from an introductory textbook on music. It illustrates the long history of antiwar music. As you read, pay special attention to the target vocabulary words in **bold**.

OPPOSING WAR THROUGH MUSIC: CLASSICAL AND MODERN EXAMPLES

1   Music has power both as a driving force in time of war and as an expression of humankind's desire for lasting peace. In fact, the power of music as a social **commentary** is perhaps the strongest in music that is inspired by war, often **inducing** powerful reactions in the listener. Music addressing specific causes, such as support for a war effort or protest against a war, may be a personal expression of the composer, but it also can reflect the feelings of a large segment of the population.

2   For centuries, music has been used for the **objectives** of inciting soldiers to war, praising its heroes, relieving the boredom of military life, and providing a **vehicle** for expressing the homesickness and loneliness typically connected to a soldier's life. However, a considerable amount of music has been composed that, instead of supporting the energies of war, focuses on hopes for peace. Most people will be aware of the antiwar **themes** in the popular music of the 1960s and 1970s, but may be surprised that such **themes** have also occurred in **classical** music and are still alive today.

FRANZ JOSEPH HAYDN: *MASS IN TIME OF WAR*

3   Europe was in the midst of conflict when the Viennese composer Franz Joseph Haydn wrote his *Mass in Time of War*. France, the center of a popular **revolution** in the 1790s, had witnessed massacres (a two-day outbreak of violence in Paris in 1792 produced casualties **exceeding** 1,200), and the guillotine became the symbol of justice. It claimed Louis XVI in January 1793, and his wife, Queen Marie Antoinette, suffered the same fate in October. Even Robespierre, a leading **revolutionary** who had demanded that the king be put to death, was himself guillotined in 1794.

4   In 1796, France was at war with Austria, and Napoleon, **proceeding** toward becoming emperor, was scoring a series of victories. The citizens of Vienna were mobilized for war and

Composer Franz Joseph Haydn

it was a **violation** of local law to talk of peace until the French were defeated. Haydn—a man in his sixties and by now the most prestigious musical presence in Vienna—wrote his first composition to reference war, *Mass in Time of War (Missa in tempore belli)*.

5   Haydn's *Mass in Time of War*, at first glance, is a typical treatment of the five main elements that **constitute**, or make up, the **principal** ceremony of the Catholic Church. Although the first part of the composition opens with a steady thumping of drums—which perhaps could be **interpreted** as the sound of marching or of cannons—the direct references to war do

not occur until the final movement. Here, the prominent use of the timpani, or kettledrums, has been identified with cannon fire and the trumpet fanfares have been associated with the military. The final movement is one of fury, with trumpet calls, rapid scales, and throbbing drums. It is an emotional cry for peace. The movement (and the composition) ends with four statements of the word *pacem,* the Latin word for *peace.* The **commentary** on war that Haydn makes in this composition is subtle to the modern ear; his use of drums to signify the cannons of war probably had a stronger impact on the ears of his contemporaries than it does on our ears, which are accustomed to the loud noises of amplified sound. Haydn's cry for peace was not to be answered in his lifetime. He died on May 31, 1809, when Vienna was occupied by enemy troops.

Composer Ralph Vaughan Williams

RALPH VAUGHAN WILLIAMS: *GRANT US PEACE*

6   Some 100 years after Haydn had died, a composer emerged in England who, like Haydn, had strong connections to his country and to concerns for citizenship. Unlike Haydn, Vaughan Williams had firsthand experience with war. In 1914, at age forty-two, he joined the medical corps in the British army and ended his service in France as an artillery officer. His **subsequent** *Dona nobis pacem*

(**Grant** *Us Peace*) expresses emotions born out of the composer's experience.

7   Vaughan Williams's favorite texts for his vocal and choral works were those by **authors** writing in the English language. His *Dona nobis pacem*, a forty-minute cantata, draws heavily upon English texts. Although its title is taken from a well-known prayer (**Grant** Us Peace), three of the six movements of this work are based on poems by the nineteenth-century American poet Walt Whitman. Whitman's text comes from a series of poems, *Drum Taps*, which the poet wrote in reaction to the American **Civil** War, a war between the Northern and Southern states. No doubt Whitman had strong personal reasons for writing these verses, for his brother was wounded in the war and Whitman himself worked as a nurse in a hospital for soldiers in Washington during the **Civil** War years (1861–1865). Whitman's words provide fertile images and sounds for elaboration by a composer—an ideal text for musical composition:

Beat! beat! drums!—blow! bugles! blow!
Through the windows—through the doors—
burst like a ruthless force, . . .

Let not the child's voice be heard, nor the
mother's entreaties,
Make even the trestles to shake the dead where
they lie awaiting the hearses,
So strong you thump O terrible drums—so loud
you bugles blow.

8   Vaughan Williams turned to other text sources for the last two movements. The fifth part of the cantata opens with a baritone solo singing words that originally were spoken by John Bright before the House of Commons during a debate on the Crimean War in 1855. Bright's **comments** refer to the Old Testament account of Passover (*"The Angel of Death has been abroad throughout the land; you may almost hear the beating of his wings. . .).* The composer then cleverly turns to several other texts to further the mood set by the opening solo. These texts all have strong, explicitly stated antiwar **themes**. Thus, compared to Haydn's **implicit** references to war and peace in *Mass in Time of War,* Williams's *Dona nobis pacem* takes a more obvious position against war.

ANTIWAR MUSIC: FROM THE 1960s TO PRESENT TIMES

9   Although **classical** music contained antiwar elements, one of the most influential periods of antiwar music occurred in the latter half of the twentieth century in the United States. During the 1960s, protest songs played a major role in expressing and shaping public opinion about the presence of the U.S. armed forces in Southeast Asia, specifically, in Vietnam. Singer-songwriters such as Bob Dylan and Joan Baez composed and sang songs against nuclear

Bob Dylan performing in 1965

weapons and the violence of war, including "Talking World War III Blues" and "Where Are You Now, My Son?" These protest songs expressed a pro-peace **ideological** perspective. They gained an audience and became hits on popular music charts in the United States. Although the music of Bob Dylan, Joan Baez, and others may not have directly stopped the Vietnam War, it supported a political antiwar movement that led politicians to finally **cease** waging war in the early 1970s. When the Vietnam War ended in 1973, **radical** protest songs generally faded from the popular music scene.

10   After an **interval** of thirty years, the war in Iraq generated a new wave of protest music. A number of artists including Stephen Smith and The Compassionate Conservatives distributed protest songs such as "The Bell" and "In the Garden of Eden" for free over their websites. They used a downloadable MP3 **format**, which allowed them to gain almost immediate access to the public rather than waiting for official release through their record labels. The Internet also provided an increasingly interconnected forum for antiwar protest; music sites were linked to the homepages of antiwar sites like the Veterans Against the Iraq War. This suggests that, in the age of **computers** and instant global communication, antiwar music may become increasingly influential in shaping public opinion about future conflicts.

Adapted from Nichols, D. C. (2001). *Musical Encounters*. Upper Saddle River, NJ: Prentice Hall, pp. 301, 305–306, 308–309, 316.

UNDERSTANDING THE READING

Respond to the following in writing. Base your responses on the reading and your own personal experiences.

1. Why is music able to inspire people to action, for example, to go to war or to protest against war?
2. Give some examples of how protest music has changed from the late-eighteenth century to present times.
3. Describe some songs about war and peace from your own country or culture. What message does each song transmit to you?

WORD MEANING

Match the words with their definitions. If you are unsure about a word's meaning, try to figure it out from context by rereading the passage on pp. 171–173. Then check your dictionary.

Set 1

_____ **1.** interval

_____ **2.** radical

_____ **3.** vehicle

_____ **4.** constitute

_____ **5.** civil

_____ **6.** proceed

_____ **7.** revolution

a. a time of great social and political change, especially the changing of a ruler or political system by force

b. relating to the people who live in the same country

c. a period of time or distance between two events, activities, etc.

d. to continue to do something that has already been started

e. supportive of thorough and complete social or political change

f. something used in order to achieve something, spread ideas, or express opinions

g. to form something from different parts

Set 2

_____ **1.** violation

_____ **2.** exceed

_____ **3.** ideological

_____ **4.** interpret

_____ **5.** author

_____ **6.** grant

_____ **7.** commentary

a. someone who writes a book, play, story, etc.

b. to consider someone's actions or behavior or an event as having a particular meaning

c. to be more than a particular number, amount, etc.

d. an action that breaks a law, agreement, or principle

e. an analysis or explanation of something such as an event or theory

f. based on a particular set of beliefs or ideas, especially political ideas

g. to give someone something they have asked for

Read the row of words below each numbered word. One word in each list is *not* a synonym for the numbered word. Cross it out.

1. subsequent
| later | following | consequent | previously |

2. cease
| stop | finish | perceive | conclude |

3. classical
| crucial | traditional | conventional | established |

4. induce
| cause | produce | conform | provoke |

5. compute
| calculate | figure | attain | estimate |

6. format

arrangement   design   policy   setup

7. principal

main   approximate   primary   fundamental

8. implicit

mutual   unspoken   implied   hidden

9. theme

subject   attitude   topic   idea

10. objective

purpose   aim   goal   recruitment

WORD TIP

▶ The word **principal** is an adjective that means "most important."

The **principal** reason for the American Revolution was that the colonists wanted a say in how they were governed.

▶ In its noun form, **principal** has the more common meaning "someone who is in charge of a school."

The **principal** is responsible for the smooth running of a school.

▶ This word is commonly mistaken for a similarly spelled word **principle**, which is a noun that means "a belief or idea on which a set of ideas is based." (See Chapter 5 for more on this target word.)

A key **principle** of democracy is free speech.

WORD FAMILIES

The table below contains word families for some of the target words in the reading. Complete the rest of the table. An *X* indicates that there is no form or that the form is not common. Sometimes there may be more than one form possible. If you are unsure about a form, check your dictionary.

Verb	Noun	Adjective	Adverb
1. commentate 2. comment	1. commentary 2. commentator	X	X
compute	1. computer 2.	computational	computationally
exceed	X	X	
X		ideological	ideologically
X	X	implicit	
interpret		interpretive	X
	1. revolution 2. revolutionary	revolutionary	X
X	X	subsequent	
X	theme		thematically
	1. violation 2. violator	X	X

Choose the correct form of the word in **bold** in sentence **a** to complete sentence **b**.
Use the word family table you just completed as a guide.

1. **a.** Many amusement parks are now based around a **theme**, for example, movies, cartoon characters, or international locations.

   b. Most libraries arrange books _____, with volumes on similar topics stored together.

2. **a.** The dominant economic **ideology** in the world today is capitalism.

   b. The politician left her party because of _____ differences.

3. **a.** Although he did not explicitly support the firemen's strike, his refusal to condemn it offered **implicit** support.

   b. After twenty years of married life, the couple knew each other's needs _____.

4. **a.** After retiring, the senator agreed to **commentate** on political events for the cable television news channel.

   b. The sports _____ suggested that the team had failed to live up to its potential.

5. **a.** At the time when the U.S. Constitution was written, the notion that governments should be answerable to the people was a **revolutionary** idea.

   b. Computer automation has _____ the way banks process and store their records.

6. **a.** The new tax was extremely unpopular, as **subsequent** riots clearly indicated.

   b. Although Henry VIII believed that only a man could rule England, his daughter Elizabeth I _____ proved to be one of Britain's strongest monarchs.

7. **a.** Some knowledge of statistics is required to **interpret** the results of most scientific research reports.

   b. The judge's _____ of the antidiscrimination law set a precedent for future law cases in that area.

8. **a.** Some people can **compute** totals on an abacus as quickly as most others can with an electronic calculator.

   b. No matter how the accountants tried to adjust the financial figures, their _____ showed that the city would be bankrupt within months.

9. **a.** The export of subsidized farm goods was a **violation** of the trade agreement.

   b. Normally, a teacher cannot be fired unless school officials can show that the teacher's actions have _____ state laws.

10. **a.** The improvement of the orchestra under the new conductor **exceeded** all expectations.

    b. The high altitude and cold weather make climbing Mt. Everest an _____ difficult task.

COLLOCATION

Each item below contains three sentences with the same collocation. Write a fourth sentence of your own using the same word partners.

1. **a.** One way to **induce sleep** is to drink a glass of warm milk before bedtime.
   b. The drug triazolam is often prescribed to **induce sleep**.
   c. Many people are turning to herbal remedies as a natural method of **inducing sleep**.

   d. _____

2. **a.** The Hubble telescope has been a **principal source** of information on the physical properties of the universe.
   b. Despite generational differences, parents remain a **principal source** of advice for their teenage children.
   c. OPEC countries are the **principal source** of petroleum for the world.

   d. _____

3. **a.** If the current rate of destruction continues, the Amazon rain forest may **cease to exist** within forty to fifty years.
   b. Czechoslovakia **ceased to exist** in 1993, splitting into the Czech Republic and Slovakia.
   c. If the earth's climate became too warm, the Gulf Stream could **cease to exist**.

   d. _____

4. **a.** Several western states received **government grants** to cover the cost of fighting forest fires caused by drought.
   b. The city used its **government grant** to pay for improving access to public buildings for disabled people.
   c. Many countries subsidize essential services, such as public transportation, by offering **government grants** to companies that provide those services.

   d. _____

5. **a.** It is a wise precaution to have health checkups at **regular intervals**.
   b. The volumes of the *Harry Potter* series were intended to be published at **regular intervals**, to fuel fresh excitement for each new book.
   c. The discovery that pendulums swing at a **regular interval** was applied to the production of more accurate clocks.

   d. _____

6. **a.** Dr. Martin Luther King Jr. was one of the key leaders in the **civil rights** movement.
   b. The consistently low percentage of U.S. citizens who exercise their **civil right** to vote is an ongoing cause for concern.
   c. Many observers fear that some of the legislation passed in response to security threats seriously erodes basic **civil rights**.

   d. _____

7. a. The **standard format** for labeling food products is to list ingredients in descending order of the amount contained in the product.

   b. Double spacing is part of the **standard format** for typing an academic paper.

   c. The **standard format** for reporting academic research includes the following sections: Introduction, Background, Methodology, Results, Discussion, and Conclusion.

   d. _____

8. a. The **political objective** of the United Nations is to restore peace to the region.

   b. Ending the U.S. military presence in Vietnam was one of the main **political objectives** of the antiwar movement of the 1960s.

   c. The principal **political objective** of the Democratic and the Republican parties should be the good of the country, not getting party candidates reelected.

   d. _____

EXPANSION

Read the statements below and indicate whether you agree **(A)** or disagree **(D)**. Then discuss your opinions and reasoning with a partner.

_____ **1.** The vast amount of nuclear material in the world **constitutes** a clear danger to the future of humankind.

_____ **2.** Famous **authors** deserve to be paid as much as famous movie stars.

_____ **3.** The world would be a better place if the use of motor **vehicles** was severely reduced.

_____ **4.** Governments should **proceed** to make tobacco illegal in the interest of public health.

_____ **5.** The wealth gap between developed and developing countries requires a **revolutionary** solution, in which developed countries voluntarily give up some of their quality of life to help those who are less fortunate.

_____ **6. Classical** music has more artistic merit than rock music.

_____ **7.** People who wear unusual clothes and have extreme hairstyles usually hold **radical ideological** beliefs.

_____ **8.** People who **violate** the law repeatedly should automatically receive long prison terms.

Choose a song or other piece of music that you equate with a social/political issue. Listen carefully to the point of view expressed by the musicians. Research the social/political issue that the music describes and write an essay on the results of your investigation. Clearly indicate whether or not you support the point of view taken in the music.

22 *Noise Hurts*

GETTING STARTED

Discuss the following questions with your classmates.

▶ Have you ever been annoyed by noise? What caused the noise, and how did the noise make you feel?

▶ What are some places that are particularly noisy? List several of them.

▶ How can you protect yourself from noise?

TARGET WORDS—Assessing Your Vocabulary Knowledge

Look at each of the target words in the box. Use the scale to give yourself a score for each word. After you finish the chapter, score yourself again to check your improvement.

1 I don't know this word.

2 I have seen this word before, but I am not sure of the meaning.

3 I understand the word when I see it or hear it in a sentence, but I don't know how to use it in my own speaking and writing.

4 I know this word and can use it in my own speaking and writing.

TARGET WORDS

_____albeit	_____convinced	_____equivalent	_____parameter
_____ambiguous	_____correspond	_____file	_____passive
_____amend	_____credit	_____formula	_____preliminary
_____clause	_____deviation	_____grade	_____protocol
_____consent	_____distorted	_____index	_____route
_____consultation	_____draft	_____integral	_____tense

The following passage is adapted from an introductory textbook on noise control in industrial settings. It discusses noise and its harmful effects. As you read, pay special attention to the target vocabulary words in **bold**.

Noise Pollution

1   People tend to have contradictory attitudes about loud noise. On the one hand, they may enjoy listening to loud rock music. At the same time, they may resent living under the flight path of an airport or working near a loud construction site, even though the noise levels may be **equivalent**. Despite such inconsistent responses to noise, there is nothing **ambiguous** about the negative effects of sound pollution. Evidence clearly indicates that high levels of noise are harmful to human well-being, and noise pollution needs to be controlled. This is particularly relevant in the industrial sector. Industrial noise pollution affects people in various ways. It causes annoyance to neighbors, particularly in residential areas where industrial plants have been built nearby, often without a community's **consent**. Perhaps more importantly, industrial noise causes actual damage to the hearing of laborers who suffer overexposure to loud sounds in the workplace. Fortunately, many victims of noise pollution have **filed** complaints in court. To protect workers, lawmakers have **drafted** noise control **clauses** into new laws and **amended** old laws to provide additional safeguards. To their **credit**, many companies have changed their practices to conform to the latest noise control legislation.

A worker wearing protective headphones

2   Short periods of exposure to excessive noise levels produce varying degrees of inner ear damage, which is initially reversible. The ear temporarily loses a degree of its ability to hear, and sounds may become **distorted** (for example, people may hear ringing or buzzing in their ears). The effect progressively lessens with time after a person leaves the excessively noisy environment. The time it typically takes to recover from this loss or **distortion** in hearing may be anything from a few minutes to days, depending upon the degree of exposure. Permanent damage occurs when exposure to excessive noise continues over a long period of time.

3   So loud noise is dangerous and a health hazard, but what exactly are the acceptable **parameters**, or limits, for exposure to excessive noise? Exposure to noise in excess of 90 dB (decibels—an **index**, or standard measure, of the power of sound) for eight hours in any twenty-four hours for five days a week can lead to permanent hearing damage if exposure continues over a period of thirty to forty years. The sound produced by the average automobile is **equivalent** to 90 dB. However, not everyone develops the same **grade**, or level, of hearing loss when exposed to the same noise. Because of the variation in the susceptibility of individual ears, the 90 dB norm will only protect up to 80 percent of the population. The remaining 20 percent may have their hearing affected by exposure to noise levels of between 80 dB and 90 dB, but obviously to a lesser extent than exposure to levels above 90 dB. Exposure to noise levels below 80 dB over any period of time is not thought to cause hearing damage. The generally recommended **parameters** for acceptable noise levels are that no person at any time should be exposed to noise levels in excess of 120 dB without proper hearing protection, and that no one should be exposed under any conditions to levels in excess of

140 dB. Exposure to noise of 150 dB or above can damage the ear beyond repair.

4   Moreover, noise does not have to be audible to be destructive. Sounds outside the normal hearing range of the human ear can also cause physical discomfort and annoyance. Sound frequencies are measured in units called hertz (Hz). Ultrasonic frequencies (above 20,000 Hz), which are used in such applications as sonar or sonograms, can seriously damage the human ear even though the ear does not register their presence. Similarly, infrasound frequencies below the human hearing range (i.e., below 20 Hz), which are used in exploring geological formations for petroleum, can affect the sense of balance and cause fatigue, irritation, and nausea, if sufficiently intense. The brain is particularly sensitive to infrasound frequencies of 7 Hz, which **correspond** with brain alpha waves. Exposure to this type of sound can prevent clear thought or concentration. An everyday example of this would be the low frequency vibrations (4–7 Hz) of a moving car causing car sickness.

5   Industrial noise, **albeit** an important factor in hearing loss, is not the only source. Blows to the head or explosive blasts near the ear may damage the ear. Disease can also affect the ear and can even physically erode parts of it, such as nerve hair cells. Compacted wax or foreign bodies in the ear can cause a hearing loss by blocking the **route** sound follows through the ear canal. Finally, like all organs of the body, the aging process has an **integral** effect on hearing. Age-related deterioration typically occurs at the higher sound frequencies at about age thirty in men and at age thirty-five in women. There is some discussion as to whether the difference between men and women is partially due to men being exposed to higher levels of noise than women both inside of and outside of the workplace.

6   The effects of noise pollution are not restricted to hearing loss, either. Other effects include changes in **integral** body functions, such as the electrical activity of the brain, heart and breathing rates, and muscle mobility. **Preliminary** studies have noted other negative effects during tests on animals, and it is likely that these same effects may be present in human beings, although they have not yet been sufficiently documented. These effects include changes in the size of glands, blood pressure changes, and narrowing of the blood vessels. Observations of fatigue, anxiety, **deviations** in sleep patterns, and reduction of appetite have also been noted in animals.

7   Apart from these physical changes, noise can cause psychological disturbances. Interruption of sleep by noise can cause people to become **tense**, irritable, and resentful about the cause of the noise, especially if they are **convinced** that the noise is avoidable. In Britain, for example, a man was jailed for digging up a speed bump outside his house because the noise caused by trucks driving over it prevented him from sleeping. In addition, speech communication can be impaired by noise, resulting in inefficiency, feelings of isolation, and more seriously, accidents. In several tests, it has been established that productivity and efficiency can be seriously affected by high noise levels and that fewer mistakes are typically made when noise levels are reduced. When a reduction in productivity occurs, it can be a direct result of the mental fatigue caused by noise, which makes people disagreeable and has been shown to be a direct cause of absenteeism.

8   Noise can therefore be the cause of hearing loss, mental illness, reduced productivity, or even loss of life. To prevent this, companies can require employees to wear devices that reduce the level of noise, such as foam earplugs and **passive** headsets. There are also active headsets available, which transmit sound waves electronically to cancel out additional noise. Companies can also offer their workers **consultations** with doctors for annual hearing tests. Instituting these standard procedures, or **protocols**, can be partially effective. Nevertheless, the best **formula** for reducing noise damage is for sound engineers to dampen as much noise as possible, preventing noise pollution at its source.

Adapted from Sound Research Laboratories Ltd. Spon, E. & F. N. (1991). *Noise Control in Industry*, 3rd ed. London, UK: Chapman and Hall, pp. 19, 24–26, 29–30, 35.

UNDERSTANDING THE READING

Respond to the following in writing. Base your responses on the reading and your own personal experiences.

1. At what point can noise levels be classified as excessive?
2. Beyond hearing loss, what are some additional effects of excessive noise?
3. What types of noise are you exposed to in your daily life? Are any of them potentially harmful to your hearing or general well-being in the short or long term? Explain.

FOCUSING ON VOCABULARY

WORD MEANING

Each of the following target words appears in the reading on pages 180–181. Use the paragraph number in parentheses to locate each word in context. Read the dictionary definitions below. Write the letter of the definition that reflects how the word is used in the reading.

_____1. **ambiguous** (1)
   a. having more than one meaning, so that it is not clear which meaning is intended
   b. difficult to understand, or not certain

_____2. **file** (1)
   a. to officially record something such as a complaint, law case, official document, etc.
   b. to keep papers with information on them in a particular place so that you can find them easily

_____3. **draft** (1)
   a. to write a plan, report, law, etc. that will need to be changed before it is in its final form
   b. to order someone to serve in their country's military, especially during a war

_____4. **clause** (1)
   a. a group of words that contains a subject and a verb, but which is usually only part of a sentence
   b. a part of a written law or legal document covering a particular subject, condition, etc.

_____5. **credit** (1)
   a. an arrangement with a bank, store, etc. that allows you to buy something and pay for it later
   b. the responsibility for achieving or doing something good

_____6. **index** (3)
   a. an alphabetical list of names, subjects, etc. at the back of a book, with the numbers of the pages where they can be found
   b. a standard by which the level of something can be judged or measured

_____7. **grade** (3)
   a. the level or degree of quality that something has
   b. one of the twelve years of school in the United States, or the students in a particular year

_____8. **correspond** (4)
    a. to write letters to someone and receive letters from them
    b. to be very similar or the same as something else

_____9. **route** (5)
    a. the pathway from one place to another, especially one that is used often
    b. a way of doing something or achieving a particular result

_____10. **deviation** (6)
    a. the difference between a number or measurement in a set and the average of all the numbers or measurements in that set
    b. a noticeable difference from what is expected or normal

_____11. **formula** (8)
    a. a method or set of principles that you use to solve a problem or to make sure something is successful
    b. a series of letters and/or numbers that represent a mathematical or scientific rule

Each sentence below contains a paraphrase or set of synonyms for a target word. Read each sentence and then select the matching target word from the box.

albeit	consultation	equivalent	preliminary
amended	convinced	integral	protocol
consent	distorted	parameters	tense

1. The mechanic found that the engine was running within its normal

    _____.
        (limits, restrictions)

2. Many people feel that moral development is a(n) _____
                                        (essential, fundamental)
    element of education.

3. The report from the chairman of the Federal Reserve Board indicated that the economy was growing, _____ slowly.
                                     (although, even though)

4. Before undergoing open-heart surgery, the patient arranged a

    _____ with another doctor to get a second opinion.
        (meeting, conference)

5. The grandmother _____ her will to include her newborn
                         (modified, revised)
    granddaughter.

6. After the man had a stroke, his voice was so _____
                                      (unclear, changed from the norm)
    that we couldn't figure out what he was trying to say.

7. The _____ round of voting narrowed the large field of
         (initial, introductory)
    candidates down to two for the main election.

8. Many mainstream doctors are not yet _____ of the
                                 (sure, certain)
    benefits of alternative medicine.

9. According to hospital _____, no more than two family
                    (procedure, set of rules)
    members at a time were allowed to visit patients in the intensive care unit.

10. It is estimated that 53,000 square miles of rain forest are destroyed each year, an area _____ to the state of North Carolina.
(comparable, equal)

11. Researchers must usually obtain the written _____ of
(agreement, permission)
subjects participating in research studies.

12. Although the Olympic swimmer looked _____ before the
(nervous, worried)
competition began, she overcame her anxiety and won the race.

WORD TIP

▶ The most common meanings of the word **passive** are related to inactivity: A **passive** person tends to accept situations without attempting to change them or prevent them.

▶ A **passive** learning style means that the student is not actively involved in learning.

▶ In this reading, **passive** takes on a technical meaning—"exhibiting no gain or control."

  Passive *headsets* block out some noise, but they have no electronic circuit that actively tries to control and lessen even more noise.

WORD FAMILIES

Study the members of the word families in the table below. Look for spelling patterns for the verb, noun, adjective, and adverb forms of the words. Complete the table. List the patterns in the spaces.

Verb	Noun	Adjective	Adverb
X	ambiguity	ambiguous	ambiguously
amend	amendment	amended	X
consent	1. consent 2. consensus	consenting	X
consult	1. consultation 2. consultant	1. consulting 2. consultative	X
convince	X	1. convinced 2. convincing	convincingly
correspond	correspondence	corresponding	correspondingly
deviate	deviation	deviant	X
distort	distortion	distorted	X
X	1. equivalence 2. equivalent	equivalent	equivalently
formulate	1. formula 2. formulation	formulaic	X
Spelling patterns			

Read each sentence and identify the part of speech of the missing word. Write an appropriate form for the target word in the blank. Use the word families table on page 184 to help you.

1. The politician's speech was intentionally _____ (**ambiguous**) so that later he could not be held accountable for specific promises.

2. Saudi Arabia holds the largest known petroleum reserves, _____ (**equivalence**) to 257 billion barrels.

3. Many people suspect that there is a _____ (**correspond**) between the violence seen on television and the violence carried out in the real world.

4. Severe chemical imbalances in the body can lead to _____ (**deviate**) behavior, but people who suffer from these disturbances can now be treated with chemical therapy.

5. Macular degeneration is an eye disease that can cause severe _____ (**distorted**) to a person's vision, including the inability to perceive fine detail.

6. The secretary general of the United Nations spoke _____ (**convince**) about the need for tighter controls on the international arms trade.

7. After the error in the treasurer's report had been corrected, the _____ (**amend**) minutes of the previous meeting were accepted.

8. Before receiving a large inheritance, it is wise to _____ (**consultation**) an accountant in order to minimize taxes.

9. The new president of the university plans to _____ (**formula**) policies designed to increase research by 50 percent.

10. There is unlikely to be peace in Northern Ireland until republicans and unionists reach a _____ (**consent**) on paramilitary disarmament.

COLLOCATION

Each item below contains three example sentences with the same target word. In each sentence, the target word is paired with a different word and forms a different collocation. In the fourth sentence, the collocation has been left blank. Choose the collocation from the examples that best fits the last sentence and write it in the blank. You may need to change the form of one of the words to fit the sentence.

1. a. The athlete insisted that there be a no-trade **clause** in his **contract** to ensure he could not be traded to a weaker team in case he was injured.

   b. There is usually a **clause** in rental **agreements** that allows a landlord to evict the renter for nonpayment of rent.

   c. In 1954, the U.S. Supreme Court held that the equal protection **clause** of the Fourteenth **Amendment** prohibits states from maintaining racially segregated public schools.

   d. The employee did not like the _____ in her _____ which required weekend work.

2. a. The sports star was quick to **give credit** to his teammates for making his success possible.

   b. The president **took credit** for the healthy economy, even though it was mainly the result of his predecessor's policies.

   c. Red Cross workers **deserve credit** for their dedication, especially since they often have to work in dangerous, war-torn locations.

   d. Scientists _____ to Einstein for radically changing the way we conceptualize time and space.

3. a. The museum was forced to **draft** a new **budget** after one of their biggest donors withdrew his support.

   b. In the United States, the president has staff whose responsibility it is to **draft** his annual **speech** to Congress known as the State of the Union Address.

   c. Mothers Against Drunk Drivers (MADD) has urged the U.S. Congress to **draft legislation** that would impose stiff penalties on drunk drivers.

   d. It is the responsibility of the Office of Management and Budget in the White House to _____ the national _____ and present it to Congress for approval.

4. a. Farmers on the river were forced to **file** a **lawsuit** to prevent other farmers upstream from using more than their share of water.

   b. The state prosecutor **filed charges** against the chemical company for dumping waste into the river.

   c. A huge number of state-controlled companies were forced to **file** for **bankruptcy** during the economic revolution in the former communist countries.

   d. The dictator _____ of treason against his opponents in order to silence the opposition to his government.

5. a. **Passive smoking**, where secondhand smoke is breathed in by nonsmokers, has been shown to be a serious health risk.

   b. Gandhi advocated various forms of **passive resistance**—including noncooperation and civil disobedience—as methods of nonviolent protest against British colonial rule.

   c. In some cultures, women are expected to accept a **passive role**, but in others they are expected to take an active part in society.

   d. Although he founded the company, he now preferred to take a _____, allowing others to handle the day-to-day management.

6. a. **Preliminary results** from the archaeological dig indicate that an ancient Roman town existed on the site.

   b. A **preliminary report** into the airplane crash suggested that engine failure was the cause, but several tests remain to be carried out.

   c. Although it is still early in the process, **preliminary discussions** on merging the two companies look promising.

   d. The _____ of the blood test were negative, which indicated that the patient was healthy.

7. a. Parents should make sure their children know a safe **escape route** from their bedrooms in case of fire during the night.
   b. The most **direct route** between North America and Europe is the Great Circle route, which follows the curvature of the earth.
   c. When East Germany closed its borders to ground traffic in 1948, the West had to find an **alternate route** to supply Berlin—thus the Berlin Airlift came about.
   d. Because of the flooding on the northbound interstate highway, drivers were advised to use a(n) _____ to the suburbs north of the city.

8. a. It was a **tense situation**, with soldiers and police on one side of the barricade and protesters on the other.
   b. In 1962, the Cuban Missile Crisis increased the already **tense atmosphere** between the Soviet Union and the United States.
   c. There was a **tense silence** in the courtroom while everyone waited for the jury to announce their verdict.
   d. Because none of the participants was willing to speak first, there was a

   _____ in the negotiating room, which was only broken by the ticking of the clock.

EXPANSION

Complete the passage by filling in the blanks with the target words in the box. Use each word only once.

albeit	corresponds	equivalent	integral
convinced	deviations	index	parameters

THE SCIENCE OF SOUND

1   Sounds are all around us; some we can hear and some are not within the

(1) _____ of human hearing (20–20,000 Hz). Humans typically

perceive sound through air, but sound can travel through any medium,

(2) _____ not in a vacuum. However, sound travels at different

speeds depending on the degree of density of the medium. The speed of sound

through air is about 345 meters per second; this is the (3) _____

of 1,100 feet per second, with (4) _____ from this depending on

the temperature. Sound travels about four times faster in water and about

fifteen times faster in solids like steel.

2   Sounds can be perceived as regular, ordered, and beautiful when played as

music. Conversely, noise seems disorganized, irritating, and unpleasant. But

both music and noise consist of sound waves. One person's music may be

another's noise as when parents are (5) _____ that their

teenager's music is really just noise!

3   Three basic characteristics are (6) _____ to the nature of
sound: frequency, amplitude, and waveform. Frequency (7) _____
to pitch (e.g., high frequencies correspond to high notes). Amplitude
determines how loud a wave sounds, as indicated by the standard measure of
sound, the decibel (8) _____. The waveform leads to a distinctive
timbre or quality of sound. For any particular musical instrument, these
characteristics combine to produce a sound distinctive to that instrument.
The same applies to human voices and even animal sounds.

EXPLORING THE TOPIC

What kinds of music do you particularly like and dislike—vocal or instrumental music,
rock, folk, or jazz? What musical qualities typify your likes and dislikes? Write a
comparison/contrast essay in which you discuss the similarities and differences
between the music you enjoy and the music you dislike. Consider what factors
influence your musical taste.

CHAPTER 23

Ultrasonics: Super Sound?

GETTING STARTED

Discuss the following questions with your classmates.

▶ Sonar is a device that uses sound to detect, or locate, underwater objects. In what ways is sonar useful to people on fishing boats or warships?

▶ Ultrasound has many medical applications. What medical tests do you know of that use ultrasound devices?

▶ What are some other ways that sound is used in the arts, in science, and in industry?

TARGET WORDS — Assessing Your Vocabulary Knowledge

Look at each of the target words in the box. Use the scale to give yourself a score for each word. After you finish the chapter, score yourself again to check your improvement.

1 I don't know this word.

2 I have seen this word before, but I am not sure of the meaning.

3 I understand the word when I see it or hear it in a sentence, but I don't know how to use it in my own speaking and writing.

4 I know this word and can use it in my own speaking and writing.

TARGET WORDS

_____accumulate	_____detect	_____inspect	_____shift
_____brief	_____enormous	_____integrity	_____spherical
_____channel	_____generating	_____medicine	_____thereby
_____chart	_____implement	_____minimal	_____uniformity
_____component	_____incidence	_____monitor	_____version
_____convert	_____inhibited	_____option	_____visualized

The following passage is adapted from an introductory textbook on physics that focuses specifically on sound. As you read, pay special attention to the target vocabulary words in **bold**.

ULTRASONICS

1   Sound surrounds us every day, from the ringing of an alarm clock and the clanking of trucks to the singing of birds and the sounds of human voices. However, a large percentage of the sound around us cannot be **detected** by the human ear. This ultrasonic sound is now being harnessed to provide an amazing range of benefits to society.

2   *Ultrasonics* refers to waves whose frequencies lie above the audible range; ultrasonic frequencies range from about 20 kHz (1 kHz = 1,000 Hz), the upper frequency for human hearing, to about 1.25×10^{13} Hz, the maximum frequency of sound waves (1 hertz [Hz] = one complete vibration per second). The table below gives the range of hearing for humans and selected animals. It becomes clear that, despite the relatively large range of sound perception in people, the hearing range of many other species extends beyond ours on the upper and/or lower ends. Many of us have used a "dog whistle," the frequency of which is too high for us to hear but still well within the range of hearing of dogs. Most of us are also familiar with the idea of bats **generating** ultrasonic frequencies to both navigate and to locate flying insects for food.

Range of Hearing for a Variety of Life Forms

Humans	20–20,000 Hz
Cats	100–32,000 Hz
Dogs	40–46,000 Hz
Horses	31–40,000 Hz
Elephants	16–12,000 Hz
Cattle	16–40,000 Hz
Bats	1,000–150,000 Hz
Grasshoppers	100–50,000 Hz
Rodents	1,000–100,000 Hz
Whales, Dolphins	70–150,000 Hz

3   Ultrasonics is one of the most rapidly growing areas of science and technology, with a large number of very important recent innovations in such diverse fields as **medicine** and high-tech industrial machining, such as metal working. The device most often used to both produce and **detect** ultrasonic waves is the *piezoelectric transducer,* a crystal made of material that can **convert** both electrical oscillations into mechanical vibrations and mechanical vibrations into electrical oscillations. Piezoelectric crystals can be formed into various shapes (e.g., flat or **spherical**) that send out ultrasonic waves in particular patterns. For example, a convex surface will spread the waves widely, and a concave surface will **channel** waves into a beam that will focus to a point.

4   One of the simplest applications of the use of ultrasound is in sonar. By sending out **brief** bursts of ultrasound and measuring the time it takes to reflect off some object, the distance to the object can be determined if the velocity of sound in the medium is known. This procedure can be used to **chart** the depth of lakes or oceans or to locate and track submarines under water. Even small boats have sonic ranging devices to warn them of shallow water and thus prevent them from running aground. Many large fishing trawlers are equipped with sonic ranging devices that aid them in locating schools of fish with great efficiency.

5   Perhaps the most significant modern applications of ultrasound lie in the field of **medicine**. Two primary applications are in diagnostic and surgical procedures. Not only does ultrasound have many technical advantages over other **medical** techniques, it often turns out to be one of the most economical techniques, due to the simplicity of the electronics required and its ease of use. Because ultrasound readily reflects off cells, it can be used to measure blood flow in places where there is no other simple procedure available. Ultrasonic devices exist that can be

readily aimed along an artery under investigation to measure blood flow, allowing immediate determination of the effectiveness of that artery. One **version** of this device uses a 3-MHz (1 MHz = 1,000,000 Hz) beam that reflects off arterial blood. Different blood flow rates will cause slight **shifts** in sound, which are processed by the device so that they can be heard directly by the physician. This technique enables doctors to diagnose and treat hardening of the arteries.

6   Perhaps the most well-known application of ultrasound among the general public is in the making of sonograms, or ultrasonic pictures, of a fetus at an early stage in its development to determine whether growth is proceeding normally. The sonogram of a fetus has in fact become virtually synonymous with ultrasound for many new parents, who observe the fetus on a video **monitor** with excitement as it moves about within the mother. Now, more than half of all pregnant women choose the **option** of having sonograms at some time during their pregnancy, an **enormous** change from the late 1960s and early 1970s, when the **incidence** of sonograms was virtually nonexistent.

7   Whereas these diagnostic applications of ultrasound involve relatively low intensity levels, surgical applications generally involve substantially higher levels. Perhaps the most well-known high intensity application involves the breakup of kidney stones, with **minimal** or no use of surgery. The focusing of intense ultrasonic beams onto small internal regions can also be used to create local heating. This technique has been used to relieve pain in joints, especially in the back and shoulder. By focusing ultrasound onto a cancerous region, creating local heating, it is believed that the cancer can be **inhibited** or destroyed while leaving the surrounding region unaffected.

8   In addition to its use in **medical** diagnostics and procedures, ultrasound has several nondestructive industrial testing applications. Because sound waves move more efficiently through metals than do X-rays, they can be used to probe more deeply. Because they reflect more readily off small faults or other changes in the material than do X-rays, they are useful in identifying relatively small structural problems, such as holes, cracks,

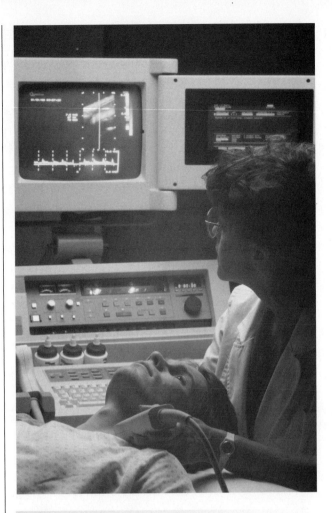

A man having a sonogram of his neck

or corrosion in materials. Ultrasound is used to **inspect** welded materials, establish the **uniformity** and quality of poured concrete, and **monitor** metal fatigue. As a result of the Three Mile Island nuclear reactor accident, an increased number of ultrasonic **inspection** procedures have been **implemented** for the structural **components** of nuclear reactors.

9   Perhaps the most widespread use of high-energy ultrasound is in ultrasonic cleaning. Ultrasonic waves are introduced into small tanks of liquid into which objects, such as jewelry, surgical instruments, or small machinery, are placed for cleaning. The bubbling of the liquid as well as the vibrations result in a powerful cleaning action, which **thereby** removes even the dirt that has **accumulated** in hard-to-reach places in the objects.

10   Ultrasonic waves are even used by industry to cut and drill materials. For example, a process known as ultrasonic drilling can be used to form

holes of virtually any shape in materials such as glass or ceramic, which are very difficult to drill using standard techniques without compromising the **integrity** of the material.

11   Many of the above applications of ultrasound were developed relatively recently. Given that ultrasound technology is constantly improving, it is not difficult to **visualize** a future in which ultrasound will be utilized even more widely than it is today.

_____

Adapted from Berg, R. E. and Stork, D. G. (1995). *The Physics of Sound*, 2nd ed. Englewood Cliffs, NJ: Prentice Hall, pp. 59–63.

UNDERSTANDING THE READING

Respond to the following in writing. Base your responses on the reading and your own personal experiences.

1. Which nonhuman life-form has the narrowest range of hearing? Which has the widest? How do these ranges compare to the range of human hearing?
2. Describe how sonar works and several ways in which it can be used.
3. List three medical uses of ultrasound. Describe how a patient might benefit from these uses of ultrasound. If you know of an actual example of someone who was helped by ultrasound, describe it.

FOCUSING ON VOCABULARY

WORD MEANING

Read the sentences below and circle the letter of the word or phrase that best matches the meaning of the target word in **bold**. Use context clues in the sentences to determine the correct meaning. Check your dictionary if you are not sure of the answer.

1. Looking directly at the sun, even for very **brief** periods, can cause serious eye damage.
   a. nearly perfect
   b. strong and easy to see
   c. continuing for a short time

2. A lot of money has been **channeled** into cancer research.
   a. communicated a message
   b. controlled or directed something toward a particular purpose
   c. subtracted from something

3. George Mason and Jeremiah Dixon were two surveyors sent from England to **chart** the border between the Maryland and Pennsylvania colonies.
   a. give reasons to support an idea
   b. make a map of an area of land, ocean, or stars
   c. observe the stars and the planets

4. The cable-based Internet network was having problems with two key **components**, the server computers that send the data and the cable modems that translate it.
   a. parts that make up a machine or system
   b. qualities related to being human
   c. tasks or pieces of work

5. It was estimated that the new taxes would **generate** $150 million in new revenue.
   a. produce or make something
   b. hide something
   c. expand something

6. The **incidence** of malaria has been rising in recent years.
   a. length of time something takes
   b. spread of infection
   c. number of times something happens

7. It is important to keep food in the refrigerator at 5°C (41°F) or colder to **inhibit** bacterial growth.
   a. improve
   b. prevent growth or development
   c. move quickly

8. Upon start-up, computers automatically do an internal check of the **integrity** of all of their components.
   a. good condition; soundness
   b. bad or faulty condition
   c. lack of unity

9. For the United States, World War I marked a **shift** from isolationism to international engagement.
   a. change or movement
   b. high point
   c. strong feeling

10. Saturn is not perfectly **spherical** in shape; rather it is quite flat at its poles.
    a. smooth
    b. rough
    c. round

11. The Black Death killed about a third of Europe's population, **thereby** creating a labor shortage and strengthening the position of working people.
    a. with everyone's agreement to something
    b. in contrast to something
    c. with the result that something else happens

12. Gymnasts often **visualize** themselves going through their routine in preparation for their actual performance.
    a. form a picture of something in the mind
    b. move something from one place to another
    c. become more interesting or exciting

Read the sentences below and use context to figure out the meaning of the target words in **bold**. Look for a core meaning that provides a general understanding of each target word. Write the meaning in your own words.

1. a. Social security is a savings system in the United States whereby taxes collected from salaries **accumulate** over time to pay retirees' benefits.
   b. As most athletes know, fatigue and cramping can occur when lactic acid **accumulates** in the muscles after a period of strenuous exercise.

   accumulate _____

2. a. You have to **convert** the distances from miles to kilometers.

   b. Photosynthesis is the process whereby plants **convert** sunlight into food.

   convert _____

3. a. Many forms of cancer can be cured if **detected** early.

   b. Hyenas can **detect** smells that humans cannot, because the odor-detecting membranes in their noses are fifty times larger.

   detect _____

4. a. The Sahara is an **enormous** desert in northern Africa.

   b. There is **enormous** pressure in the deepest parts of the ocean: 16,000 pounds per square inch at a depth of 35,813 feet.

   enormous _____

5. a. The new company president was expected to **implement** the plan his predecessor had developed.

   b. The government wanted to **implement** the committee's recommendations on urban transportation but lacked the resources to do so.

   implement _____

6. a. Divers had to swim under the ship in order to **inspect** it for damage after the collision with the iceberg.

   b. Customs officials **inspect** the goods brought into a country in order to stop illegal substances and biological pests from entering.

   inspect _____

7. a. Today's doctors can cure many previously untreatable illnesses, but the cost of cutting-edge **medicine** is sometimes prohibitive.

   b. Modern **medicine** dates from the beginning of the seventeenth century when William Harvey confirmed the heart's role in circulating blood.

   medicine _____

8. a. The Nepalese government strives to ensure that mountain climbers have a **minimal** impact on the environment.

   b. In World War II, Allied bombs caused only **minimal** damage to the German submarine fleet, because it was protected by concrete structures when at harbor.

   minimal _____

9. a. A good boss will **monitor** the performance of his employees and provide them with additional training where necessary.

   b. American U2 spy planes were able to **monitor** the movements of Soviet missiles during the 1962 Cuban missile crisis.

   monitor _____

10. a. For consumers, the best **option** is often to pay more initially for a higher quality product than to pay less for a product that is likely to fail.

   b. The chief executive officer (CEO) had the **option** of taking either a cash bonus or additional company stock.

   option _____

11. **a.** The **uniformity** of operating protocols in large multinational companies ensures that business practices will be similar in different parts of the world.

    b. Although some countries pride themselves on their cultural **uniformity**, discussions on sensitive issues still bring out a wide variety of opinions.

    uniformity _____

12. **a.** The latest **version** of the software program is twice as fast, but also requires twice as much memory.

    b. Most film critics consider Alfred Hitchcock's original **version** of the movie *Psycho* to be superior to more recent remakes.

    version _____

WORD FAMILIES

Read the sentences below. Some of the target words have been used correctly, but in six sentences a wrong word form has been used. If the wrong form has been used, cross it out and write the correct form. If the form is correct, put a checkmark (✓).

1. The **spherical** geodesic dome is the lightest, strongest structure ever devised.

   _____

2. Many of the lyrics and **visualization** images that accompany popular songs are about love. _____

3. Researchers sometimes analyze newly discovered plants for their potential **medicinal** value. _____

4. The politician's **convert** to the strikers' cause was seen as opportunistic.

   _____

5. Even world-class athletes may be overwhelmed by the **enormously** of an event like the Olympics. _____

6. Some parents choose to limit their career moves when their children are young in order to **minimal** disruption to their children's lives.

   _____

7. The U.S. Supreme Court affirmed the right of Congress to withhold federal funds from states that did not adopt a **uniform** minimum drinking age of twenty-one. _____

8. Universities now have access to software that can **detection** plagiarism.

   _____

9. The amount of pollution **generation** by factories must be controlled.

   _____

10. There was a marked **shift** in public opinion toward the city council's decision to install closed circuit television (CCTV) camera surveillance systems.

    _____

COLLOCATION

Match each target word in the box with the group of words that regularly occur with it. If the (~) symbol appears before a word in a list, the target word comes before the word in the list. In all other cases, the target word comes after the word in the list.

brief	chart	implement	monitor
channel	component	integrity	option

1. _____
~ money
~ resources
~ funds
~ energy

2. _____
~ history
~ mention
~ sojourn
~ introduction

3. _____
~ progress
~ performance
~ compliance
~ standards

4. _____
~ policy
~ recommendations
~ strategy
~ reforms

5. _____
attractive
easy
preferred
safe

6. _____
structural
territorial
scientific
financial

7. _____
essential
key
basic
vital

8. _____
~ a career path
~ a course for
~ the direction of
~ the journey from

EXPANSION

How much do you know about sound, music, and hearing? Take the following trivia test and see how many little-known facts you know about these topics. Compare your results with a partner.

SOUND TRIVIA

1. Beats are periodic **shifts**, or variations, in the _____ of a sound.
   a. softness
   b. echoes
   c. loudness

2. _____ cannot **detect** some of the high-pitched sounds that humans can hear.
   a. Dogs
   b. Whales
   c. Elephants

3. The **incidence** of deafness in the United States is about one person per _____ people.
   a. 150
   b. 300
   c. 450

4. The first **versions** of metal trumpets appeared around _____.
   a. the fifteenth century B.C.
   b. A.D. 100
   c. A.D. 1100

5. The best medium for **inhibiting** the transmission of sound is a

   _____.
   a. 4-inch brick wall
   b. 4-inch wood panel
   c. vacuum

6. Antonio Stradivari (1644–1737), the famous Italian violin maker, made an **enormous** number of stringed instruments in his lifetime. His **accumulated** output was about 1,100 to 1,200 instruments, of which _____ still survive today.
   a. 450
   b. 650
   c. 850

7. Certain creatures, such as _____, rub parts of their bodies together, **thereby** creating songlike sounds.
   a. insects
   b. birds
   c. bats

8. Ultrasound techniques cannot be used to **inspect** _____.
   a. space shuttle wings
   b. lungs of medical patients
   c. cast iron

 Research other interesting facts about sound, music, and hearing. Write a trivia test of your own and exchange it with a partner.

Strategy Practice

USING YOUR DICTIONARY—Example Sentences as Writing Models

In order to use academic words correctly and effectively in your own writing, you should pay close attention to how the words are used in context. Notice how words are used in the texts you read, and consult your dictionary often. Dictionaries often give one or more example sentences for a word entry to help learners understand a word's meaning, usage, and placement in a sentence. These example sentences provide you with good models for your own writing.

Suppose you are writing a sentence that contains one of the target words in this book, and you know your sentence needs improvement. You could look the word up in a dictionary and scan the entry for a model sentence. Based on the dictionary's model sentence, you could rephrase, reorder, and correct the words in your sentence to create a better sentence. Below is an example of how one English language learner used a dictionary model sentence to improve a sentence with the word *cease*.

Poor sentence:

Celebration of the holiday long ago *cease*.

Dictionary model:

*By noon the rain had **ceased**.*

Better sentence:

Long ago, celebration of the holiday had *ceased*.

PRACTICING YOUR DICTIONARY SKILLS

Below are eight example sentences from the *Longman Advanced American Dictionary*. Use these dictionary models to write sentences of your own for each of the target words in **bold**. Try to imitate some of the word order, usage, and phrasing of the models. The first two sentences have been done for you.

1. *The soldiers developed leprosy **subsequent** to leaving the army.*

   The child developed an allergy subsequent to playing with the cat.

2. *Cather's novel has been made into a beautiful, **albeit** slow-paced, musical.*

   The story conveyed a somewhat humorous, albeit tragic, tone.

3. *A **clause** in the contract states when payment must be made.*

   _____

4. *What is happening in California **corresponds** to what happened in New England in June.*

_____

5. *He redesigned the process, **thereby** saving the company thousands of dollars.*

_____

6. *There is a higher **incidence** of suicide among women than men.*

_____

7. *Music should be an **integral** part of children's education.*

_____

8. *The youngest player in the league has far **exceeded** his coaches' expectations.*

_____

STRATEGY—Using the Keyword Technique

One of the most effective ways to remember words is the *keyword technique*. Language researchers have found that it is more effective than many other strategies, such as rote repetition, using synonyms, and placing words in a meaningful sentence. Of course you will not be able to use it for every word, but it is a useful strategy worth learning. You have already been briefly introduced to the technique on page xiii of To the Student.

The initial step is finding a word in your first language that sounds like the second language word you want to remember. If you are a German speaker learning the English word *clog* ("wooden shoe"), you might use the German word *klage* ("complain") as the keyword. The next step is to make a mental image combining the two concepts ("complaining" and "shoe"). You might think of a Dutch girl complaining that the store sent her wooden clogs that are too big.

When you hear the word *clog*, it will trigger the keyword image, which will allow you to access the meaning of *shoe* from the image. Be creative when making a keyword image; the more unusual the image, the more likely you are to remember it.

Now select several words from this unit and try using the keyword technique with them.

The basic verbs *do, make,* and *take* are used with hundreds of other words, including academic words. Examples include *make a **purchase*** and *take **medicine***. Often, more than one of these basic verbs can be used with an academic word, although each combination has a different meaning:

- The company decided to *do* a **survey** to determine how well their new product might sell. (meaning: "ask people for their opinions")
- The archaeologists decided to *make* a **survey** of the area to see if the ancient Roman settlement they were looking for existed below the surface. (meaning: "make a physical examination")

However, in most cases a particular one of the verbs *do, make,* or *take* is preferred:

- The author *did* a brief **draft** of her essay while riding the train.
- A member of the audience raised her hand to indicate that she wished to *make* a **comment**.
- The politician *took* the **objectives** of the protesters seriously.

For each sentence, decide which of the verbs *do, make,* or *take* is most appropriate and write it in the blank. The first one has been done for you.

1. Companies who _____*make*_____ **investments** in their employees' training have a much better chance of retaining their skilled workers.

2. They decided to _____ the scenic **route** home even though it was a little longer.

3. After college, many young people may initially work at jobs that do not require a college degree. This _____ **interpreting** graduate employment statistics rather tricky.

4. The small no-frills airlines _____ a different **approach** to flying than their larger competitors, and many are increasingly successful.

5. A good education enables people to _____ a **contribution** to society.

6. After collecting wind tunnel data, the engineer was ready to _____ a preliminary **design** of the new car's shape.

7. The company designed the new building in the winter, but hoped to _____ the **construction** during the summer when the weather was favorable.

8. Many cities encourage people to _____ public **transportation** instead of driving.

9. The chair asked the secretary to _____ a brief **summary** of the main points of the meeting.

10. People who always _____ the easy **option** may find themselves missing out on many opportunities.

UNIT
7

Animal Nature

CHAPTER

25

Endangered Elephants

GETTING STARTED

Discuss the following questions with your classmates.

▶ What are some species of animals and plants that are in danger of extinction?

▶ What are some ways that individuals and governments can protect endangered animals and plants? If you know of a specific effort to save an endangered species, describe it.

▶ Does your culture use ivory? What kinds of things are or have been made from ivory?

TARGET WORDS — Assessing Your Vocabulary Knowledge

Look at each of the target words in the box. Use the scale to give yourself a score for each word. After you finish the chapter, score yourself again to check your improvement.

1 I don't know this word.

2 I have seen this word before, but I am not sure of the meaning.

3 I understand the word when I see it or hear it in a sentence, but I don't know how to use it in my own speaking and writing.

4 I know this word and can use it in my own speaking and writing.

TARGET WORDS

____accommodate	____enforcement	____mechanism	____resolution
____appendix	____financial	____pose	____restore
____automatic	____ignorance	____prime	____scheme
____committed	____incentive	____rational	____scope
____compensate	____initially	____recovery	____suspend
____displace	____irrelevant	____registration	____welfare

The following passage is adapted from a textbook about international efforts to preserve the African elephant. As you read, pay special attention to the target vocabulary words in **bold**.

Saving THE AFRICAN ELEPHANT: USING INTERNATIONAL LAW AND TRADE

1   The elephant is perhaps the best-known and most visible symbol of African wildlife. However, it continues to face two serious threats to its existence—the ivory trade and habitat loss. For the conservationist, trade is a double-edged sword. The trade in endangered species of fauna and flora can push, and has pushed, many species to the edge of extinction. Some have been pushed beyond. There is little doubt that the international trade in ivory was largely responsible for the radical decline in elephant populations between 1979 and 1989. Demand for ivory in Japan and the West forced up ivory prices; high prices created an **incentive** to poach (illegally catch or kill animals, birds, or fish); and poaching devastated the population.

The endangered African elephant

Poaching is more dangerous than habitat loss in the sense that it can devastate populations with extraordinary speed. It was the **prime** reason for the death of approximately 700,000 animals in a single decade—fully half of the world's African elephants. To combat this, the Convention on International Trade in Endangered Species (CITES) placed the elephant on its list of protected animals (the CITES **Appendix** 1 endangered list), which created a ban on the ivory trade. It is clear that placing elephants on the **Appendix** 1 list played a vital role in closing down demand for ivory, in reducing the **incentive** to poach elephants, and in the precarious population **recovery** that has followed.

2   If poaching **posed** the only threat to the African elephant, the case would be open and shut; the ivory ban has worked well, and it should be continued. Poaching is controllable because it is driven by demand for a product that is **irrelevant** to the necessities of life. The ivory trade succeeds only if **enforcement** agencies are too weak or corrupt to stop it.

3   Habitat loss **poses** more ominous problems for the elephant, and the **scope** of this problem is great. Loss of land occurs slowly. The annual population growth of sub-Saharan Africa is approximately 2.1 percent per year. Loss of elephant habitat is, very roughly, comparable. It attracts almost no media attention. It has no villains. The problems it presents cannot easily be turned into a bumper-sticker campaign. The Africa of the Western imagination—endless savannahs full of game with virtually no people—will largely be gone before today's young Africans have grown old, most likely never to be **restored**.

4   To save the land on which the African elephant lives, people must understand that more income can be generated—and more people fed—if the land is kept free of farms or settled communities so that the elephants can roam. If the elephants are allowed to wander across the land, money can be generated through

the tourist trade, limited sport hunting, and a tightly-controlled harvest of ivory. Commercial enterprises like these, if properly managed, could generate a **financial incentive** to protect the elephant and its habitat, as long as the people who must pay the costs of supporting the animal and its range are the same people who benefit from the commercial use of the elephant.

5   Various **schemes** have been proposed for saving the African elephant and its habitat. The simplest solution would be to ban the ivory trade forever, but ask countries and organizations that wish to conserve the elephant to pay some sort of **compensation** to local communities. The best system would likely be one in which local landowners, public or private, were paid a price—at least equal to the value of each animal's ivory—for every elephant kept alive in its original habitat. "Willingness to pay" surveys apparently indicate that the general public in Western Europe and North America might be willing to take on that burden. Strangely, however, no **mechanism** for doing this has yet been suggested.

6   Another option for saving the African elephant would be an exclusive marketing **scheme** for the trading of ivory. The core of such a system would have to be an agreement between exporting countries that are **committed** to managing their elephant herds at sustainable levels, and importing countries that are both willing and able to **enforce** import controls; such controls would only allow the importation of ivory from approved exporting countries. Ivory could be taken for **registration** to a single point of export controlled and supervised by CITES. The CITES center would accept ivory only from places deemed to have met strict conservation criteria. Once exported, ivory samples would be randomly tested at regular intervals to determine their place of origin. Ivory from anywhere other than CITES-approved states would be confiscated and the importing nation fined in the first instance, and **suspended** from the **scheme** in the case of repeated offenses. This **scheme** might be small **initially** but it could be expanded later if it were successful. Such expansion could be implemented by a **resolution** within the CITES framework.

7   One problem is that actual **enforcement** of such plans is by no means **automatic**.

Considerations like the corruption or powerlessness of officials, **ignorance**, and apathy must be fully addressed in order to successfully implement such a program.

8   If **schemes** like these are not put into place, what is the future of the elephant? The **Appendix** 1 listing for the elephant will create a **welfare** environment for elephant conservation in Africa. Those countries that support the ivory ban will, for a time, find themselves richly **compensated** by various Western groups. Those countries that defy the ivory ban will lose the revenues offered to the more compliant nations; they will not be able to offset this loss by a gain in ivory trade, because there will be no market for ivory.

9   Thus a pattern will emerge as time goes by. In East Africa, where countries generally support the ban, the great parks will prosper, as will the elephant populations within their confines. However, elephants outside the park fences will disappear almost altogether. In southern Africa, where the ban is often looked upon with skepticism, the opposite will happen. Poaching, once almost defeated, will grow again—becoming a major problem. The parks, once the pride of Africa, will become less effective due to lack of revenue. Beyond the parks, however, the decline of the elephant will be slower. So long as private sport hunting is allowed (and profitable), farmers and communities will put an effort into protecting the elephants that live on their land.

10   In the end, however, the charity of Western donors toward elephant preservation will be outbalanced by the massive human population growth in Africa. The parks, even in countries that have **accommodated** Western interests, will become embattled because of the human need for land. Many parks will be lost and their elephants **displaced**.

11   The elephant will not become extinct (it is too visible a symbol of the natural world for that), but by the end of the first quarter of the twenty-first century, the great herds that could still be seen in many parts of Africa in the 1990s will largely be gone. Much of this will have come about largely through a failure to see the effect to which a **rational** use of international trade and law could have been put.

Adapted from Harland, D. (1994). *Killing Game: International Law and the African Elephant*. Westport, CT: Praeger Publishers, pp. 167–175.

UNDERSTANDING THE READING

Respond to the following in writing. Base your responses on the reading and your own personal experiences.

1. How has the CITES ivory trade ban helped to save the African elephant?
2. In what ways can tourism help to preserve endangered animals and their habitats?
3. Do you support a total ban on the ivory trade, or do you feel that controlled trade is a better option to save the elephant? Give reasons for your point of view.

FOCUSING ON VOCABULARY

WORD MEANING

Match the words with their definitions. If you are unsure about a word's meaning, try to figure it out from context by rereading the passage on pp. 203–204. Then check your dictionary.

Set 1

_____ **1.** committed

_____ **2.** registration

_____ **3.** ignorance

_____ **4.** resolution

_____ **5.** accommodate

_____ **6.** compensate

_____ **7.** suspend

a. the act of recording names and details on an official list

b. to officially stop something from continuing, especially for a short time

c. willing to work very hard at something

d. a formal decision or statement agreed on by a group of people, especially after a vote

e. to pay someone money because they have suffered injury, loss, or damage

f. lack of knowledge or information about something

g. to accept someone's opinions or needs and try to do what they want, especially when your ideas differ

Set 2

_____ **1.** recovery

_____ **2.** enforcement

_____ **3.** pose

_____ **4.** irrelevant

_____ **5.** financial

_____ **6.** welfare

_____ **7.** appendix

a. relating to money, or the management of money

b. not useful in or not relating to a particular situation

c. money paid by the government to people who are poor, do not have jobs, are sick, etc.

d. a part at the end of a book or paper containing additional information

e. making someone obey a rule or law, especially by punishing those who do not obey it

f. to exist in a way that may cause a problem, danger, or difficulty

g. the process of returning to a normal condition after a period of trouble or difficulty

Read the row of words and phrases below each numbered word. One word or phrase in each row is *not* a synonym for the numbered word. Cross it out.

1. **automatic**
   certain | desired | sure | guaranteed

2. **displace**
   take | move | relocate | transfer

3. **incentive**
   encouragement | permission | motivation | reason

4. **initially**
   at the start | to begin with | at the outset | in a small way

5. **mechanism**
   ruling | procedure | system | method

6. **prime**
   major | chief | simple | principal

7. **rational**
   reasonable | economical | logical | sensible

8. **restore**
   reestablish | return | bring back | develop

9. **scheme**
   method | association | system | plan

10. **scope**
    focus | range | extent | reach

WORD TIP

▶ There is a considerable difference in how the British and Americans use the word *scheme*. In British English, the typical meaning is "an official plan intended to help people in some way."

   Unfortunately, the National Health Insurance *scheme* of 1911 did not cover all workers.

▶ In American English, *scheme* has a much more negative meaning: "an intelligent plan, especially to do something bad or illegal."

   Young came up with a *scheme* to pass phony checks.

WORD FAMILIES

The table below contains word families for some of the target words in the reading. Complete the rest of the table. An *X* indicates that there is no form or that the form is not common. Sometimes there may be more than one form possible. If you are unsure about a form, check your dictionary.

Verb	Noun	Adjective	Adverb
accommodate		accommodating	X
compensate	compensation		X
displace	displacement		X
	1. finance 2. financing	financial	financially
ignore	ignorance		X
X		irrelevant	irrelevantly
	rationalization	rational	rationally
register	1. registration 2. register		X
restore		restored	X
suspend		suspended	X

Choose the correct form of the word in **bold** in sentence **a** to complete sentence **b**. Use the word family table you just completed as a guide.

1. **a.** The views of the two parties in the dispute were so far apart that any chance of **accommodation** seemed impossible.
   b. The petitioners had expected the committee to be in a more

   _____ frame of mind, so they were surprised when their proposal was voted down.

2. **a.** The court ordered the company to **compensate** the community with a payment of $5 million for polluting the water supply.
   b. In the United States, if you are injured on the job you have the right to

   Workers' _____.

3. **a.** A **displaced** person is someone who has been forced to leave his or her own country and live somewhere else, often because of war.

   b. The _____ of the Cherokee people from their homelands to a reservation in Oklahoma is one of the most shameful episodes in U.S. history.

4. **a.** Most people do not have enough money to buy their home in cash, so they **finance** the purchase with a mortgage.

   b. In order to be _____ secure in one's old age, it is best to start building up investments and a pension early in life.

5. a. **Ignorance** of the law is no excuse for not obeying it.

   b. Although people from all backgrounds in the United States now join in celebrating ethnic holidays such as Cinco de Mayo and Chinese New Year, many are _____ of the origins of these festivals.

6. a. For many young people in Europe, the old monarchies are an **irrelevance**.

   b. The student's composition on the causes of the American Civil War included an _____ paragraph about women's fashion during that period.

7. a. There is still no **rational** explanation for some of the unsolved UFO phenomena.

   b. Some people _____ their refusal to exercise by saying that they are trying to avoid any possibility of physical injury.

8. a. U.S. citizens have to **register** in order to vote.

   b. The _____ numbers of U.S. aircraft begin with the letter *N*, Canadian numbers begin with *C*, and British numbers begin with *G*.

9. a. The **restored** table from the period of Louis XIV was in fine condition and was expected to attract high bids at the auction.

   b. Classic car _____ clubs exist throughout the United States.

10. a. The driver had his license **suspended** for one year after receiving his fourth speeding ticket.

   b. The negotiated cease-fire required the _____ of all military activity by both sides at midnight.

COLLOCATION

Each item below contains three sentences with the same collocation. Write a fourth sentence of your own using the same word partners.

1. a. Students who see no connection between what they are learning and their career goals have **little incentive** to study hard at school.

   b. In countries with surplus energy there is **little incentive** to develop alternative fuel sources.

   c. Farmers have **little incentive** to grow crops for export if they can't sell the crops for a profit.

   d. _____

2. a. Groups who act as watchdogs by monitoring the output of the media serve as a **feedback mechanism** for journalists, forcing them to defend their practices.

   b. Quality management systems rely on effective **feedback mechanisms** to direct comments and ideas from employees to management.

   c. Student questionnaires are the most common **feedback mechanism** used in universities.

   d. _____

3. **a.** Many patients consult their doctors on environmental, psychiatric, and religious matters, which are **beyond the scope of** a medical education.

   b. Teachers should design activities that are not **beyond the scope of** even their weakest students.

   c. A full discussion of first-language acquisition is **beyond the scope of** this book.

   d. _____

4. **a.** Broadly categorizing all **welfare recipients** as members of the underclass prevents us from understanding the full range of circumstances that lead to poverty.

   b. Limited access to transportation makes it difficult for **welfare recipients** to attend job interviews or commute to work.

   c. In 2003, there were approximately 5 million **welfare recipients** in the United States compared to 1.75 million in Canada.

   d. _____

5. **a.** The United Nations Committee on the Rights of the Child **adopted a resolution** urging countries to address all issues of social discrimination against children.

   b. The International Civil Aviation Organization **adopted a resolution** calling for a more coordinated approach to the problem of aircraft noise.

   c. The European Parliament **adopted a resolution** to set up the Temporary Committee on Improving Safety at Sea.

   d. _____

6. **a.** The accounting profession needs to develop a comprehensive program of **standards** and **enforce** it vigorously.

   b. It is the responsibility of utilities boards to both set and **enforce** water **standards**.

   c. The National Traffic and Motor Vehicle Safety Act authorizes the government to **enforce** safety **standards** for the automotive industry.

   d. _____

7. **a.** Sufferers of addiction have a better chance of **sustained recovery** if family members attend associated family therapy programs.

   b. There was some seasonal improvement in the second quarter of the year, but firm evidence of **sustained recovery** in the housing market has yet to appear.

   c. The greatest threat to **sustained** economic **recovery** is excessive government borrowing over the medium term.

   d. _____

8. **a.** Because of its poor performance, the local branch of the company was a **prime candidate** for closure.

   b. New graduates are **prime candidates** for entry-level jobs because companies can train them in their own systems.

   c. Picnickers who eat food that has been left out in the hot sun for hours are **prime candidates** for food poisoning.

   d. _____

Read the statements below and indicate whether you agree **(A)** or disagree **(D)**. Then discuss your opinions and reasoning with a partner.

_____ **1.** Governments should cut defense spending and use that money to fund better **welfare** programs.

_____ **2.** Sometimes the **appendices** contain the most interesting information in a book or article.

_____ **3.** If antiwar protesters are truly **committed** to their cause, they should be willing to go to jail for their beliefs.

_____ **4.** The **initial** impression that a person gives to others has a long-term effect on other people's opinions of him or her.

_____ **5.** If a **scheme** to make money sounds too good to be true, it probably is.

_____ **6.** Anyone convicted of involvement with illegal drugs should **automatically** be given a prison sentence.

_____ **7.** It is possible to **compensate** for a lack of talent or ability by working harder than others.

_____ **8.** The disparity in wealth between the world's developed and developing countries **poses** serious problems for today's world.

The reading in this chapter was originally written in 1994. Research the current state of the elephant population in Africa. Investigate whether any of the ideas put forward in the reading have been implemented. If yes, have they been successful? If no, what is being done instead? Write an essay in which you describe and evaluate efforts to save the African elephant.

26 *Animals: How Human?*

GETTING STARTED

Discuss the following questions with your classmates.

▶ Think of an animal—a pet, a farm animal, or an animal in the wild. What characteristics does this animal have? Is it intelligent? Playful? Loyal? Describe what the animal is like.

▶ Anthropomorphism is the practice of describing or thinking of animals in terms of human characteristics or feelings. Why might it be a problem to view animals in human terms?

▶ What key characteristics distinguish human beings from other animals?

TARGET WORDS—Assessing Your Vocabulary Knowledge

Look at each of the target words in the box. Use the scale to give yourself a score for each word. After you finish the chapter, score yourself again to check your improvement.

1 I don't know this word.

2 I have seen this word before, but I am not sure of the meaning.

3 I understand the word when I see it or hear it in a sentence, but I don't know how to use it in my own speaking and writing.

4 I know this word and can use it in my own speaking and writing.

TARGET WORDS

_____ abstract	_____ funding	_____ migrate	_____ revise
_____ coherent	_____ institute	_____ paradigm	_____ scenario
_____ context	_____ intelligence	_____ physically	_____ sequence
_____ drama	_____ intrinsic	_____ previously	_____ simulate
_____ erode	_____ investigation	_____ publish	_____ submit
_____ focus	_____ invoke	_____ reverse	_____ successive

The following passage discusses the abilities and behaviors of chimpanzees. As you read, pay special attention to the target vocabulary words in **bold**.

CHIMPANZEES: OUR CLOSEST RELATIVE

1   Recent documentaries and news articles reporting on ape language may **invoke** visions of the classic *Planet of the Apes* movies. In this series of films, humans use the capacity of apes to learn and perform tasks to train them to be slaves. The apes eventually revolt and win control of the planet. They then go on to develop a society that looks both **physically** and socially very much like nineteenth-century human civilization. At the time the films were made, the fact that the apes could all speak English appeared to be just another Hollywood special effect to add to the **drama** of the films. However, research relating to language and other skills is forcing us to **revise** our understanding of primate capabilities and to examine more carefully the evolutionary links between them and us.

2   Humans have always had a special interest in apes because of our **intrinsic** similarities. We have, nonetheless, continued to regard apes as separate from ourselves and in so doing justify our domination over them and all the rest of the animal kingdom. The strongest arguments for keeping humans and apes separate have always revolved around a theory of the mind. The emphasis on the mind as a symbol of the difference between species became even stronger after genetic research revealed that humans and chimpanzees share 98.6 percent of the same DNA. The chimpanzee is closer to the human than to its other primate cousin, the gorilla.

3   When we look at what are commonly thought to be the products of the human mind—language, rational thought, music, art, and culture—we can see that research on chimpanzees has begun to **erode** this difference. A number of governmental science foundations and university research **institutes** have supplied the necessary **funding** to examine more carefully whether or not chimpanzees are in fact capable of a number of behaviors **previously** considered to be unique to humans.

These include the ability to:

- use rational and logical thought
- learn and use language
- intentionally teach their offspring
- develop culture

4   With regard to rational thought, humans have often been defined as the only species able to make tools to a set and regular pattern. In 1960, Jane Goodall went to Lake Tanganyika on the border between Tanzania and the Congo to study the behavior of chimpanzees living in the wild. While observing two male chimpanzees fishing for termites, she made the discovery that not only could chimpanzees use tools, these two chimpanzees were altering twigs by stripping off their leaves to make them more useful for the purpose of fishing. Other researchers have since **published** reports of tool-making behaviors among other groups of chimpanzees, including using or modifying sticks or rocks to open nuts, or crumpled leaves to soak up drinking water that is hard to get to.

5   The question of chimpanzee **intelligence** was **submitted** to more controlled **investigation** by Sarah ("Sally") Boysen and the chimpanzee Sheba at the Chimpanzee Center at Ohio State University. Sheba has demonstrated throughout **successive** studies the ability to count and to understand the **abstract** concept of zero. Sheba was first taught to associate paper cards with Arabic numerals on them to corresponding amounts of gumdrop candies presented to her. After many tests to establish that she clearly understood the concept of numbers, she was given a further task to determine whether she could perform addition. Zero to four oranges were placed at various sites around the lab and her number cards were placed on a table. Sheba was required to move among the food sites and then go back to the table and select the Arabic numeral that represented the total number of oranges in the lab. Sheba successfully completed the task on the very first attempt.

She and other chimpanzees at the center have gone from learning simple counting procedures to more advanced numerical concepts like subtraction and fractions.

Sally Boysen studying chimpanzee intelligence

6   Another line of research aims to discover whether apes have the capacity to learn language. Early research, in which chimpanzees were taught sign language, **focused** on the animals' ability to produce language. This research followed behaviorists' views on how humans learn languages; a **paradigm** shift in the study of human language has enabled new approaches to research in the area of ape language. Current research **focuses** on comprehension of language. Researchers at Georgia State University have found that young chimpanzees can learn to use symbols for communication simply by watching their mothers use these symbols. The question these researchers have to answer is whether this communication is evidence of real language use or some other behavior.

7   An important difference between Goodall's original tool discovery and the language and numerical competence research is that the first was conducted by observing the behavior of chimpanzees in the **context** of their natural environment. **Investigations** of ape language and mathematical capabilities have only been conducted with chimpanzees who have been placed in a human environment or in zoos or reserves that can only **simulate** a natural habitat. Studies of chimpanzee culture, on the other hand, have been conducted both at zoos and in the wild.

8   Determining whether or not chimpanzees have culture depends first on agreeing on a **coherent** definition of *culture*. Among humans, behavioral diversity is considered to be one aspect of culture. Primate researchers have found clear evidence of diversity in primate use of tools—some chimpanzees use stones to crack open nuts while others do not; some use sticks to fish for termites while others do not. When chimpanzees **migrate** from one group to another, there is some evidence that behaviors may be transferred. Diversity alone, though, is not thought to be sufficient to claim that chimpanzees have culture. Whether chimpanzees pass these behaviors on through teaching is seen to be an essential issue.

9   Experiments have been conducted to compare chimpanzees' learning with human children's learning. In one such experiment, an adult human demonstrated to groups of chimpanzees and two-year-old children the use of a rake-like tool to enable them to reach food and other objects outside of their normal reach. Both groups learned to use the tool, but while the human children worked to reproduce the exact technique of the demonstrator, the chimps did not. They appeared to use individualized learning strategies. The children's imitation required not just noticing the **sequence** of actions of the demonstrator, but also understanding the intention behind those actions. The more functional learning of the chimpanzees **focused** on the end result rather than on the process. This has led some researchers to conclude that although chimpanzee cultural traditions may exist, they are qualitatively different from and therefore not linked to human cultural traditions.

10   While a *Planet of the Apes* **scenario** seems unlikely, the research to date indicates that many of the differences separating humans from chimpanzees may be more a matter of degree than a clear-cut difference. For any who are worried that this may lead to further blurring of the lines between the species, Jane Goodall's words indicate the **reverse** is true. "Only when we are clear about the similarities between chimpanzee and human will we be able to recognize the real differences."

UNDERSTANDING THE READING

Respond to the following in writing. Base your responses on the reading and your own personal experiences.

1. What are the primary differences, both known and hypothesized, between humans and primates?
2. Why is it important to distinguish between chimpanzee behaviors observed in the wild and those observed in human environments?
3. If researchers can prove that chimpanzees are capable of rational thought, language ability, intentional teaching, and culture, how might treatment of these animals change? Describe some potential consequences.

FOCUSING ON VOCABULARY

WORD MEANING

Each of the following target words appears in the reading on pages 212–213. Use the paragraph number in parentheses to locate each word in context. Read the dictionary definitions below. Write the letter of the definition that reflects how the word is used in the reading.

_____ 1. **invoke** (1)
   a. to use a law, principle, or theory to support your views
   b. to make a particular idea or image appear in people's minds

_____ 2. **physically** (1)
   a. in relation to the body, rather than the mind or soul
   b. done using violent or forceful body movements

_____ 3. **drama** (1)
   a. a movie, television program, play, etc. that is serious rather than humorous
   b. an exciting and unusual situation or set of events

_____ 4. **publish** (4)
   a. to make generally known
   b. to have your research printed in journals or books for people to read

_____ 5. **intelligence** (5)
   a. the ability to learn, understand, and think about things
   b. information about the secret activities of foreign governments or militaries

_____ 6. **submit** (5)
   a. to give a plan, piece of writing, idea, etc. to someone for them to consider or approve
   b. to agree to obey a person, group, set of rules, etc. or to agree to do something, especially because you have no choice

_____ 7. **abstract** (5)
   a. existing only as an idea or quality rather than as something real you can see or touch
   b. a short written statement of the most important ideas in a speech, article, etc.

_____ **8. paradigm** (6)
   a. a particular way of doing something or thinking about something which is generally accepted or copied
   b. an example or pattern of a word showing all its grammatical forms, like "child, child's, children, children's"

_____ **9. focus** (6)
   a. to pay special attention to a particular person or thing instead of others
   b. to change the position of the lens on a camera, telescope, etc. so that you can see something clearly

_____ **10. context** (7)
   a. the situation, events, or information that is related to something and helps you to understand it better
   b. the words and sentences that come before and after a particular word that help you understand the meaning of the word

_____ **11. sequence** (9)
   a. the order that events or actions happen in or are supposed to happen in
   b. one part of a story, movie, etc. that deals with a single subject or action

_____ **12. reverse** (10)
   a. a defeat or a problem that delays your plans, as in "financial reverses"
   b. the exact opposite of what has just been mentioned

Each sentence below contains a paraphrase or set of synonyms for a target word. Read each sentence and then select the matching target word from the box.

coherent	institute	migrate	scenario
erode	intrinsic	previously	simulate
funding	investigation	revise	successive

1. The ability to develop _____ and convincing
   (clear, reasoned)
   arguments is one of the most challenging elements of good academic writing.

2. Cuts in government _____ for the arts are forcing
   (money, financial support)
   some museums to look elsewhere for support.

3. High rates of inflation can dramatically _____ the
   (wear away, eat into)
   buying power of retirees' fixed incomes.

4. Annual changes in the weather are the stimulus for millions of birds to
   _____; the Arctic tern makes the longest journey of
   (travel, journey)
   all, flying from the Arctic Circle all the way to South America or even
   Antarctica.

5. The Smithsonian _____ sponsors a number of the
   (organization, association)
   most popular museums in Washington, D.C., including the Air and Space
   Museum.

6. Chimpanzees turned out to be more capable of using tools than was

_____ assumed.
(formerly, up to that time)

7. After a careful _____ of fingerprints and other
(examination, study)

evidence at the crime scene, the police arrested two suspects.

8. Dinner plates and other items salvaged from the *Titanic* have little

_____ value, but their historical interest makes
(natural, fundamental)

them priceless.

9. The government was forced to _____ its growth
(change, modify)

forecasts downward when the economy did not improve.

10. The Japanese economy peaked in the early 1990s, but then it became

increasingly troubled in _____ years.
(subsequent, following)

11. Airline pilots _____ emergency situations in regular
(suggest, imitate)

training sessions so that they can react quickly if a real emergency occurs.

12. In science fiction, aliens invading Earth is a common

_____ .
(situation, set of circumstances)

WORD TIP

▶ When you use *migrate, immigrate*, or *emigrate*, be sure to choose the correct word.

▶ Use *immigrate* about people who are entering a country in order to live there.
   Jae-won *immigrated* to the United States last year.

▶ Use *emigrate* about people who have left their country in order to live in another one.
   My grandparents *emigrated* from Germany.

▶ Use *migrate* about birds or animals that go to another part of the world in the fall and the spring. You can also use *migrate* about people who move from one place to another, especially to find work.
   Monarch butterflies in North America **migrate** twice a year.
   After World War II, many African Americans *migrated* to cities in the North to get jobs.

WORD FAMILIES

Study the members of the word families in the table below. Look for spelling patterns for the verb, noun, adjective, and adverb forms of the words. Complete the table. List the patterns in the spaces.

Verb	Noun	Adjective	Adverb
cohere	coherence	coherent	coherently
erode	erosion	1. eroded 2. erosive	X
X	intelligence	intelligent	intelligently
investigate	1. investigation 2. investigator	1. investigative 2. investigatory	X
migrate	1. migration 2. migrant	migratory	X
publish	1. publisher 2. publication	published	X
revise	revision	revised	X
simulate	1. simulation 2. simulator	simulated	X
submit	submission	submitted	X
succeed	1. succession 2. successor	successive	successively
Spelling patterns			

Read each sentence and identify the part of speech of the missing word. Write an appropriate form of the target word in the blank. Use the word families table above to help you.

1. The speaker spoke persuasively and _____ (**coherence**) about the dangers of global warming.

2. Soil _____ (**erode**) is a major problem in many dry and windy parts of the world.

3. In Mali, south of the Sahara desert, _____ (**migrate**) is a necessity for agricultural workers who must leave and work elsewhere during the dry season and return home to farm during the rainy season.

4. Many animal psychologists believe that on average pigs are more

   _____ (**intelligence**) than dogs.

5. Lewis and Clark were sent to _____ (**investigation**) the western lands that the United States had bought from France in the Louisiana Purchase of 1803.

6. The _____ (**publish**) of the former first lady's memoirs was eagerly awaited by the media.

7. Journal articles typically go through several _____ (**revise**) before they are published.

8. Some driver education programs use a _____ (**simulate**) so that students can get accustomed to the controls before beginning lessons in a real car.

9. The negotiators hoped to agree to a treaty in time for _____ (**submit**) to the current United Nations General Assembly.

10. The thirteen original states ratified the United States Constitution in quick

_____ (**successive**) between December 1787 and May 1790.

COLLOCATION

Each item below contains three example sentences with the same target word. In each sentence, the target word is paired with a different word and forms a different collocation. In the fourth sentence, the collocation has been left blank. Choose the collocation from the examples that best fits the last sentence and write it in the blank. You may need to change the form of one of the words to fit the sentence.

1. a. Cubism is a type of **abstract art**.
  b. Mathematics can be difficult because it is basically concerned with understanding **abstract concepts**.
  c. **Abstract nouns** describe feelings, qualities, or states, rather than objects, animals, or people.

  d. Love is an _____ that most people can easily comprehend.

2. a. Crime and the causes of crime must be considered within their **social context**.
  b. The Cuban missile crisis took place in a specific **historical context**—the Cold War between the United States and the Soviet Union.
  c. The closure of the factory was a setback, but not a major one in the **wider context** of the generally buoyant economic recovery.
  d. The value of newspaper advertising must be judged within the

  _____ of a firm's overall promotion strategy.

3. a. In recognition of the **intrinsic value** of higher education, many countries do not charge tuition fees at state-run universities.
  b. Most people would like to believe that the **intrinsic nature** of humanity is good.
  c. The most important **intrinsic property** of a diamond is its hardness; its financial value, on the other hand, derives from its desirability and limited supply.
  d. Intense competitiveness is part of the _____ of most world-class athletes.

4. **a.** U.S. presidents can **invoke** special **powers** under the National Railway Act of 1925 to declare a sixty-day cooling-off period before a union strike takes place.

   b. If one country feels it is being discriminated against in trade, it can **invoke** anti-trade **rules** against the offending country.

   c. **Invoking** economic **sanctions** against a country is one way of putting pressure on it to reform without going to war.

   d. If the payment of fines does not deter an offender, the state may

   _____ criminal _____ and send that person to prison.

5. **a.** Most doctors recommend 30 minutes of moderate **physical activity** every day as part of a healthy lifestyle.

   b. The ancient Greeks believed that the **physical world** is made up of four elements: earth, fire, air, and water.

   c. The mission of the organization San Francisco Beautiful is the improvement of the city's **physical environment**, which ranges from removing graffiti to planting trees.

   d. The committee concluded that overcrowding at the prison led to an

   unsanitary and unsafe _____.

6. **a.** The higher court **reversed** the **decision** of the district court.

   b. The rising cost of living and a disappointing stock market may **reverse** the **trend** toward early retirement.

   c. During the daytime, winds generally blow in from the sea to the land; at night they generally blow in the **reverse direction**.

   d. The revolt during the stockholders meeting forced the board to

   _____ their _____ to cut dividends by 50 percent.

7. **a.** During the Cold War period, a devastating nuclear holocaust was always a **possible scenario**.

   b. Unless global warming is halted, the flooding of vast areas of low-lying coastal land is an increasingly **likely scenario**.

   c. Extinction would be the **worst-case scenario** for many species of fish that are now being overfished.

   d. The _____ for the entire staff actually happened when the company was forced to sell all of its assets and declare bankruptcy.

8. **a.** A person's ability to remember a **random sequence** of numbers is one of the best predictors of how well he or she can learn a second language.

   b. The reasoning in an academic paper should form a **logical sequence**—that is, each argument should build on the previous one.

   c. Archaeological evidence has confirmed that human tools were made in the following **chronological sequence**: stone, bronze, and then iron.

   d. Novels typically tell a story in a _____, although flashbacks are also a commonly used device.

Complete the passage by filling in the blanks with the target words in the box. Use each word only once.

abstract	dramatically	funded	paradigm
coherently	focus	institute	previous

KANZI: A CASE STUDY OF APE LANGUAGE DEVELOPMENT

1   The Language Research Center at Georgia State University is a research (1) _____ that was originally set up and (2) _____ to teach language to severely retarded children. A keyboard full of symbols was developed in order to enable communication with and between these children. The work with the keyboard was then extended to chimpanzees in order to determine whether or not they were capable of humanlike communication through language.

2   New research with both children and chimpanzees seemed to suggest that language acquisition develops out of a combination of the context of daily life, social interaction, and social expectancy. Language learners need to understand that (3) _____ symbols (or words) can serve as replacements for real objects and events. A (4) _____ shift was occurring in ape language research as the (5) _____ changed from production to comprehension.

3   An important breakthrough in this new area of investigation came with an infant chimpanzee named Kanzi who lived with his mother at the Language Research Center. Kanzi's mother received training on understanding the keyboard symbols, but Kanzi was not trained because he was too young. When he was around three years old, the researchers wanted to begin language instruction. To their surprise, Kanzi spontaneously used the keyboard to consistently and (6) _____ communicate his desires for food or play to the researchers. Because Kanzi had had no (7) _____ training, the researchers had to carry out scientific tests to confirm what they thought was happening. Kanzi refused to submit to the standard tests used with other apes, so the researchers were forced to disguise the tests as games and daily activities. These daily activities were carried out in the Language Research Center's fifty-five acre forest. Many of the tasks involved traveling between food locations and playing games and therefore provided a natural motivation for a young chimpanzee to communicate with his human companions.

4   Kanzi's learning environment is (8) _____ different from that of other chimpanzees who have been trained in laboratories or raised in

human homes. Kanzi and the researchers at Georgia State are demonstrating that social interaction and activity in a context that is much more like a real ape environment may provide appropriate stimuli for the development of intentional language use in a nonhuman primate.

Based on Savage-Rumbaugh, S. and Lewin, R. (1996). *Kanzi: The Ape at the Brink of the Human Mind*. New York: John Wiley and Sons.

EXPLORING THE TOPIC

Human rights for animals may sound far-fetched, however there are legal professionals who are taking this point very seriously. In 1999, a bill to grant human rights to great apes was even put before New Zealand's parliament. Although the bill was rejected, it does raise a number of issues.

 With a partner, consider the implications of granting human rights to chimpanzees and other great apes. What would be some of the implications of such a policy? Could it possibly be carried out? What might the impact be for both humans and apes? Organize your ideas and present them to the class. After the class discussion, write your ideas up in an essay.

CHAPTER

27 Living Together: Advantage or Disadvantage?

GETTING STARTED

Discuss the following questions with your classmates.

▶ Do you like being alone, or do you prefer to be part of a group? Why?

▶ What are some of the advantages of being alone? Of being a group member?

▶ Which of the benefits of being solitary or social might apply to animals as well as human beings? Explain.

TARGET WORDS—Assessing Your Vocabulary Knowledge

Look at each of the target words in the box. Use the scale to give yourself a score for each word. After you finish the chapter, score yourself again to check your improvement.

1 I don't know this word.

2 I have seen this word before, but I am not sure of the meaning.

3 I understand the word when I see it or hear it in a sentence, but I don't know how to use it in my own speaking and writing.

4 I know this word and can use it in my own speaking and writing.

TARGET WORDS

_____aggregate	_____coordinate	_____intervene	_____prospect
_____analogy	_____definite	_____likewise	_____ratio
_____circumstance	_____depress	_____logical	_____react
_____commence	_____hierarchy	_____offset	_____release
_____conceive	_____hypothesis	_____phenomenon	_____temporarily
_____concurrent	_____imposing	_____positive	_____unified

The following passage is adapted from an introductory textbook on animal behavior. As you read, pay special attention to the target vocabulary words in **bold**.

THE COSTS AND BENEFITS OF SOCIAL BEHAVIOR

1   Why do some animals live together in "social" groups, while others are solitary? According to recent research, there are **concurrent** costs and benefits to living in social groups. We human beings are social creatures who live in largely **hierarchical** societies, where people perform certain cooperative roles according to their rank and in order to preserve the community. As humans, we like to flatter ourselves into believing that our social behavior is the "most advanced" way of life, and by **analogy**, also the best kind of behavior for animals. It may be difficult for us to **conceive** of a situation in which social living is not advantageous. However, although it is true that living and cooperating with others has a variety of benefits, we will see that social behavior is not inherently superior to solitary behavior in the animal kingdom.

2   Sociality gives certain creatures **definite** advantages. Black-headed gulls, for example, capture food more easily when they hunt in flocks rather than forage by themselves. A pride of lions acting in a **unified** manner can better defend a hunting territory than a single lion can. A pair of birds can often care for its young better than a single parent can; one parent can guard the nest while the other is

Musk oxen assuming a defensive position

temporarily **released** from this responsibility in order to gather food. And social animals that are preyed upon by others can often **coordinate** their efforts to repel an enemy more effectively than solitary animals can.

3   But if sociality is so beneficial, why are social species so few and far between in most species of animals? Perhaps because there are many ecological conditions for which the negative effects of living together exceed the **positive** ones. There is no doubt that social life can create extra competition for food, as well as the risk that social foragers will be exploited by others within the group, as is true with lions. **Likewise**, animals that live together often face reproductive competition from other group members. For example, the destruction of eggs is a regular **phenomenon** within societies of the acorn woodpecker, a bird that forms groups containing as many as three breeding females and four breeding males. The females place their eggs all in the same nest, from which individuals remove and destroy the eggs of their "cooperatively breeding" companions, as females try to maximize the chances of their own offspring!

4   Still another cost of sociality is the increased **prospect** of *brood parasitism*, as the cliff swallow demonstrates. This bird nests in groups ranging from a couple of breeding pairs to over 3,000 individuals, with the swallows building their mud nests side by side under overhanging cliffs, bridges, and culverts. The females sometimes slip into neighboring nests to lay eggs. The neighboring swallow usually **reacts** to this intrusion by tending the extra egg, the presence of which apparently **depresses** her own egg-laying rate. The probability of occurrence of this form of brood parasitism is dramatically greater in large colonies than in groups with fewer than ten nesting females.

5   Cliff swallows have to deal with a different kind of parasite as well, the swallow bug, a bloodsucking relative of the notorious bedbug. Here too, a positive correlation exists between

the risk of parasitic infestation and the size of cliff swallow colonies. In large nesting groups, there is a greater chance that an infested adult will be present to seed the colony with these rapidly reproducing pests. Swallow bugs do most of their reproductive damage to cliff swallows by drinking the blood of swallow babies. When nestlings were weighed and the number of bugs attacking them counted, it was found that the higher the **ratio** of bugs per bird, the less a ten-day-old nestling weighed. In colonies where the **aggregate** parasite loads were extreme, the survival rate of the young declined by as much as 50 percent.

6   Cliff swallows illustrate that social living is far from an absolute blessing. If sociality is to evolve, special ecological conditions must **intervene** so that the many costs of associating with others will be **offset** by certain benefits to social individuals. The primary benefit of social life may be improved success in dealing with predators.

7   Consider the social bluegill sunfish and its close relative, the solitary pumpkinseed sunfish. Bluegills become **temporarily** social during the breeding season, when groups of 50 to 100 males **commence** building their nests (depressions in a sandy lake bottom) side by side. Although it is possible that bluegills nest together in part because some places are better than others for nest building, males in the colony derive a **definite** benefit in terms of a reduction in predator pressure on the eggs deposited in their nests by spawning females. For example, by defending overlapping territories, social males "cooperate" in offering a united front against egg-eating catfish.

8   But social bluegills pay a price for their antipredator benefits. An individual that nests in a group must **intervene** to deter his neighbors (and other non-nesting bluegills attracted to the group) from consuming the eggs in his nest, which he has fertilized. Moreover, fungi that destroy eggs may be transmitted from nest to nest in a dense colony. These costs reduce the net benefit enjoyed by social bluegills.

9   In contrast to their bluegill relatives, pumpkinseed sunfish do not breed in colonies. Whereas bluegills have small, delicate mouths designed for "inhaling" small soft-bodied insects, pumpkinseeds have more **imposing** jaws adapted for picking up, crushing, and consuming heavy-bodied mollusk prey (e.g., snails and mussels). Thus, although a bluegill cannot pick up a snail and cart it away from the nest, pumpkinseeds are easily able to do this (and may consume their egg-loving enemy to boot). In addition, a bluegill's bite does little damage to a nest-raiding bullhead catfish, but a pumpkinseed's attack packs considerably more wallop. The fact that pumpkinseeds are relatively free from nest predation and are solitary, whereas bluegills are more vulnerable to nest predation and are social, supports the **hypothesis** that social living is adaptive only when certain benefits can counterbalance the clear costs of sociality. Pumpkinseed sunfish are in no way inferior or less well adapted than bluegills because they are solitary; they simply face different ecological **circumstances**, under which colonial nesting would yield reduced individual success. As with all animals, it is only **logical** to be social if the benefits outweigh the costs.

Adapted from Alcock, J. (1993). *Animal Behavior: An Evolutionary Approach*, 5th ed. Sunderland, MA: Sinauer Associates, pp. 501–506.

UNDERSTANDING THE READING

Respond to the following in writing. Base your responses on the reading and your own personal experiences.

1. What is the primary benefit of social living among animals? Describe an animal that benefits from leading a social life.
2. In what ways can social living be a risk for certain animals? Describe an animal that pays a price for its sociality.
3. For human beings, do the benefits of social living outweigh the costs? Explain your point of view.

WORD MEANING

Read the sentences below and circle the letter of the word or phrase that best matches the meaning of the target word in **bold**. Use context clues in the sentences to determine the correct meaning. Check your dictionary if you are not sure of the answer.

1. Her **aggregate** income from stocks, bonds, and property rental was over $4,000 per month.
   a. amazing
   b. large
   c. total

2. The teacher made an **analogy** between the wave movement of light and the wave movement of water.
   a. comparison of two things that seem similar
   b. confirmation that something is true
   c. something that appears to be difficult

3. The criminal received a five-year jail term for one robbery and a three-year term for another, but he only spent a total of five years in prison because the terms were served **concurrently**.
   a. before something else
   b. at the same time
   c. after something else

4. Support for the **hypothesis** that the earth was round came partly from astronomical observations made possible by the telescope.
   a. a suggested, but unproved explanation for something
   b. a way of doing something
   c. the weakest part of an argument

5. Language aptitude is a key predictor of achievement in second language learning; age, motivation, and use of learning strategies are **likewise** important.
   a. unusually
   b. similarly
   c. basically

6. Given that the student performed exceptionally well during her undergraduate studies, it was **logical** to assume she would also do well in her graduate studies.
   a. extremely interesting
   b. unusual
   c. seemingly reasonable and sensible

7. Cell phones are a relatively new **phenomenon**, but they may soon make landlines obsolete.
   a. something that happens or exists
   b. something that is wasteful
   c. something that is difficult to see

8. Having a college education increases a person's **prospect** of finding a good job.
   a. a difficult choice
   b. several things working together
   c. the chance of something happening

9. The criminal was **released** from jail after serving his prison sentence.
   a. temporarily removed
   b. set free
   c. looked at carefully

10. It is difficult to **conceive** of the vastness of the universe.
   a. imagine what something is like
   b. control something completely
   c. change something for the better

11. The Eiffel Tower was originally meant to be only a **temporary** attraction for the International Exhibition of Paris of 1889, yet now it is the symbol of Paris.
   a. not permanent
   b. as a result of great effort
   c. unusual

12. By conquering all the other warlords, Hideyoshi Toyotomi was able to **unify** Japan and set up a central government based in Tokyo.
   a. combine to make a single unit
   b. have doubts about something
   c. have something and not give it back

Read the sentences below and use context to figure out the meaning of the target words in **bold**. Look for a core meaning that provides a general understanding of each target word. Write the meaning in your own words.

1. a. The **circumstances** surrounding the person's death were suspicious, so the police began a murder investigation.
   b. The vice president can only take over from the president under very specific **circumstances**.

   circumstances _____

2. a. Construction work on the new high school will **commence** in three weeks.
   b. Once the opening ceremonies of the games were finished, the sporting competitions could **commence**.

   commence _____

3. a. Interior decorators **coordinate** the colors in a room for a pleasing effect.
   b. The air traffic control system at Chicago's O'Hare airport must **coordinate** approximately 2,590 takeoffs and landings every day.

   coordinate _____

4. a. In terms of efficiency, the internal combustion gasoline engine was a **definite** improvement over previous external combustion steam engines.
   b. The unions were tired of the employers' vague responses and demanded a **definite** answer to their questions within seven days.

   definite _____

5. a. An oversupply of skilled workers often has the effect of **depressing** wages.
   b. Lack of sleep **depresses** many brain functions including reaction time, making driving particularly dangerous.

   depress _____

6. **a.** In the **hierarchy** of the U.S. Army, a colonel ranks higher than a captain.
   b. The top court in the American judicial **hierarchy** is the U.S. Supreme Court.

   hierarchy _____

7. **a.** When it was built, the Empire State Building was a singularly **imposing** structure, but now it is one among many tall skyscrapers in New York City.
   b. Although Mt. Everest is higher, K2, on the China-Pakistan border, is one of the most **imposing** mountaineering challenges in the world.

   imposing _____

8. **a.** The United Nations has **intervened** militarily in various countries to help suppress civil war.
   b. Before World War II, the United States leaned toward isolationism and largely refused to **intervene** in affairs beyond the North American continent.

   intervene _____

9. **a.** Successful students often mirror their parents' **positive** attitudes toward education.
   b. The patient showed a **positive** response to the experimental medicine.

   positive _____

10. **a.** The drop in oil prices was completely **offset** by the new tax; therefore, the price of gasoline to the consumer remained the same.
    b. In the quest to feed the world, improvements in crop yields have been partially **offset** by an increase in population.

    offset _____

11. **a.** The **ratio** of hydrogen atoms to oxygen atoms in water is 2:1, thus the formula H_2O.
    b. In 2001, the **ratio** of women's weekly earnings compared to men's was 76 percent, up from 63 percent in 1979.

    ratio _____

12. **a.** The country **reacted** to the sudden increase in the number of immigrants by closing its borders.
    b. In order to best help their patients, medical personnel must learn not to **react** emotionally to their patient's condition, however distressing.

    react _____

WORD TIP

▶ Academic words sometimes appear in a reading alongside informal expressions. For example, "The Costs and Benefits of Social Behavior" contains the following informal expressions in paragraph 9:

　　to boot (meaning: "in addition to everything else you've mentioned")
　　wallop (meaning: "a hard hit")

▶ If you can't figure out the meanings of such words and expressions from context, look them up in your dictionary.

WORD FAMILIES

Read the sentences below. Some of the target words have been used correctly, but in six sentences a wrong word form has been used. If the wrong form has been used, cross it out and write the correct form. If the form is correct, put a checkmark (✓).

1. There are many cases of **analogy** behavior between humans and animals, for example the use of tools by chimpanzees. _____

2. Taxes introduced as **temporary** measures to deal with specific situations have a habit of becoming permanent. _____

3. The world's **react** to the disaster was immediate, and soon planeloads of badly-needed supplies were making their way to the affected region.

    _____

4. There is a great deal of controversy over whether psychic **phenomena** actually exist, or whether they can be accounted for by natural explanations.

    _____

5. During the Great **Depress** of the 1930s, employment, income levels, and industrial output dropped dramatically in the United States.

    _____

6. The **unify** of Germany was one of the most dramatic events of the late twentieth century. _____

7. The **intervene** of the Japanese Central Bank helped support the value of the dollar. _____

8. Sonograms can give **prospect** parents peace of mind that their unborn child is healthy. _____

9. If "All men are created equal," then it **logically** follows that every person should have equal opportunities and protection under the law.

    _____

10. According to the medical evidence, we can **definitely** say that smoking is harmful to health. _____

COLLOCATION

Match each target word in the box with the group of words that regularly occur with it. If the (~) symbol appears before a word in a list, the target word comes before the word in the list. In all other cases, the target word comes after the word in the list.

aggregate	commence	coordinate	positive
circumstances	conceive	hypothesis	release

1. _____	2. _____	3. _____	4. _____
support the	~attitude	certain	~activities
speculative	~results	exceptional	~work
alternative	~response	normal	~efforts
~predicts	~effect	economic	~policy

5. _____

~proceedings

~work

~production

~trading

6. _____

difficult to

possible to

~of a situation

~of the possibility

7. _____

~prisoners

~energy

~tension

~information

8. _____

~demand

~supply

~amount

~value

EXPANSION

Living together is not automatically the best choice for animals. Read the statements about animal behavior in the following chart. Evaluate each statement. Is it an advantage or disadvantage of living together, or is it neutral? Place a checkmark (✓) in the appropriate box. If the factor makes no difference, place a checkmark (✓) in the "Does not matter" box.

Factor	Advantage of living together	Disadvantage of living together	Does not matter
1. Musk oxen **react** to predators by forming a circle and protecting their young inside.			
2. The **ratio** of males to females in the animal population is 1:1.			
3. Lions maintain a **hierarchy** in which some males are more dominant than others and only the dominant males breed.			
4. Living in a large herd can **offset** a weak individual's vulnerability to predators.			
5. Dominant members can **impose** their will upon the whole group.			
6. In social groups, there is increased competition for a breeding partner; **likewise**, rivals may mate with one's partner.			
7. Penguins jump into the ocean **concurrently** in order to minimize the danger of any one individual being eaten by seals.			
8. Migrating birds **coordinate** their flight patterns into "V"s, which enables the birds toward the rear to work less hard.			

Choose a wild animal and investigate its social behavior. Write a descriptive essay in which you clearly identify how much time that animal spends alone or in groups. Identify the factors that determine whether the animal is primarily solitary or social. Discuss whether its solitary or social behavior is a benefit or a risk.

CHAPTER 28

Strategy Practice

USING YOUR DICTIONARY AND THESAURUS—Synonyms

As you use your expanded vocabulary in academic writing, you will want to improve and vary your choice of words. Using precise synonyms is one way to add variety and clarity to your writing. Synonyms are words that have the same basic meaning. Although many English words are close in meaning, very few are truly interchangeable. Shades of meaning, tone, grammar (e.g., is the word followed by a preposition?), and collocation are some of the factors that differentiate synonyms from one another. Knowing the differences between synonyms is particularly important for academic writing.

CHOOSING THE RIGHT SYNONYM

There are a variety of sources you can use to locate an accurate synonym for a particular word, including a regular dictionary, a dictionary of synonyms, or a thesaurus. In addition, most word processing programs include a thesaurus for quick access to synonyms.

Suppose you want a synonym for the word *commence* in the sentence below.

> EXAMPLE: Jury deliberations will **commence** after the jury hears the closing arguments of the prosecution and the defense.

You consult a thesaurus and find the following synonyms: *begin, embark (on or upon), start, kick off.* You try each of these words in the sentence and ask yourself these questions:

- Can the synonym replace the original word without changing the meaning or tone of the sentence?
- Can the synonym replace the word without changing the grammar of the sentence?

Embark and *kick off* change the meaning of the sentence. *Embark* does not work grammatically within the sentence, and *kick off* has an informal tone that is inappropriate. You are not sure whether to use *begin* or *start,* so you look *commence* up in the *Longman Advanced American Dictionary.* After the dictionary entry for the word, you read the usage note about subtle shades of difference between *commence, start,* and *begin.* (See the top of the next page.)

com•mence /kəˈmɛns/ v. [I,T] FORMAL to begin or to start something: *Work will commence on the new building immediately.* | *They will commence production in April.* | [+ **with**] *Volume 2 of the biography commences with Picasso at age 25.* | [**commence doing sth**] *The planes commenced bombing on Wednesday.*

Usage Note: Commence, Begin, Start

FORMALITY

Commence is a very formal word that is used much more often in written language than in spoken. People use **start** in written language also, but it is the word most people use in spoken language. **Begin** is the most common word to choose in written language.

Based on your findings, you decide that although *start* and *begin* both work as synonyms, *begin* would be the best choice in this context. *Begin* replaces *commence* without changing the meaning or tone of the sentence, it works grammatically within the sentence, and it is more appropriate than *start* for written text.

PRACTICING YOUR DICTIONARY SKILLS

Use a regular dictionary, a thesaurus, or a dictionary of synonyms to determine whether any of the synonyms given can replace the target word in **bold** in each sentence. Circle the letter of the synonym that fits. Make sure the synonym fits the meaning and tone. Be ready to explain your decision.

1. Passing the magnetic strip on a credit card through a card reader initiates a **sequence** of automated steps to determine whether the amount of the purchase is under the cardholder's credit limit.
   a. series   **b.** cycle   **c.** chain

2. The city government instituted several new **financial** policies.
   a. monetary   **b.** pecuniary   **c.** fiscal

3. Queen Isabella of Spain refused to allow natives of the New World to become slaves and so forced Columbus to **release** the natives he used as servants.
   a. free   **b.** let go   **c.** cut loose

STRATEGY—Using Meaning Networks

Linking words together into meaningful groups is a useful way of developing your understanding of the range of topics or contexts in which a word can occur.

Work with a partner. Sort these fifteen target words from Unit 7 into three topic areas. Since some academic words come under more than one topic area, you may decide to write some of the words in more than one column. One word in each list has been done for you.

automatic	displace	migrate	reverse	suspend
circumstance	enforce	mechanism	simulate	temporarily
commit	investigate	restore	successive	welfare

Population/Migration	Machinery	Law and Order
migrate	automatic	commit

Now look over your lists. Circle any words that you wrote in more than one column. Compare your lists with another pair of students. Are your lists the same? Discuss your reasons for placing specific words in specific columns.

WORD KNOWLEDGE—Academic Verb Collocations

Academic verbs can often take a number of collocations. For example, you can *file* for bankruptcy, *file* a lawsuit, *file* charges, *file* a report, *file* a complaint, etc.

In the following items, four words collocate with the academic verbs and one does not. Circle the letter of the word that does not. The first one has been done for you.

1. What kind of things might you **cease**?
   a. production
   b. trading
   c. operations
   d. dating
   e. hostilities

2. What kind of things might you **accumulate**?
   a. wealth
   b. surprises
   c. points
   d. money
   e. knowledge

3. What kind of things might you **amend**?
   a. punishment
   b. the Constitution
   c. the law
   d. a statement
   e. records

4. What kind of things might you **inspect**?
   a. documents
   b. repairs
   c. damage
   d. someone's work
   e. years

5. What kind of things might you **distort**?
   a. reality
   b. facts
   c. the truth
   d. talent
   e. data

6. What kind of things might you **detect**?
   a. a presence
   b. a difference
   c. marketing
   d. a change
   e. a disease

7. What kind of things might you **monitor**?
   a. movies
   b. progress
   c. performance
   d. the situation
   e. changes

8. What kind of things might you **chart**?
   a. a course
   b. communication
   c. the future
   d. progress
   e. growth

9. What kind of things might you **attain**?
   a. status
   b. objectives
   c. a goal
   d. a certain weight
   e. the world

10. What kind of things might you **assess**?
    a. needs
    b. effects
    c. damage
    d. thought
    e. the value of something

Index of Academic Words

The following is a list of academic words and the chapter in which each word is introduced.

A

abandon 14
abstract 26
access 10
accommodate 25
accompany 5
accumulate 23
accuracy 7
achieve 7
acknowledge 5
acquire 6
adapt 11
adequate 15
adjacent 14
adjustment 6
administrative 9
advocate 18
affect 2
aggregate 27
aid 13
albeit 22
allocate 9
alter 7
alternative 13
ambiguous 22
amend 22
analogy 27
analytic 11
annual 14
anticipate 15
apparent 2
appendix 25
appreciate 5
approach 9
appropriate 6
approximately 11
arbitrary 13
aspect 2
assemble 17
assess 11
assign 9
assistance 3
assume 6
assure 17
attachment 5
attain 15
attitude 2
attribute 7
author 21
authority 10
automatic 25
available 3
aware 15

B

behalf 19
benefit 14
bias 18
bond 5
brief 23
bulk 18

C

capable 15
capacity 1
category 6
cease 21
challenge 7
channel 23
chart 23
chemical 13
circumstance 27
cite 14
civil 21
clarify 15
classical 21
clause 22
code 9
coherent 26
coincide 18
collapse 17
colleague 19
commence 27
commentary 21
committed 25
commodity 15
compatible 18
compensate 25
compile 19
complement 13
complex 1
component 23
compound 19
comprehensive 19
comprise 13
compute 21
conceive 27
concentration 9
concept 2
conclude 10
concurrent 27
conduct 14
confer 2
confine 13
confirm 10
conflict 2
conform 2
consent 22

consequences 1
considerable 9
consist 3
consistent 7
constantly 6
constitute 21
constraint 17
constructed 17
consultation 22
consume 3
contact 2
contemporary 1
context 26
contracted 11
contradictory 10
contrary 18
contrast 1
contribute 3
controversial 5
conventional 10
conversely 3
convert 23
convinced 22
cooperate 3
coordinate 27
core 17
corporate 10
correspond 22
credit 22
criteria 13
crucial 10
cycle 9

D

debate 9
decade 9
decline 1
deduce 19
definite 27
demonstrate 7
denote 17
deny 7
depress 27
derive 7
design 5
despite 13
detect 23
deviation 22
device 6
devote 14
differentiate 10
dimension 7
diminish 14
discrete 15

discriminating 11
displace 25
display 10
dispose 6
distinction 2
distorted 22
distribute 5
diverse 1
document 2
domain 17
domestic 3
dominance 2
draft 22
drama 26
duration 14
dynamics 5

E

element 1
eliminate 9
emerge 7
emphasis 5
empirical 19
enable 15
encounter 1
enforce 25
enhanced 9
enormous 23
ensure 15
environment 1
equate 19
equipment 10
equivalent 22
erode 26
establish 11
estimate 1
ethics 18
ethnic 2
evaluation 2
eventually 1
evidence 1
evolve 1
exceed 21
exclusion 9
exhibition 10
expansion 14
expert 14
explicit 17
exploit 15
export 15
expose 7
external 18
extract 13

F

facilitate 9
factor 6
features 5
federal 13
file 22
financial 25
finite 18
flexibility 9
fluctuate 15

focus 26
format 21
formula 22
forthcoming 18
foundation 6
framework 17
function 3
fundamental 5
funding 26
furthermore 1

G

gender 2
generating 23
generation 1
global 1
grade 22
grant 21
guarantee 13
guideline 19

H

hence 11
hierarchy 27
highlight 13
hypothesis 27

I

identical 19
ideology 21
ignorance 25
illustrate 6
image 5
immigrate 17
impact 5
implement 23
implication 17
implicit 21
imply 13
imposing 27
incentive 25
incidence 23
inclination 17
incorporate 11
index 22
indication 10
induce 21
inevitable 14
infer 19
infrastructure 18
inherent 13
inhibited 23
initially 25
initiate 6
injured 11
innovation 10
input 14
insert 15
insight 6
inspect 23
instance 7
institute 26
integral 22
integration 18

integrity 23
intelligence 26
intensity 7
interact 1
internal 11
interpret 21
interval 21
intervene 27
intrinsic 26
investigation 26
investment 17
invoke 26
involve 6
irrelevant 25
isolation 3
issues 5
item 1

J

journal 19
justify 13

L

label 13
labor 3
layer 13
legislation 18
levy 18
liberal 19
license 17
likewise 27
locate 3
logical 27

M

maintain 3
manipulate 1
margin 18
mature 17
maximum 9
mechanism 25
media 2
mediate 19
medicine 23
mental 7
methods 10
migrate 26
military 11
minimal 23
minimize 14
ministry 18
minority 3
mode 6
modify 6
monitor 23
motivate 7
mutually 15

N

negative 3
network 3
neutral 1
nevertheless 14
nonetheless 15
norm 6

notion 17
notwithstanding 19
nuclear 3

O
objective 21
obtain 6
obviously 10
occupation 6
occur 14
oddness 17
offset 27
ongoing 6
option 23
orient 18
outcome 14
output 18
overall 11
overlap 11

P
paradigm 26
parallel 11
parameter 22
participants 7
passive 22
perceive 7
percent 9
period 11
persist 2
perspective 7
phase 9
phenomenon 27
philosophy 18
physical 26
policy 5
portion 18
pose 25
positive 27
potential 10
practitioner 18
preceding 11
precise 15
predict 14
predominate 13
preliminary 22
presumably 10
previously 26
primary 5
prime 25
principal 21
principle 5
prior 7
prioritize 18
proceed 21
process 2
prohibitive 14
promote 3
proportion 13
prospect 27
protocol 22
psychologist 10
publish 26

purchase 3
pursue 19

Q
qualitatively 18
quote 17

R
radical 21
random 13
range 2
ratio 27
rational 25
react 27
recovery 25
refine 18
region 14
registration 25
regulate 13
reinforce 6
rejection 7
release 27
reluctance 17
rely 3
residential 10
resolution 25
resource 3
response 10
restore 25
restrain 19
restrict 9
retain 2
reveal 19
revenue 5
reverse 26
revise 26
revolution 21
rigid 2
route 22

S
scenario 26
scheme 25
scope 25
sector 15
secure 15
seek 9
selection 6
sequence 26
series 11
shift 23
significant 2
simulate 26
site 15
sole 6
somewhat 10
source 1
specify 17
spherical 23
stability 7
statistics 19
status 9
straightforward 19
strategies 5

stressful 11
structure 3
style 2
submit 26
subordinate 17
subsequent 21
subsidy 17
substitute 19
successive 26
sufficient 11
summarize 19
supplement 15
survey 10
survive 19
suspend 25
sustain 15
symbol 1

T
technical 10
temporarily 27
tense 22
terminate 14
theme 21
theory 11
thereby 23
trace 9
traditional 9
transfer 6
transform 1
transition 3
transmit 11
transport 15
trend 3
trigger 7

U
ultimate 14
undergo 11
underlying 5
undertake 19
unified 27
uniformity 23
unique 13
utilize 15

V
validity 17
vary 2
vehicle 21
version 23
via 5
violation 21
virtually 14
visible 5
vision 7
visualized 23
volume 14
volunteer 11

W
welfare 25
whereas 13
whereby 5
widespread 9

Credits

Text

Pages 3, 12, 20, *Sociology*: *A Global Introduction*, Macionis and Plummer, Copyright 1997. New York: Prentice Hall Europe. adaptation/condensation of pages 64–75, 139–141, 164. Page 23, Popenoe, David, *Sociology*, 10th ed., Copyright 1995. Reprinted by permission of Pearson Education, Inc., Upper Saddle River, NJ, pp. 310–313. Page 38, 57, *Consumer Behaviour: A European Perspective*, 2nd ed. Solomon, Bamossy, Askegaard, S., Copyright 2002. New York: Prentice Hall Europe. adaptation/condensation of pages 13–17, 189–191. Page 46, Schiffman, Leon and Kanuk, Leslie, *Consumer Behavior*, 7th ed., Copyright 2000. Reprinted by permission of Pearson Education, Inc., Upper Saddle River, NJ, pp. 277–279, 282–283. Page 71, Robbins, Steven P., *Organizational Behavior*, 9th ed., Copyright 2001. Reprinted by permission of Pearson Education, Inc., Upper Saddle River, NJ, pp. 456–459. Page 80, From *The Chair: Rethinking Culture, Body, and Design* by Galen Cranz. Copyright 1998 by Galen Cranz. Used by permission of W.W. Norton & Company, Inc, pp. 54–59. Pages 91, 98, Kroemer, K.H.E., Kroemer, H.B., and Kroemer-Elbert, E., *Ergonomics: How to Design for Ease and Efficiency*, 2nd ed., Copyright 2001. Reprinted by permission of Pearson Education, Inc., Upper Saddle River, NJ, pp. 350, 404–406, 409–411, 413, 415–416. Page 114, Micklin, P.P. "Desiccation of the Aral Sea: A Water Management Disaster in the Soviet Union." A. Goudie, *The Human Impact Reader*. Copyright 1997. Blackwell, pp. 130–142. Page 122, Thurman, Harold V. and Trujillo, Alan P., *Essentials of Oceanography*, 7th ed., Copyright 2002. Reprinted by permission of Pearson Education, Inc., Upper Saddle River, NJ, pp. 155–157. Page 124, Adapted from J.A. Allan. *Avoiding War Over Natural Resources*. 11 January 1998. ICRC. Page 139, Adapted from Atkins, P. and Bowler, I. Copyright 2001. *Food in Society*. Arnold Press, pp. 274–280, 297–298, 301–304. Page 148, Adapted from Blake, F. (1990). *Organic Farming and Growing*. The Crowood Press, pp. 9–12. Page 158, Adapted from Batzing, B.L. (2002). *Microbiology: An Introduction*. Brooks/Cole-Thomson Learning, pp. 661–662, 672. Page 171, Nichols, David C., *Musical Encounters*, 1st ed., Copyright 2001. Reprinted by permission of Pearson Education Inc., Upper Saddle River, NJ, pp. 301, 305–306, 308–309, 316. Page 180, Adapted from Sound Research Laboratories Ltd. Spon, E. & F.N. (1991). *Noise Control in Industry*, 3rd ed., pp. 19, 24–26, 29–30, 35. Page 190, Berg, Richard E. and Stork, David G., *The Physics of Sound*, 2nd ed., Copyright 1995. Reprinted by permission of Pearson Education, Inc., Upper Saddle River, NJ, pp. 59–63. Page 203, Adapted from Harland, D. (1994). *Killing Game; International Law and the African Elephant*. Praegar Publishers, pp. 167–175. Page 220, Based on Savage-Rumbaugh, S. and Lewin, R. *Kanzi: The Ape at the Brink of the Human Mind*. New York: John Wiley and Sons. Page 223, Adapted from Alcock, J. (1993) *Animal Behavior: An Evolutionary Approach*, 5th ed. Sinauer Associates, pp. 501–506.

Photos

Page 1, © Strauss/Curtis/Corbis; page 3, © Photo Archives of the South Tyrol Museum of Archaeology; page 13, Digital Vision/Getty Images; page 23, © Paul Barton/Corbis; page 24, © Keren Su/Corbis; page 36, © Image 100 Ltd.; page 38, © James Marshall/Corbis; page 39, left: AP/Wide World Photos; right, © Amy Etra/PhotoEdit; page 46, © Thinkstock; page 47, Photodisc Red/Getty Images; page 48, Digital Vision/Getty Images; page 57, © Bill Aron/PhotoEdit; page 69, © David Katzenstein/Corbis; page 71, © Bill Varie/Corbis; page 72, © Royalty-Free/Corbis; page 80, Ryan McVay/Photodisc Green/Getty Images; page 81, left, Ryan McVay/Photodisc Green/Getty Images; page 81, right, Balans Variable, designed by Peter Opsvik, photo courtesy of Tollefsen; page 91, Davies/Stringer/Topical Press Agency/Getty Images; page 103 © Lester Lefkowitz/Corbis; page 105, Anthony/ Masterson/Botanica/Getty Images; page 115, © David Turnley/Corbis; page 124, © Freelance Consulting Services Pty Ltd./Corbis; page 137, © Royalty-Free/Corbis;

page 139, © Dave Bartruff/Corbis; page 148, © Ed Young/Corbis; page 158, © Gianni Dagli Orti/Corbis; page 159, © Dave Bartruff/Corbis; page 169, © Royalty-Free/Corbis; page 171, Scala/Art Resource, NY; page 172, © Bettmann/Corbis; page 173, © Bettmann/Corbis; page 180, © Bob Rowan, Progressive Image/Corbis; page 191, © Steve Chenn/Corbis; page 201, © Daniel Aubry NYC/Corbis; page 203, AP/Wide World Photos; page 213, © Liss Steve/Corbis; page 223, David E. Myers/Stone/Getty Images.

Illustrations

Page 92, Neil Stewart, based on original figures by Chaffin and Andersson © 1984 *Occupational Biomechanics*. This material is used by permission of John Wiley and Sons, Inc. pages 114, 121, 122, Burmar Technical Corporation. page 141, Paige, David M., and Theodore M. Bayless, *Lactose Digestion: Clinical and Nutritional Implications*, p. 33, Figure 3.9, © 1981. Johns Hopkins University Press. page 199, Steve Attoe.